The Oracle Universal Content Management Handbook

Build, administer, and manage Oracle Stellent UCM Solutions

Practical knowledge and breakthrough shortcuts to Oracle UCM expertise

Dmitri Khanine

[PACKT] enterprise 器

PUBLISHING   professional expertise distilled

BIRMINGHAM - MUMBAI

The Oracle Universal Content Management Handbook
Build, administer, and manage Oracle Stellent UCM Solutions

First published: August 2010

Production Reference: 1040810

Published by Packt Publishing Ltd.
32 Lincoln Road
Olton
Birmingham, B27 6PA, UK.

ISBN 978-1-849680-38-7

www.packtpub.com

Cover Image by Dr. José Eugenio Gómez Rodríguez (jegomezrdz@gmail.com)

Credits

Author
Dmitri Khanine

Reviewer
Billy Cripe

Acquisition Editor
Amey Kanse

Technical Editor
Bhavesh D. Bhasin

Indexer
Monica Ajmera Mehta

Graphics
Nilesh Mohite

Editorial Team Leader
Gagandeep Singh

Project Team Leader
Lata Basantani

Project Coordinators
Poorvi Nair

Shubhanjan Chatterjee

Proofreaders
Chris Smith

Claire Cresswell-Lane

Production Coordinator
Adline Swetha Jesuthas

Cover Work
Adline Swetha Jesuthas

Foreword

Enterprise Content Management (ECM) is getting a lot of attention in corporations around the world today. Corporations create a large amount of unstructured content in the form of documents, scanned content, videos, audio, photos, images, and so on. Some statistics show that more than 80 percent of a corporation's intellectual property exists in the form of unstructured data. If that much of a corporation's intellectual property exists in an unstructured format how much time do employees spend searching the corporate network to locate and gather information? How much disk space do we consume saving copy after copy, revision upon revision of content only so we can find it later just to find we forgot where we put it?

This is where ECM system comes in to play. They are designed to manage unstructured content, provide search tools, enforce content security rules, web publishing, provide repository services to business systems, and many other functions depending on product offerings and corporate needs.

This book focuses on the ECM products offered by Oracle. In 2007 Oracle acquired Stellent, and has been working to integrate the Content Server into the entire Oracle product line. Oracle's vision is to offer a complete application stack integrating all the applications any organization needs to operate from top to bottom. Oracle has taken the Content Server core and plugged it into the Fusion Middleware stack giving repository services capability to all the enterprise business systems Oracle owns.

As UCM grows in adoption in organizations administrators are faced with managing a system that may be rapidly growing in usage creating a huge demands for UCM services. Understanding Oracle UCM, how it works, how to set it up and administration is essential to having an ECM system that performs and provides services expected by the end users.

There are many books about ECM and ECM systems in general but very few that cover Oracle Content Management products. If you want to learn about the Oracle Content Management system you would need to attend training classes or pour over the Oracle documentation to find out the information you need to install and set up UCM. This book condenses the Oracle documentation into short and understandable descriptions, and step by step instructions about how to set up, configure, and understand the workings of Oracle UCM version 10gR3. The language used by the author is very understandable and each topic is explained in plain talk, which makes the context of the book easy to understand by new as well as experienced administrators and users. This book does not cover hardware configurations and setup which is an entirely separate topic that depends on your organizations preferences for OS types, hardware manufacturer, and requirements but it will get you up and running and ready to manage your content once the hardware resources have been installed and configured to run in your organizations environment.

I don't understand what this sentence is trying to say!! All you need to do is open it up to any page and start reading. If you are an experienced administrator you will see how informational the book is. If you are a new to Oracle UCM you will enjoy getting right to the workings of Oracle UCM and quickly get to setting up your new UCM environment.

Allan Hoof,

Oracle UCM expert and President of the IOUG
Oracle Content Management Special Interest Group

Allan Hoof has been focused on implementing technology since the mid 90's. He started in the data management area focusing on the data files for the 3D CAD system Pro/ENGINEER. In 1997 he transitioned into the Enterprise Content Management field using Stellent products and continued with the Oracle Content Management products after the Oracle acquisition of Stellent. In his current position he manages the ECM environment which houses over 2 million content items in the ECM system. Allan also volunteers as the Oracle Content Management Special Interest Group (OCM SIG) President and as a COLLABORATE Conference Committee Content Management Track Manager with the Independent Oracle Users Group (IOUG).

About the Author

Dmitri Khanine is one of the most respected names in Oracle UCM. He is among the two people in the world who is recognized as leading community enthusiast and advocate in the field of Content Management - with a prestigious Oracle ACE award. He also runs the Independent Oracle UCM Knowledge Center.

Dmitri is available for a limited number of training, speaking and consulting engagements. You can reach him at: `dk@stellentExperts.com`.

> I want to thank Hellen, my beautiful wife and my lifetime companion, for her loving support and being by my side no matter what, and my lovely kids—Gaby and Nathan—for bringing joy and energy into my life.

About the Reviewer

Billy Cripe is currently the Vice President of Marketing for Oracle E20 Partner, Fishbowl Solutions (`http://www.fishbowlsolutions.com`). Prior to this position Billy was the Director of Product Management for Oracle ECM and E20. Billy has over 11 years of experience in the ECM industry as a client, developer, consultant, and product strategist. He has been involved with the architecture, development, and implementation of key information management systems at clients from large multi-national corporations to local municipalities and small businesses.

Billy Cripe is co-author of the book "Reshaping Your Business with Web 2.0" (McGraw-Hill 2008) along with Oracle VP of Product Management Vince Casarez, Oracle SE Philipp Weckerle and Web 2.0 Guru Jean Sini. Billy is also the author of the eBook, "Two Types of Collaboration and Ten Requirements for using them" (Smashwords, 2010).

Billy has traveled all over the world speaking and meeting with customers on the importance, value, and strategy of enterprise information management. He has been widely published online and in print on Enterprise 2.0 and Social Enterprise Information Management. You can keep up with him on Twitter at: @billycripe or on his blogs `http://cfour.fishbowlsolutions.com` and `http://www.enterprise20.tv`.

Acknowledgement

I would like to thank Dmitri Khanine and the Independent Oracle ECM Knowledge Center for inviting me to participate in this work. Dmitri's easily accessible writing style and his ability to distill the complexities of enterprise content management into those core capabilities that people actually need is refreshing.

I would also like to thank the team at Fishbowl Solutions for supporting my work on this and similar projects. This reflects our core belief that a healthy ECM community is maintained and enriched through participation with others who share our passion even as we compete for business.

I would be remiss if I failed to offer my thanks to Packt Publishing for bearing with my schedule with the grace and gentleness they consistently offered.

Finally, thanks to my wife and kids for giving up evenings with Dad as I worked with Dmitri on this project.

Table of Contents

Preface

If you ever wanted to learn Oracle UCM, successfully deliver a project, or take your career to the next level—this will be the most important book you ever read. Why? Because the text you're looking at right now is a lot more than just a book.

Your complete Oracle UCM mastery system

That's right, this IS your complete Oracle UCM mastery system—the book itself is just a component. And this system will take you to where you need to b fast. Let me show you in more specific details the actual components, that work together to get you there:

- **The book chapters** will give you the much needed knowledge, insider information, and shortcuts that you can use to slash days, weeks, and even months off your learning curve, and your project schedule. Its "you and me talking" style makes learning effortless and fun—even if you are a "slow learner".

- **8 hour Quick Start** will give you a rocket boost to help you get comfortable with Oracle UCM in a hurry. If you are "under the gun" to decide whether your project can be accomplished with UCM or you found yourself on a deep end of the pool of a UCM implementation—this section will be your helping hand.

- **Your Free Critique Certificate** entitles you to having me personally review and comment on your architecture document, security or metadata model, or any other Oracle UCM-related matter that you can describe in one email. We routinely charge no less than $100 to $200 per critique, so this is a very real $100 to $200 value. It's probably the only time in your life you'll ever buy an inexpensive book and find $100 stuck inside it! And it's very possible that redeeming it will prove even more valuable to you.

- **Extensive Resource directory** — your Oracle UCM "Yellow Pages" that gives you instant access to the most comprehensive collection of resources you can use to keep yourself up to date or get help with your current project. You will find anything from a listing of UCM blogs to a directory of professional services firms that specialize in Oracle UCM space.

- And finally, your free Newsletter Subscription that gets you important updates on this book's content, (especially timely and critical now, when the new UCM 11g is just about to be released) and keeps you abreast of the new tools, features, and techniques. It will force-feed critical information that you need to continue improving your UCM skills without putting any effort into it.

Not only these unique components will help you achieve your professional goals, over time, they will take you straight to Oracle UCM mastery and get you to the top ranks of your team, your company and, maybe even your industry.

And now let me pause for a second and describe the ideal audience — people, who will reap maximum benefits from The Oracle UCM Handbook and this Complete Oracle UCM Mastery System.

What this book covers

In this section I'll quickly guide you through the chapters of the book itself, and show you what each of them will help you achieve.

Chapter 1, Getting Up and Running, is a deluxe walkthrough that takes you over building your personal "sandbox", downloading free unlimited evaluation software, and completing the installation. It also "shows you around the house" to get you instantly familiar with core UCM Document Management.

Chapter 2, Major Controls, guides you through all major controls of Content Server in time it takes to have lunch. Get instantly familiar with operations, diagnostics, and troubleshooting, and also learn how to manager users.

Chapter 3, Metadata, helps you master standard and custom metadata, and learn how to quickly perform complex customizations on Check In, Content Info, and Search screens without a single line of code.

Chapter 4, Understanding Security, gets you a crystal clear understanding of UCM Security Model and how to get it right, the first time around, to avoid costly redesigns.

Chapter 5, Understanding Workflows, explains what UCM workflows can do for you and how to use them. It includes tutorial for advanced workflow design that shows you how to use jumps, sub-workflows, basic and criteria workflows, tokens, and aliases.

Chapter 6, Understanding Virtual Folders and WebDAV, tells you all about Virtual Folders. It is a detailed walkthrough that shows how to set up and use folder structures, so you can bring alive your shared drives and other existing content.

Chapter 7, Under the hood, is an in depth review of the file system, content store, and important utilities (for managing System Configuration and Process Administration), also discover how Content Server is designed to be so lightning-fast.

Chapter 8, Backup, Restore, and Content Migration, shows you how to backup and restore the Content Server like a pro — to avoid devastating data losses. Also learn to use Archiver — to remove inactive content, migrate items to other servers, and mass-update metadata. (This tip alone can white-out days of mind-numbing manual labor from your life's chart).

Chapter 9, Migrating Configuration, shows you how to transfer just the changes you want from Development to Testing and Production environments. Avoid the quicksand of manually applying the same changes to multiple environments.

Chapter 10, Customizing Oracle UCM, introduces you to all the tools and techniques available for altering UCM interface and behavior. It also shows you how to smoothly integrate into your overall organization's infrastructure and avoid dreaded manual data re-entry and multiple "source of truth" repositories that spell disaster for content management systems.

Chapter 11, Web Content Management and Collaboration, is your complete step by step walkthrough of creating killer websites with Site Studio Designer. It walks you through the server-site set up, and how to best use templates, regions, and fragments.

Appendix A, Exploring Oracle UCM Product Offering, gives you an in-depth review of the entire Oracle UCM Product Offering, insider tips, strongest sides, and the caveats you need to be aware of—when using dozens of products and components within the UCM Suite (and how to avoid missing the cut by picking a wrong tool for the job).

Appendix B, Detailed Oracle UCM Resource Directory, is your instant access to many valuable print and online resources, trusted system integrators, UCM training providers and more. Here're just a few categories of resources you will find in *Appendix B*:

- **Free online resources**—a comprehensive listing of UCM-specific and general content-management related blogs, review, and article sites. Many of these hidden gems are not actively promoted and you won't pick them up from a Google search.

- **Best recommended publications**—the few UCM-related books and whitepapers you may find really useful some even indispensable.

- **Trusted System Integrators**—a small list of time-tested, good track record Oracle Partners that specialize in the UCM space.

- **Trusted Training Providers**—just like the System Integrators, this is a small list of vendors you can start with if you're looking for official or customized Oracle UCM training.

- **Value-Added Products and Services**—a list of products that may help you avoid expensive customizations or save you time on content migration and other time consuming initiatives.

Be sure to check your Resource Directory when you are done reading the chapters.

And now let's see what kind of hardware and software you will need to run the examples and follow the tutorials from this book.

What you need for this book

If you want to build your own local copy of the Content Server, to run the examples and follow the tutorials in this book, you will need a Windows (2000, XP, Vista, or Windows 7) desktop or laptop with 5 GB of free disk space and at least, 1GB of RAM. You can also use your existing development or sandbox environment running Oracle Content Server v.10g R3, in which case all you need on your local machine is a web browser.

And now let's get right into the Eight-hour Quick Start System.

Eight-hour quick start system

Welcome to the eight hours quick start! This section is different—it's here to give you a rocket boost to help you get comfortable with Oracle UCM in a hurry. If you are "under the gun" to decide if your project can be accomplished with UCM or you found yourself on a deep end of the pool of a UCM implementation—this section will be the helping hand you need.

Even though the book you're reading right now is the fastest way to master Oracle UCM I know about, this may still not be "fast enough" for what you're trying to accomplish. So how do we force-feed the UCM expertise directly into your brain? The answer may shock and delight you.

We will rely on the famous 80/20 rule. 80 percent of what you really need to learn only takes 20 percent of time to master. The rest of the time is spent on the remaining 20 percent of knowledge!

In this section I'll help you identify the knowledge you need and help you find it within this book at maximum speed.

Ready? Let's get into it. But first, I want to tell you something that will help you get even better results.

Five reasons to feel excited about learning Oracle UCM

I want you to feel this way because you picked a very good product to master. Here's why:

- Oracle is a great company, leader in the marketplace, and offers great support.

- The UCM itself has been around for 14 years, has thousands of happy customers and you'll come to appreciate its speed, simplicity, and reliability.

- I actually challenge you to find an enterprise level UCM solution that can run completely on 512 MB of RAM, fit on a 1 GB flash drive, and run on an outdated laptop! And offer comparable response speed. Most of the tools today are bloated, take an enormous amount of hardware and are slow. Not every laptop or even desktop will let you run a copy or SharePoint 2007. Certainly, not—if you have 2 GB or RAM!

- It doesn't take a lot of effort to configure and learn, which you can actually see by the size of this book! It's not that another thousand page volume with a hundred of pages of dedicated to installation and configuration.

- And it doesn't take two weeks just to get up and running. (In fact, in the first chapter I'll show you how to build and configure your own Content Server in a short afternoon).

So let's take a look at your eight-hour Quick Start System.

What are you going to learn?

There are two types of facts you'll be acquiring today. The basic concepts behind Oracle UCM, that unlock the rest of the knowledge for you, and additional stuff that your project at hand may urgently require.

Required information that you must internalize

No matter what you're planning on doing with Oracle UCM, you need to start with the Content Server. All major UCM modules, such as Document Management, Web Content Management, and Records Management are all based on it.

The best way to get started and understand the base Content Server paradigms is by reading the introduction in *Chapter 1*. Easily enough, it's called "Here's an easy way to understand the Content Server".

> If you're in a rush, don't install your local copy of Content Server at this point. Just flip through the pages and focus on introductions, summaries, headers, and illustrations.
>
> Not sure what this sentence is trying to say! When you're learning at a maximum speed, you need to go for the "bird eye" view of all of the content.

Once you have a feel for how it works, take it a bit deeper and learn more about metadata and security. These are the two most important aspects of any Content Server implementation, and the one that you must understand in order to succeed.

I'm not asking you to carefully read and study the chapters at this point. You're after the "what" question, not the "how". Flip through the pages and see:

- What metadata is used for

- What's involved in creating a metadata model

- What are the basic concepts of Content Server Security
- How different security components fit together

At this point, you will find yourself a lot more comfortable and ready to focus on your specific UCM assignment.

Other stuff you might find useful

If you plan on doing some hands-on Content Server administration, review *Chapter 2, Major Controls*. This will get you instantly familiar with operations, diagnostics, and UCM troubleshooting, and show you how to manage users.

If you are planning on customizing Oracle UCM, skim *Chapter 7* and *Chapter 10*. This will give you important insights about the inner workings of Content Server, its key file formats and all the tools, and choices you have for customizing its interface and behavior.

And if you are working or planning to work with a vendor then be sure to review the section called *Five ways to maximize results and avoid disaster when working with a UCM vendor* in *Chapter 10*. These street-tough project success tips will help you reduce your risk and avoid severe penalties to your budget, timeline, and your system functionality.

And last, but not least, I urge you to scan through *Appendix A* and get yourself familiar with the entire Oracle UCM product line up. Not only you will see how other modules integrate with Content Server, you will see what other tools and integration options you have at your disposal.

That's it. How did you do? Still have a bit of time left of your eight hours? Then how about some activity? Why not have a little fun with actually installing your own local copy of the Content Server? Or you can simply skim *Chapter 1* and see what it takes to install.

Quick start summary

Congratulations! You've just accomplished something that a vast majority of technical people cannot even dream possible. You've got yourself a solid understanding of Oracle UCM—in just under eight short hours. I agree, you may not be ready to take over a high volume production environment, but I'm sure, you can find your way around it.

So now, let's pick up everything we've left off in the first reading. Let's get some practice and get you bumped up to next level of Oracle UCM mastery.

And before I see you in *Chapter 1*, let's take one quick important step that will literally put your learning on auto-pilot and help you achieve your career objectives faster than you ever dreamed possible.

Your fastest way to Oracle UCM mastery

You will soon be finished with the book material, but it doesn't mean you will not continue to benefit from it for years to come, and I don't mean re-reading the chapters when you need a refresher. That goes without saying...

What I do mean is the fact that any book is limited in what the author can relate to you. And you need a steady flow of insider information to keep you up in the top ranks of your chosen filed, any field. And Oracle UCM is no exception.

That's why, to thank you for investing in this book, I've set aside your own private and personal spot in the **Independent Oracle UCM Knowledge Center**. Claim it and you will accomplish these three critical objectives:

- You will receive important updates to this book's content. Those will be especially timely and critical now, when the new *UCM 11g is just about to be released*. I'll keep you in the loop on how what you've just learned will apply to the new version, and what new features you can use to get things done better and faster.

- You will stay abreast of the new tools, features and techniques, no matter whether or not they were covered in this book at all. And the most precious gift I can give you is the fact that...

- You will stay motivated about mastering Oracle UCM and reaping the maximum benefit it can give your organization and your career.

Imagine waking up in the morning feeling yourself on the top of your profession. Going to work, mentally repeating to yourself "I'm the best! In my team... In my company... I'm the best!", and knowing in your heart of hearts, **IT'S TRUE!**

Few people are really motivated to learn anything. Even fewer are keeping their skills updated on a regular basis. Just a tiny number of brave souls can keep themselves on top—week after week, month after month...

A few short months from now you can easily be considered a top Oracle UCM expert in your team, your company and, maybe even your industry.

And here's the secret of...

How to quickly get on top and stay there

Feel at ease and relaxed when everyone else is painfully grinding out every little bit of knowledge they acquire. And the secret (and the fastest) way to the top is simply *to be on the right bus!*

Let me explain. It's tough to make yourself learn something new every day, and many people run out of enthusiasm almost immediately. So why not try the other way? Why not simply subscribe to an e-mail list and let the publisher do the hard work? All you need to do is look over the tips, tricks, and trade secrets you receive right in your in-box, and use them to your advantage.

One day I'll ask you to read a short article. The other day, it will be a three minute screen cast video, and before you know it, you will find yourself in the top ranks of Oracle UCM.

Don't miss your bus. Stop by www.stellentexperts.com/handbook and pick up your free subscription. This elite community of professionals is not open to just anyone. I don't want the tire-kickers and wannabes as subscribers. That's why I'm keeping this subscription page hidden.

Your subscription will also help you get the most of this book's content and digest it even faster. So don't delay. These great insider tips, tricks, in-depth articles, and exclusive special offers are only e-mailed once and will not be repeated. Why is this important?

Let me give you an example. The all-new UCM 11gR1 has just been released, and while most of this book's content still applies to the new version, a few specific areas (such as installation and user management) have been changed. I'll be covering those in a series of articles. But if you miss out on, say the one covering the installation — you will have to study the Installation Guides and make your own mistakes, and you don't need to waste your days on trial and error!

I've already seen this mistakes being made and have the solution ready for you. All you need to do is simply this: go to www.stellentexperts.com/handbook and claim your free Oracle UCM continuing education.

Sincerely,

Dmitri Khanine

Dmitri Khanine

P.S. You are not risking anything by subscribing to this free exclusive newsletter. Your email address will never be sold, traded or misused, and you can unsubscribe at any time. You have nothing to lose and everything to gain. Don't risk missing out on this great career booster. Subscribe now, while this information is still fresh in your mind.

Who this book is for

This book and this system is for all IT professionals — who would like to win an unfair advantage of Oracle UCM mastery for their project and their jackpot career, and for Oracle Stellent UCM Users, Administrators, and Developers who're ready to jump up to the next level of expertise.

Conventions

In this book, you will find a number of styles of text that distinguish between different kinds of information. Here are some examples of these styles, and an explanation of their meaning.

Code words in text are shown as follows: "Close all of your browser windows and re-login to Content Server as sysadmin."

A block of code is set as follows:

```
<html>
<body>

Hello <strong><$UserFullName$></strong><br/>
Your login name is <$UserName$>,<br/>
your roles are <$UserRoles$><br/>
and your accounts are <$UserAccounts$>

</body>
</html>
```

When we wish to draw your attention to a particular part of a code block, the relevant lines or items are set in bold:

```
<table border="0">
   <tr valign="top">
     <td>
         <!--SS_BEGIN_ELEMENT(region1_element1)-->
```

```
<!--$ssIncludeXml(SS_DATAFILE,region1_element1 &
    "/node()")-->
```

Any command-line input or output is written as follows:

```
C:\oracle\ucm\server\bin>IdcCommand.exe -f c:\Temp\create_folder.hda -u
sysadmin  -l c:\Temp\log.txt -c auto
```

New terms and **important words** are shown in bold. Words that you see on the screen, in menus or dialog boxes for example, appear in the text like this: "They were moved to the **Trash** folder".

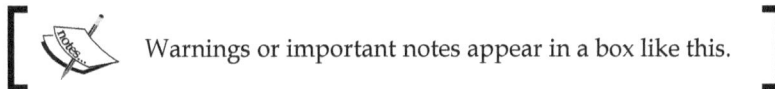

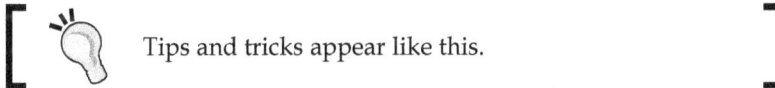

> Warnings or important notes appear in a box like this.

> Tips and tricks appear like this.

Reader feedback

Feedback from our readers is always welcome. Let us know what you think about this book—what you liked or may have disliked. Reader feedback is important for us to develop titles that you really get the most out of.

To send us general feedback, simply send an e-mail to feedback@packtpub.com, and mention the book title via the subject of your message.

If there is a book that you need and would like to see us publish, please send us a note in the **SUGGEST A TITLE** form on www.packtpub.com or e-mail suggest@packtpub.com.

If there is a topic that you have expertise in and you are interested in either writing or contributing to a book, see our author guide on www.packtpub.com/authors.

Customer support

Now that you are the proud owner of a Packt book, we have a number of things to help you to get the most from your purchase.

Errata

Although we have taken every care to ensure the accuracy of our content, mistakes do happen. If you find a mistake in one of our books—maybe a mistake in the text or the code—we would be grateful if you would report this to us. By doing so, you can save other readers from frustration and help us improve subsequent versions of this book. If you find any errata, please report them by visiting http://www.packtpub.com/support, selecting your book, clicking on the **let us know** link, and entering the details of your errata. Once your errata are verified, your submission will be accepted and the errata will be uploaded on our website, or added to any list of existing errata, under the Errata section of that title. Any existing errata can be viewed by selecting your title from http://www.packtpub.com/support.

Piracy

Piracy of copyright material on the Internet is an ongoing problem across all media. At Packt, we take the protection of our copyright and licenses very seriously. If you come across any illegal copies of our works, in any form, on the Internet, please provide us with the location address or website name immediately so that we can pursue a remedy.

Please contact us at copyright@packtpub.com with a link to the suspected pirated material.

We appreciate your help in protecting our authors, and our ability to bring you valuable content.

Questions

You can contact us at questions@packtpub.com if you are having a problem with any aspect of the book, and we will do our best to address it.

Getting Up and Running

1

In this chapter you will accomplish two important objectives — you will build your own portable **Oracle Universal Content Management** (**Oracle UCM**) environment and you will understand the basics of the Content Server and major Content Management paradigms. More specifically, you will learn:

- How to obtain your free unlimited evaluation version of Oracle UCM products

- How to set up the Content Server in just an hour or two, and how to steer clear of nasty installation problems

- A maximum speed introduction to Content Server that will make you instantly familiar (and comfortable) with it

- Required knowledge and basic principles you must internalize — about Content Management in general, that will help you avoid devastating losses, no matter what CMS tool you use

Ready? Let's get started with a quick overview.

Installation overview

A few years ago, we made a mistake during a server upgrade and had to spend two days restoring from a tape backup. Technology changed since then and you can avoid our mistakes. Now you have more memory in a basic laptop than we had in our servers!

You can have a copy of your entire production environment run on a single machine and you can "dry-run" important upgrades and installations, before you even consider applying them to your live production servers.

And it doesn't even take a lot of resources. So why not put your spare RAM to good use? Let's bring up Oracle Content Server in a **virtual environment**.

What do I mean by "virtual environment"? Let's see this in more detail.

Quick primer on virtual environments

A Virtual Machine (a VM) is "an efficient, isolated duplicate of a real machine."
    Source: Wikipedia

It's an image of a physical machine. For example, if you use Microsoft Virtual PC, it runs in its own process and looks like a window on the desktop—like a Remote Desktop Connection window.

It has its own virtual hard disk or two, its own virtual network connections, and much more. You can even run a web server on a VM and browse it from your desktop.

The physical machine running VMs is called a **host machine**.

You can in fact back up your server or your workstation and restore that image into a VM, and run that virtual machine on your laptop or desktop computer.

You can have multiple machines running at the same time or you can have the entire server farm running off your laptop (as shown in the following screenshot).

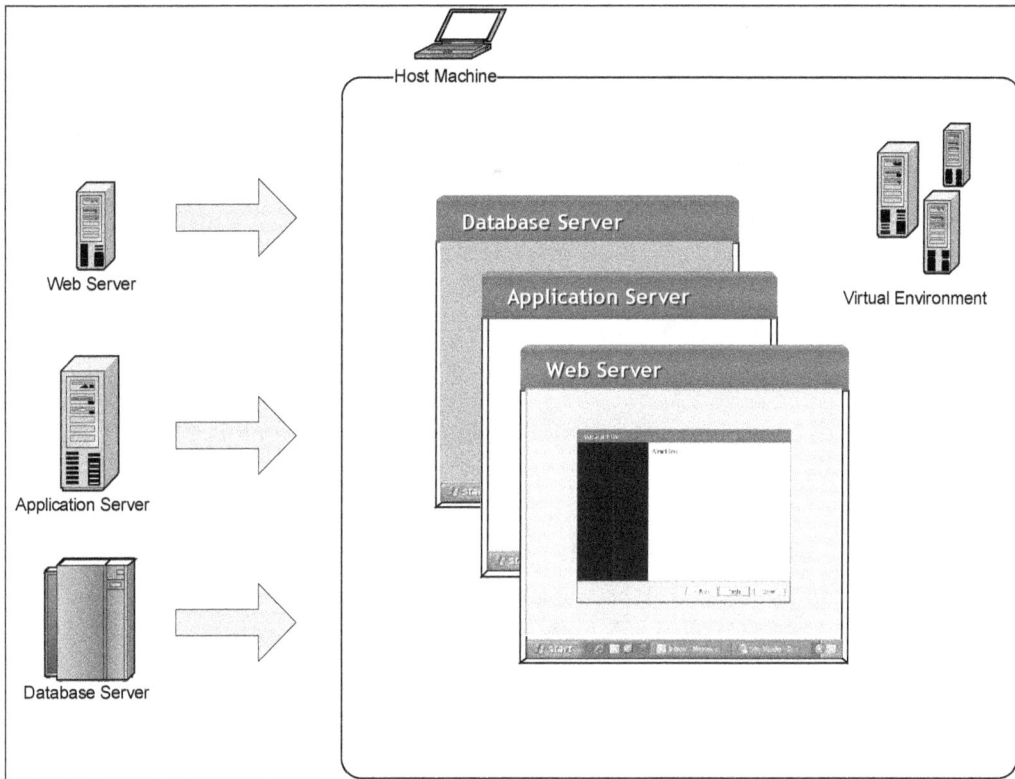

We will be using this feature in the following chapters.

Running Oracle Content Server in a virtual environment offers you some important benefits that can slash days and even weeks off your learning curve:

- You can always undo anything that went wrong.
- **Guest OS**, the VM's Operating System has absolutely no affect and may even have no access to your host. Even if you're running a deadly virus on your VM you may be completely safe.
- You'll be able to take the VM with you; moving it to another machine is a simple file copy operation.

I hope I have you convinced. And now it's time to get our tools ready.

Get your tools ready

Let's get ready to install Oracle UCM.

Content Server can work with a number of different databases. I suggest we use Microsoft SQL Server. Why?

Because chances are that you are running Windows and familiar with basic administration. Also, Microsoft offers an evaluation version of SQL Server, so you won't have to spend time installing the OS and a database server.

You can download SQL Server 2005 on Windows 2003 Server — installed and pre-configured for you in a virtual environment. It's ready to use.

All you need to do is get Oracle Content Server, and install it on this VM. In fact, I am going to walk you through the process.

Download your test VM

I'm not giving you the exact link because links change quite often. Type these words in Google: **download SQL server VHD**.

> What's **VHD**?
> It's an extension of Virtual Hard Disk files that you can run with Microsoft Virtual PC.

Find a link from a Microsoft site and download your virtual machine.

You will need Microsoft Virtual PC to run it. Again, right now, the current version is 2007. It's a free download from Microsoft site.

Type into Google: **download Microsoft virtual PC**. You'll get the download link.

Install Virtual PC on a machine where you will be running your VMs.

> **How much RAM should you have?**
> I recommend that you have at least 512 MB of RAM that you have to spare on top of your daily essentials. 1 GB on the host is the minimum.

Once you have the VHD unzipped and Microsoft virtual PC 2007 installed on your machine — you're ready to run your VM.

The last thing you need is the actual copy of the Content Server.

Getting a copy of Oracle UCM

To get the Oracle UCM follow these steps:

1. Go to `http://edelivery.oracle.com/`. Here you will get a page as shown in the following screenshot; click on **Continue**:

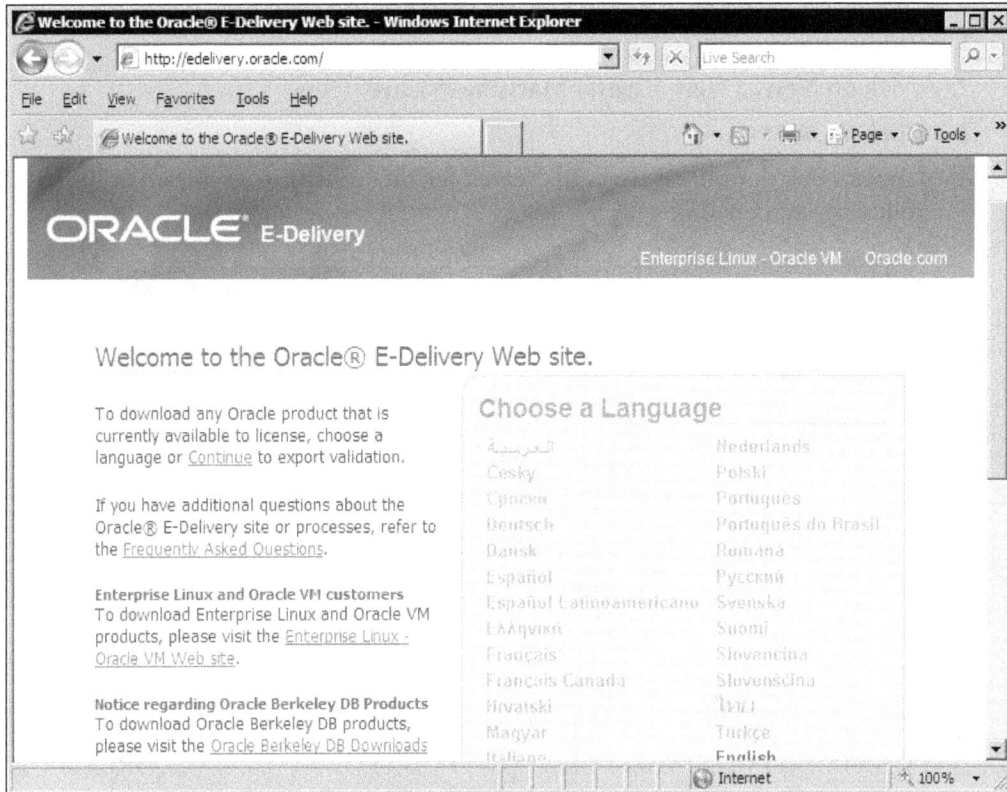

2. Enter your first and last name and your company information. Accept the terms and click on **Continue** to proceed.

3. In the next page, select **Oracle Fusion Middleware** as the product pack and **Microsoft Windows (32 bit)** as platform and click on **Go**.

4. Pick **Oracle® Enterprise Content Management 10g Release 3 (10.1.3) Media Pack** and click on **Continue**.

5. Now out of the available options download **Oracle Content Server 10gR3 (10.1.3.3.3) for Microsoft Windows (32-bit)**.

While your Content Server is downloading, we can use the time for getting the VM ready.

Getting the VM ready for Content Server

In this section I'll walk you through the steps of using MS Virtual PC 2007 to run the VHD file you've just downloaded, and how to configure it best to save time when you will be installing the Content Server.

Let's get started:

1. Run Virtual PC 2007.

2. Click on **New...**; **New Virtual Machine Wizard** opens.

3. Click on **Next**.

4. Choose **Use default settings to create a virtual machine** as shown in the following screenshot:

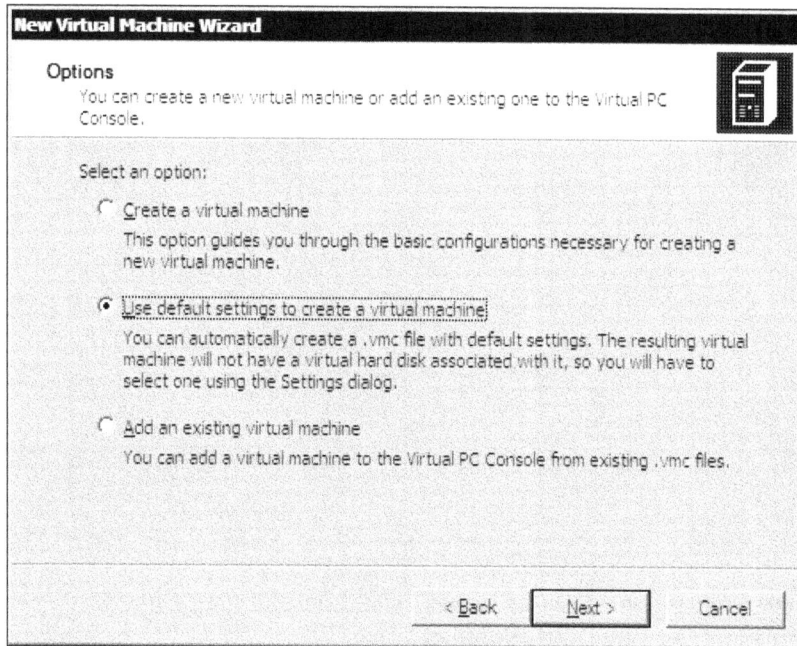

5. Give the VM a name and a location.

How to save a few gigabytes of disk space

I recommend putting a VM in an *NTFS compressed* folder. The default location is My Virtual Machines in My Documents folder. You can compress that to save a few gigabytes. Remember, VMs are the images of actual machines. Files get pretty large.

6.   Click on **Next**.

7.   Click on **Finish**. Virtual Machine settings dialog opens.

8.   Give your VM 512 or 1024 MB of RAM depending on how much RAM you have to spare.

9.   Select **Hard Disk 1** as shown in the following screenshot:

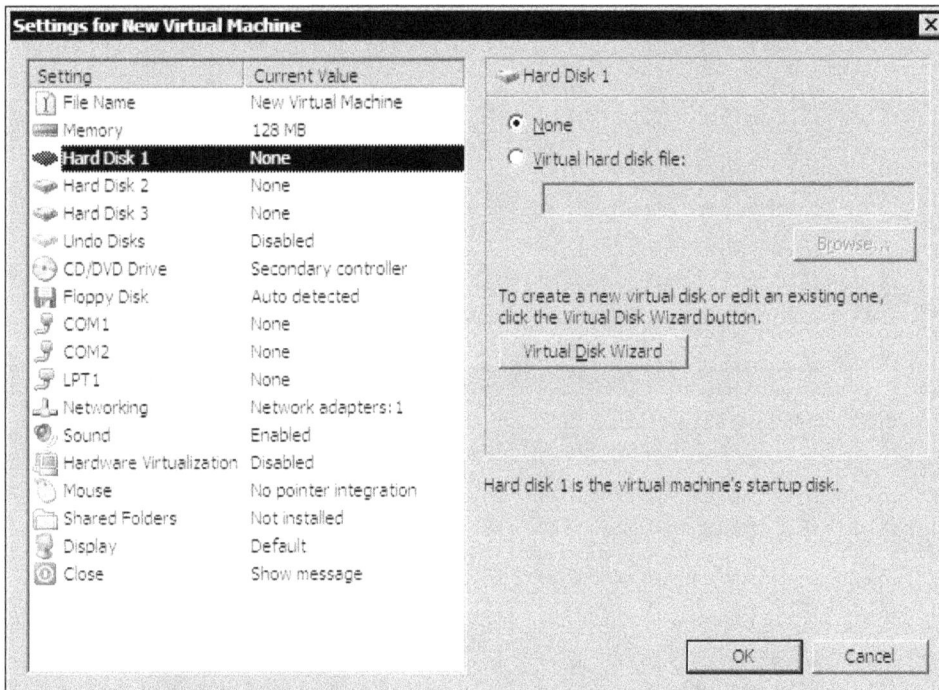

10.   Click on **Virtual Disk Wizard**.

11.   Click on **Next**; leave **Create a new virtual disk** selected.

12.   Pickle **A virtual hard disk** and click on **Next**.

13. Pick a location. I recommend putting it in the same folder where you created your VM. See the following screenshot:

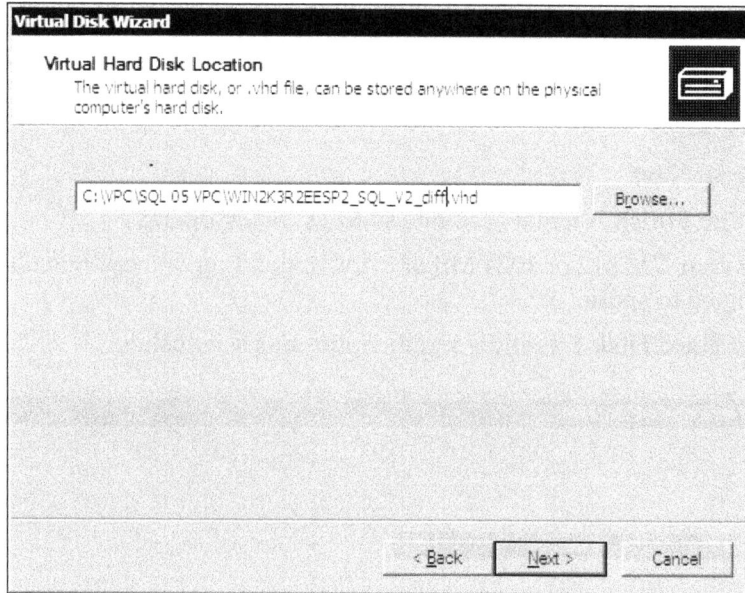

14. Now click on **Next**.

15. Pick **Differencing** as shown in the following screenshot:

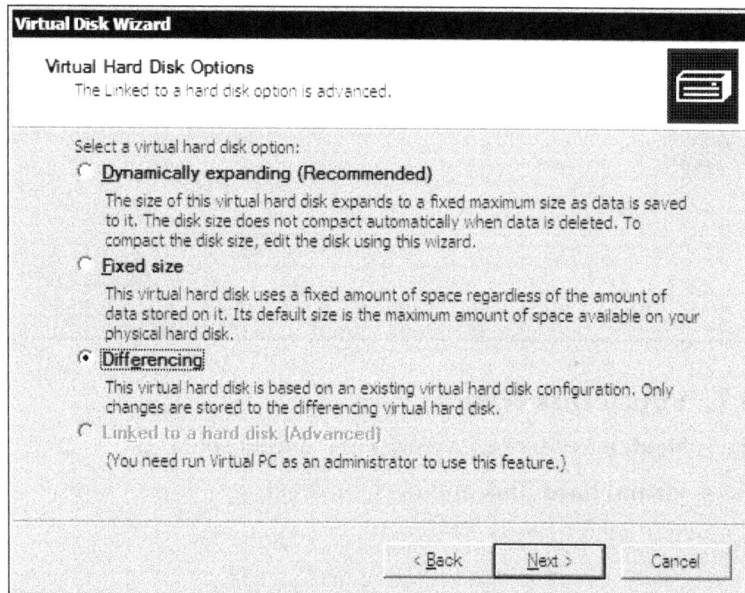

16. Pick the parent VHD file—the one you downloaded from Microsoft.

17. Keep **Undo Disks** disabled for now.

18. Click on **OK** to close settings dialog.

19. On a Virtual PC Console click on **Start** button.

Watch your VM start... Aren't you excited yet?

1. Once the VM displays a login prompt—log in with `Administrator` and a password from `Readme.htm` that came with the VHD. Mine was `Evaluation1`.

2. Open SQL Server Management Studio.

3. Click on **Connect**.

4. Expand **Security Logins** on the tree view on your left.

5. Right-click on **Logins**. Pick **New Login**.

6. Create a user that your Content Server will use to connect to SQL Server. Make sure you use **SQL Server authentication** and **Enforce password expiration** is off.

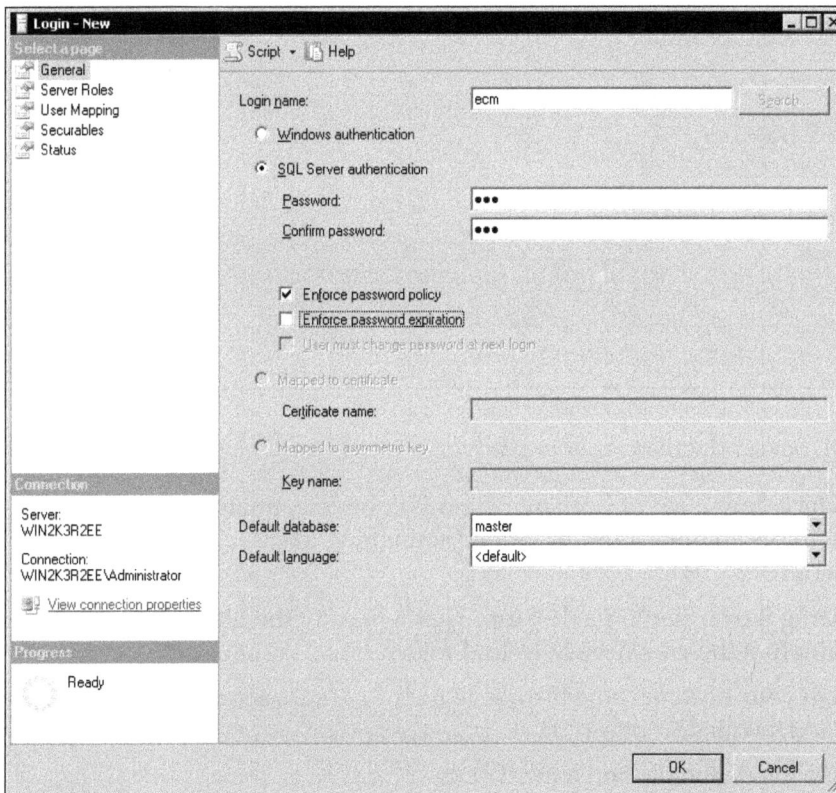

7. Right-click on **Databases** and pick **New Database**.

8. Give it a name. Make sure you specify the user you've just created as database owner:

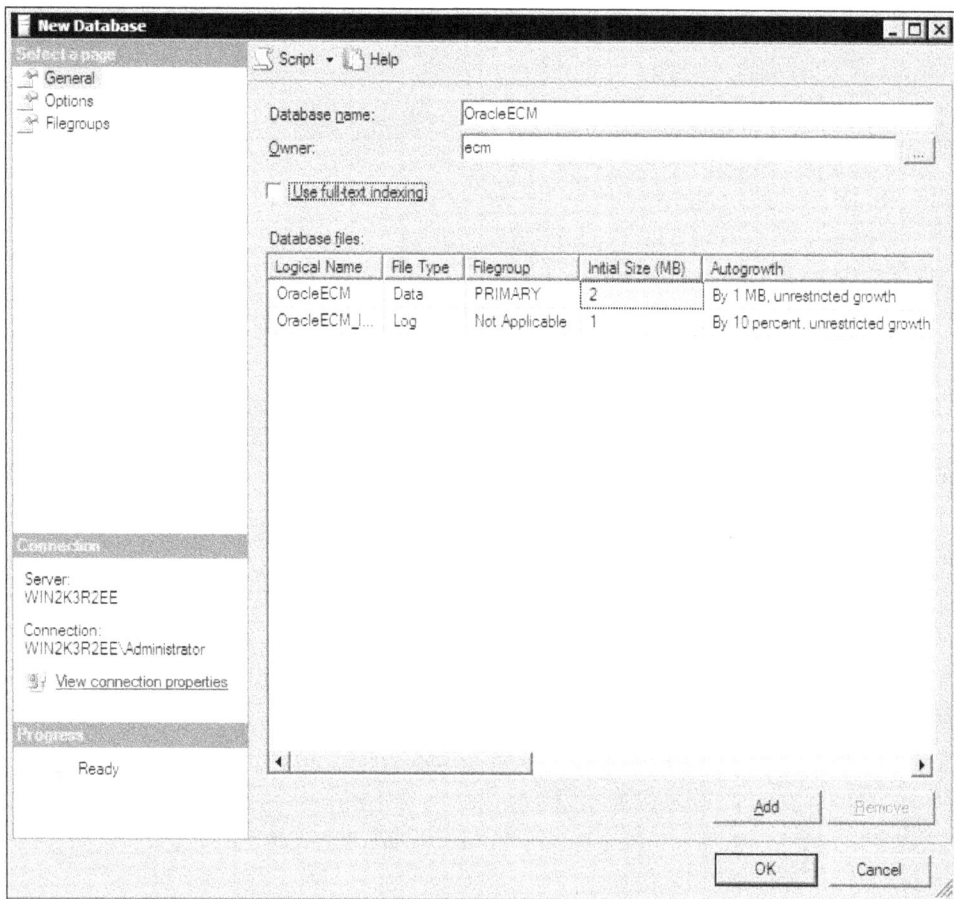

Your SQL Server database is now ready.

1. Once download of Content Server is complete, unzip the file. You will see an inner ZIP file, named something like: `ContentServer_Windows_10gR3_20080807.zip`.

2. Drag it over the VM's desktop. That will copy the file over to the VM. Unzip it there to an easy-to-find folder, like `c:\install`.

3. On your host machine browse to `http://jtds.sourceforge.net/`. Go Download. Save `jtds-1.2.x-dist.zip`.

4. Go inside the file and extract `jtds-1.2.x.jar`.

5. Drag the `.jar` (NOT `.zip`) file over to your VM. Place it into the installation directory.

The installation directory on your VM should look something like this:

Great! You've now completed all the pre-work and are ready to install a copy of Content Server.

Wait! There's something else I want you to do. I bet you'll like the next step.

In case you make a mistake and would like to re-run the installation—I don't want you to go through all the steps you just completed. Virtual PC gives us the power to save you from doing that.

1. Click on Windows **Start** button and shutdown your VM.

2. Once it stops running, go the **Settings** and enable **Undo Disks**.

3. Start the VM.

Now you can always get back to the "Ready to install" step in just a few seconds!

Suppose you made a mistake and would like to start over. Just click on the X on the top right corner of the VM window and pick **Turn off and delete changes**. When you start the VM, it will be back in the state in which it last started!

Say, your VM with Undo Disks enabled was infected and completely destroyed by a virus. All you need to do is **Turn off and delete changes** (as shown in the following screenshot)! Love it! The power of Undo Disks...

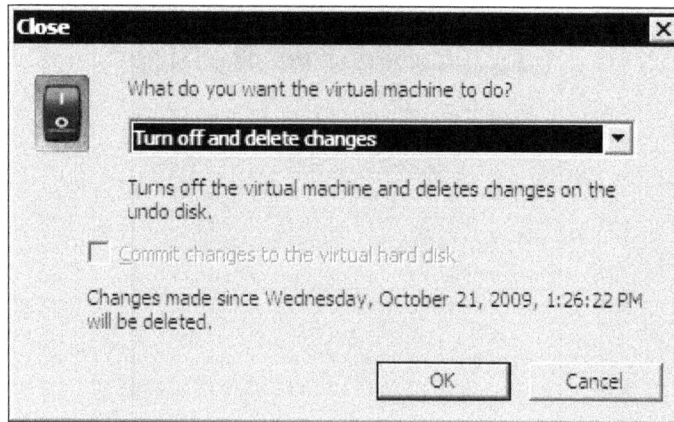

> Don't pick **Turn off and delete changes** unless you really want to go back. You can lose your work!

I hope you're not out of steam yet! It was a long prep-work. Normally, if you just install the UCM on a physical server, you'll be starting in the Lab 1 section. Just trust me, getting your VM ready was time well spent. You'll thank me later!

Lab 1: Install content server

Welcome to the actual Content Server installation process! It's time to benefit from all that prep work:

1. Start the VM.
2. Once it is started, in your installation directory there go to
   `UCM\ContentServer\win32`.
3. Start `installer.exe`. The Installer opens as shown in the following screenshot:

```
C:\Download\UCM\ContentServer\win32\Installer.exe                    _ □ ✕

Please select your locale from the list.
            1. Chinese-Simplified
            2. Chinese-Traditional
            3. Deutsch
          *4. English-US
            5. English-UK
            6. Español
            7. Français
            8. Italiano
            9. Japanese
           10. Korean
           11. Nederlands
           12. Português-Brazil
Choice?
```

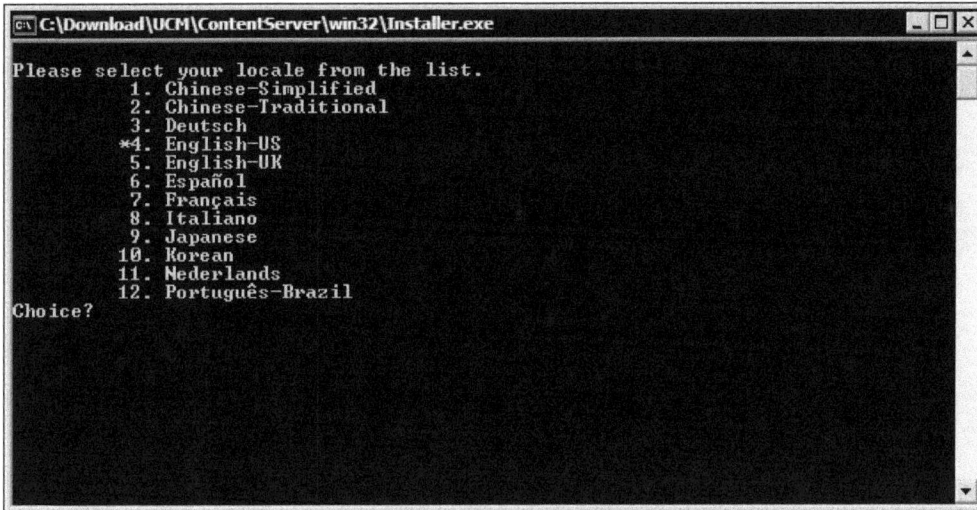

Installer is a cross-platform application. It looks the same on UNIX and Windows. It takes a few seconds to get used to, but it has its own advantages....

In case you didn't guess, an asterisk designates a currently selected option. If you're OK to proceed just press *Enter*. If you need to change the option, type in the new choice and then press *Enter*.

4. `*1. Install new server`—just press *Enter*. The default choice is fine.

5. Hit *Enter* to install in a default directory.

6. Hit *Enter* to go with `default JVM`.

7. Just keep on pressing *Enter* to accept default choices for all directories.

8. Hit *Enter* to pick default option that is `*1. Configure as a master server`.

9. Keep going with defaults until you see a database selection prompt. It reads `"Please select a database from the list below to use with the Content Server. Content Server Database"`.

10. Type 2 then hit *Enter*. You're choosing Microsoft SQL Server 2005.

11. JDBC driver `classname []:`—use `net.sourceforge.jtds.jdbc.Driver`.

12. JDBC connection string `[]`—use `jdbc:jtds:sqlserver://Win2k3R2EE:1433/OracleUCM`; I assume your machine name is `win2k3R2EE` and your database name is `OracleUCM`.

13. `Database User ID`—type up the user ID you picked for your database. If you followed the screenshots, you should have UCM for yours.

14. Specify the DB password.

15. `JDBC driver .jar file path []` — type the path to the JAR file that was inside that ZIP folder you downloaded from SourceForge. If you followed my instructions — use `C:\install\jtds-1.2.4.jar`.

16. Go with defaults to `Copy JDBC driver files`, `Attempt to create database tables` and `Use Unicode text fields`.

17. The installer asks you to select components to install. Hit 1 then *Enter* to select Content Folios. Also select `Folders_g`. Hit *F* and then *Enter* to continue.

18. Pick `default` under `Configure the Administration Server service`.

19. Pick 2 to say `No` to `Configure the admin service to run as a specific user`. This will have a service run as a Local System on Windows.

20. Continue with the default `No` for `Configure admin service to be dependent on another service`.

21. Default to Configure the Content Server service. `*1. Install service and start automatically` is fine.

22. Pick 2 to say `No` to `Configure the service to run as a specific user`.

23. Continue with default choices but **don't proceed with the install yet**.

Right before you proceed be sure to check the content of `C:\oracle\ucm\server\install\log.txt`. Right-click on it and open it with WordPad. as shown in the following screenshot:

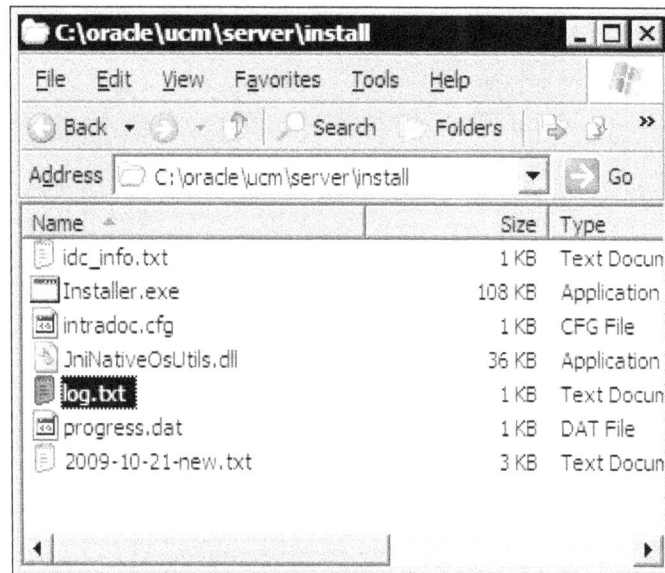

Oops! You bet I'm happy I didn't go ahead now. I've accidentally added a space in my JDBC connection string as shown in the following screenshot:

If you see errors in `log.txt` — choose **Change Configuration** and correct the mistakes. It will be even easier this time around. All the choices you made are still there and you'll just have to keep on pressing *Enter*.

Choose **Proceed** to continue with the installation.

Once install is complete, check the log file once again. Search for the word `Error`. If you see errors, you'll know what went wrong and what to expect from the installation.

> We just completed installation of a fresh instance of Content Server. You can later use a similar procedure for upgrades. You can also install additional Content Server instances on the same machine.

How to hold on to your success

Hopefully, you have no errors in your `log.txt` file and your installation was successful. Now it's a good time to take a snapshot of your VM. Why?

So you can feel safe about playing with it. You'll always be able to get back to this "just installed" state.

Here's how you do it. Click on Windows Start button on your VM and shut it down. When shutdown is complete, you have a choice of committing or discarding the changes you made to the machine since the last save. Pick **Commit changes to the virtual hard disk** as shown in the following screenshot:

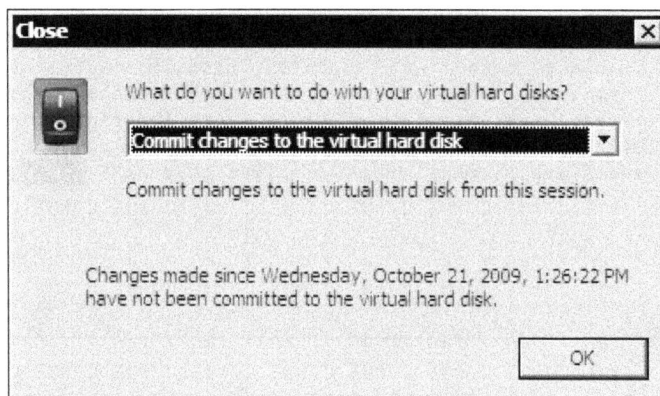

Congratulations! You've just completed your installation. Now let me show you around.

Here's an easy way to understand the Content Server

Oracle Content Server is the foundation of Oracle Universal Content Management Suite. It's the center product. Other major UCM modules, such as Web Content Management and Document Management are built on top of it.

Think of the Content Server as a central database for storing content. A database analogy is the easiest way to understand it.

In fact, you can think of a Content Server as one huge table that can store millions of records.

And the only major difference between Content Server and a database server is the fact that every record in it has revisions and can go through the workflow.

Every row in the table would be a single **content item**. Every field in that row would be a **metadata field** — just like in a table in SQL Server or Oracle or MySQL, or any other database you are comfortable with.

And just like a row in a table you can add and remove fields to fit your organization's requirements.

Every database, as you know, has standard or system fields. And just the same way Oracle Content Server has pre-defined metadata fields; the **system metadata** fields. It also has **custom metadata** fields.

Let's take a quick look:

1. On your VM, go to `http://localhost/idc`. You'll see a login screen as seen in the screenshot below.

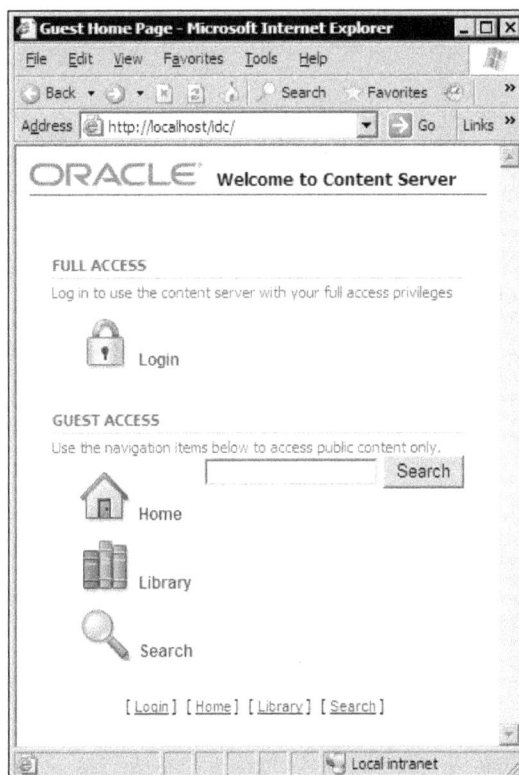

2. Click on the **Login** link. Type **sysadmin** for user name and **idc** for the password. Your Content Server Home page loads as shown in the following screenshot:

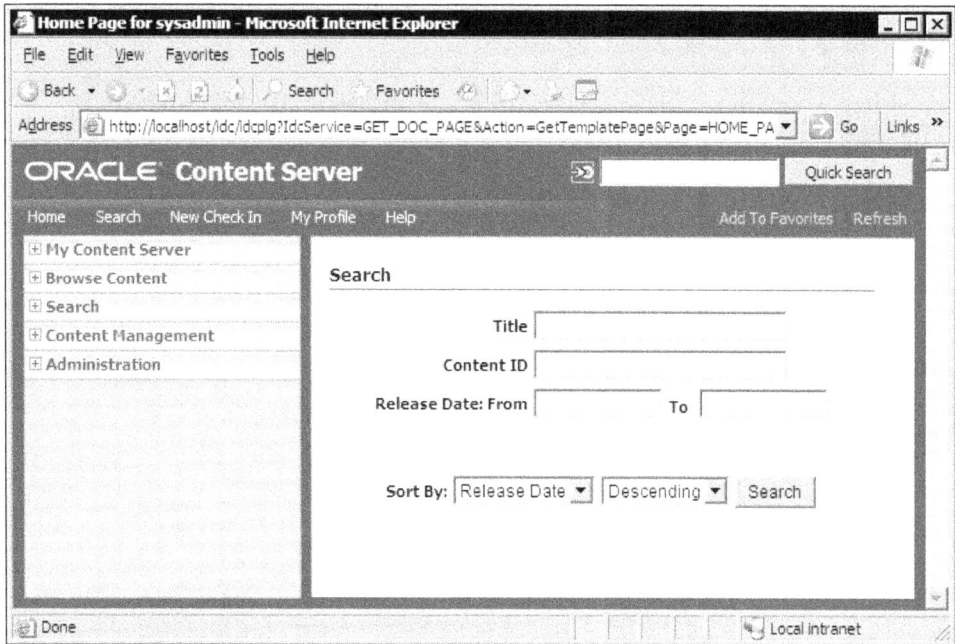

3. Now click on **New Check In**. The check-in form loads as shown in the following screenshot:

Ugly, isn't it? Imagine getting your end users to fill a form like this every time they have a document to check in! The good news is that you can easily personalize this form with custom rules and only show the fields you want your users to see.

Did you notice that some of the field names have an asterisk in front of them? Yes, those values are required, but in our case, those are system fields. Here's a quick description of some of the major metadata fields you'll be sure to deal with:

- **Content ID**: A unique identifier of the content item in the system.
- **Type** (content type): A built-in metadata field that allows you to specify a broad category for this content item, such as "Vendor Invoice", "Human Resources", or "Project Plan".
- **Security Group**: A metadata field that controls an item's security. I will give you later in the following chapters.
- **Comments**: A place for extra info about the content item. This filed is *custom* or *extended* metadata.
- **Release Date**: The date this item is "released" into the system. In most cases, that would be the date of its original check in.

Custom metadata fields are the ones that you can define and manage and even delete if you wish. System metadata fields, such as content ID or title, are part of the system and are required for Content Server to function properly.

You can use metadata values to find content in the database and you can search by any combination of fields. Content Server even has a simple, almost SQL-like query language. Or you can search by individual field just like in Windows Explorer you can search files by name or modification dates.

But that's where the similarity ends. Unlike Windows Explorer, you don't necessarily have a folder structure in Content Server. The actual content store is flat like a database table.

But most organizations prefer to use hierarchies such as shared drives, file plans, retention schedules, and so on. Can you continue to use them with Content Server? Yes, you can!

Your users can continue benefiting from taxonomies, from the knowledge your organization has accumulated, and you can continue using that filing system if it still works well for business folks.

Each content item may be associated with a **virtual folder**. Remember, the content is not physically stored in that folder. It is just linked to it so that users can also find it that way—in addition to using the search feature.

Virtual folders provide users a convenient and familiar metaphor for storage and classification. Content Server folders may be browsed just like other, familiar systems.

We will have a longer discussion on Virtual Folders once we get to *Chapter 7, Under the Hood*.

How to get content in

If you click on the quick search button on the top right of your screen, you will see that your Content Server is empty. Let's check something in.

On the check-in screen find the **Primary File** field and click on the **Browse** button. Pick any small file, like readme.htm. Specify values for the required fields and click on the **Check In** button at the bottom. The **Check in Confirmation** dialog is displayed as shown in the following screenshot:

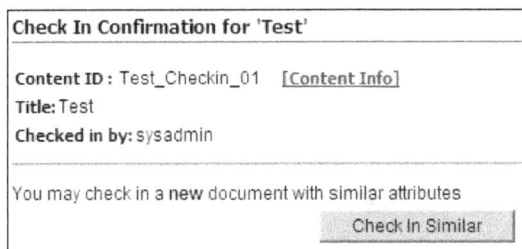

Now wait for 30 seconds or so for the new file to get indexed. Click on the **Quick Search** button at the top right corner. Your newly checked-in content should appear in the search results:

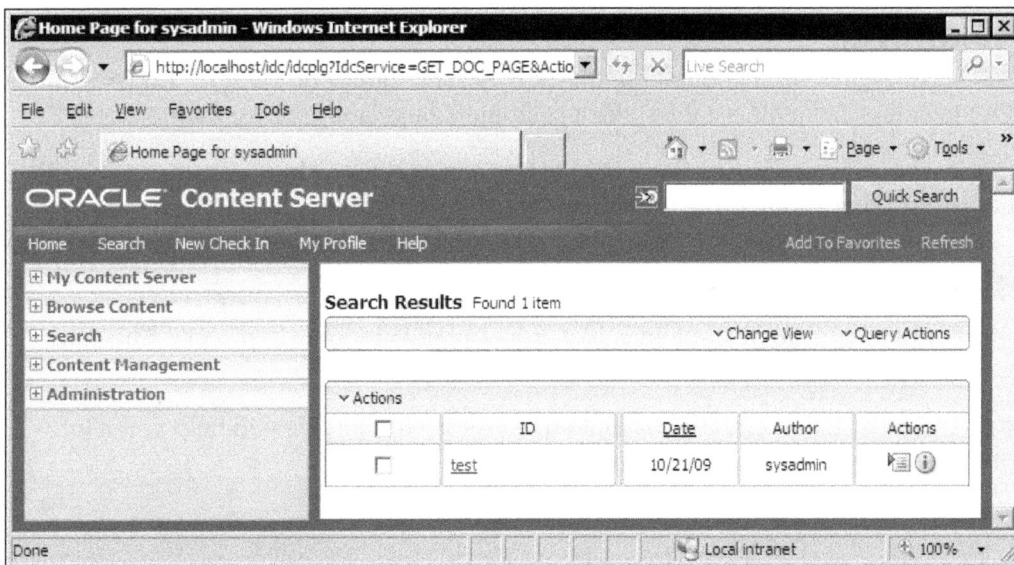

There are multiple ways to contribute content. Using the check-in form is one of the most popular.

Remember, you can make the check-in form look almost any way you like with just a few minutes of simple configuration. And you can have multiple versions of the form—for different types of content you check in... We will take a deeper look at the Metadata in *Chapter 4, Understanding Security*.

The building blocks of a content management system

I mean, important things you need to understand, even if you use SharePoint, Open Text, or Interwoven, there're some things all ECM systems have in common.

I'm not going to bore you with a long tutorial in ECM. Let me just give you the core concepts you need to understand and keep in mind when designing your system.

Storage paradigms

Storage paradigms are how your data is represented in the system. How your users interact with it. How they find content.

There are two major storage paradigms; Relational and Hierarchical. Let's take a look at these one by one.

Relational

This is your conventional database like SQL Server, Oracle or MySQL. Tables can refer to values from other tables like a customers table and table of their orders.

This is what Content Server Store is like. Don't expect the values to "propagate from the parent", that's something the other storage paradigm would do.

Hierarchical

This is what a typical file system is like. Remember Windows Explorer... This goes back to our discussion of virtual folders earlier in this chapter.

Just remember that hierarchy in Content Server is *virtual*. This will help you a lot when planning metadata and permissions.

Metadata

Metadata is the description of data. When you buy a book, you want to know the author, the title, and publication date. This is metadata. The title of the movie and names of the actors are metadata. The names of the songs you see in your CD player are metadata. Without it, you won't be able to pick a book by its title, won't know who's playing in the movie until you have watched it, and won't know the title of the song you're listening to.

Metadata is extremely important. In *Chapter 4*, I'll show you how to define and use custom fields, and how to make your check-in form look exactly the way you want it.

And the last building block I want you to look at is the Content lifecycle.

Content lifecycle

Here's what Content Management really mean. Your business can only benefit from an ECM system when these four stages of content lifecycle are in place:

Contribution

The system cannot manage content that it doesn't know about. So you need to ask your system to take in a document or a web page before it becomes **managed** content. This is what a process of Check In does for you.

Once checked-in, the content item is in storage.

Storage

The system stores the content in its repository, or links it to external content store. In any event, each record in the repository, each content item has metadata associated with it.

Once stored, the content item is ready for consumption.

Consumption

This is when your content begins to bring business value. If you have a Word document in the repository and would like that content to display on a web page, Dynamic Converter, a Content Server component, can create a web-viewable rendition.

If you'd like a PDF version to send out to customers, a PDF Converter component will do just that. And you don't need to update three different copies. One document can have many renditions.

Once the content reaches the end of its life cycle, it's ready for disposition.

Disposition

When an employee terminates, his or her profile needs to be taken out of the company directory. Old files that are no longer used are wasting your disk space and indexing cycles.

When a corporate deal is complete, you don't want to keep your records longer than required by law. Some of the files may have information that, in case of a lawsuit, you'd much rather had been destroyed. But people forget and the content may still be there. A delight for an opposing party's law firm!

So Content Server gives you expiry and archiving controls (We'll be looking at those in *Chapter 4* and *Chapter 10, Customizing Oracle UCM*). If you need more functionality, Oracle offers a Content Server add-on for a DOD 5015.2-compliant Records Management System.

Top 3 common rollout mistakes that spell "failure" in any UCM project

These are more fundamental mistakes than security flaws and bad hardware choices. I'm talking project killers, things that are sure to take your project under. And the worst thing of all is when your new Oracle UCM is not accepted by your organization. If that happens—your project is finished! When people don't like your system, they won't be using it. When they are not using the system, no one can benefit from it. End of story.

Now, let's look a little deeper. What does it take to get people to use it? Let's consider the requirements.

Integration into organization culture

Oracle UCM just like SharePoint, Vignette, BroadVision, you name it, is just a framework. All it does is allow you, the designer, to quickly and easily automate business processes. Eliminate paper. Help them find the information faster. Destroy when it has to be destroyed.

You need to adjust your content collection, management, and presentation systems to the processes and demands of your organization. That's the real goal, not the software installation!

So guess what comes first?

If you misunderstand your organization's culture, processes, and business requirements, no system out there will save your project.

Take the time to understand the real needs of business people. Understand the goals of your enterprise. Then go ahead and automate them. You won't be stuck trying to automate a *bad* process! (Be sure to read about Iterative Development later in this chapter.)

Another fatal mistake commonly found in failed UCM rollouts is bad Metadata design.

Metadata design

Once you've identified your business clients and spent time understanding their needs, you're ready to reflect your knowledge in a content management system. And you do this through metadata design and workflows.

As you've seen earlier in this chapter, metadata design is all about creating custom fields. Fields that describe various types of content you'll be storing in the system.

For example, if you store Project Plans, you might like to add a project manager's name, completion date, and expense account number.

And remember, if users don't understand the purpose of a metadata field, they'll skip it, put wrong stuff in there, or just type up some garbage, so the system lets them submit the form.

Here are some tips for successful metadata design, expensive to ignore.

Don't ask for all of your fields every time

If they check in an employee record and you're asking them for PM name, guess what kind of name you'll get. It must make sense. And it also must be as quick and painless as possible. Business people are busy and many perceive content management as a "necessary evil", even "pain in the neck", so if you don't have to ask them for a specific field value don't.

Now if you don't need a user's input on a specific field, consider hiding it. On the other hand, if you do need their input, consider using validation.

Another great thing you can do is take advantage of features that let you pre-populate metadata values, features such as Content Profiles (covered in detail in *Chapter 4*), Content categorizer (see Appendix A), or the Multi-Field Configuration Utility from Fishbowl Solutions (www.FishbowlSolutions.com/StellentSolutions).

Beware of the snowball effect

This is what happens when you ignore the previous rule.

Picture yourself having a nicely configured system with clean data. Every document has correct meta values. Now you begin asking for a field that doesn't make sense.

Your contributors will begin putting garbage there and they'll be putting garbage in other fields as well! How?

Once you have put garbage in one field, say 'asdf', it becomes very easy to simply put that in the rest of the fields all the way down the form. The system will soon become polluted and you might end up losing the meta values for your entire repository. Why?

You won't know which records have the real values and which just garbage.

Soon enough you won't be able to trust the data anymore!

Keep an eye on what content is getting entered and always keep communicating with your business users.

Know this single, most expensive type of UCM activity

The single most expensive UCM activity is manual Cleansing and Matching. Unless you have an army of data analysts looking for stuff to do, I don't recommend letting your project get to this point. You must prevent it almost at any cost.

And here is one more common way organizations kill their content management projects. It's by ignoring the principles of iterative development.

Iterative development

You can still afford to delay the rollout until you have all the knowledge you need to design your new system. It doesn't have to be chunked into large and expensive phases—expensive and vulnerable to scope creep.

You can easily implement a useful system while you're still acquiring knowledge. The key here is to have a live working system in the hands of your business people as soon as you possibly can.

All you need to do is make small incremental changes such as adding different types of documents, new modules, new workflows, and so on.

And listen to feedback. If business is happy you did great. If not all you have to undo is just a small change! So don't try to bite off more than you can chew. (If you need more info on agile and iterative development processes, Wikipedia (www.wikipedia.org) is a good place to start. Just search for "Agile software development". Congratulations!

Summary

You now have a fully functional instance of Oracle Content Server. You've checked in your first document and you know what metadata is all about.

You've seen the main reasons why so many UCM rollouts fail.

In the next chapter I'll give you a deluxe tour of Content Server. We will look at all the major controls and learn the frequently used features.

2
Major Controls

By the end of this chapter you will find yourself feeling a lot more comfortable with Content Server, and much closer to becoming independent of any outside consulting help.

You will learn the core administration and operations of content server. More specifically, you will learn:

- How to check and update server configuration, what configuration settings are available, and which ones do you need to look at for your task at hand
- How to troubleshoot Content Server and where to find vital diagnostic information
- How to add and remove users from the system and how to update user information
- What other ways you can use to bring in new content

Before you know it, this chapter will take you to the next level of understanding of Oracle Content Server. It won't take you nearly as long as Content Server installation! Let's get into this.

Where to start?

Before we get into turning the knobs and pulling on the levers let me mention that there are two major groups of controls out there, **Administration** and **Operations**. Content Server doesn't draw a clear border between them. The reason I focus on this is simple—Administration deals with changing the way things work, while Operations deals with keeping things up and running. It pays to keep those separate.

If you didn't already do so then log into your Content Server and expand the Administration tray on the left (as shown in the following screenshot):

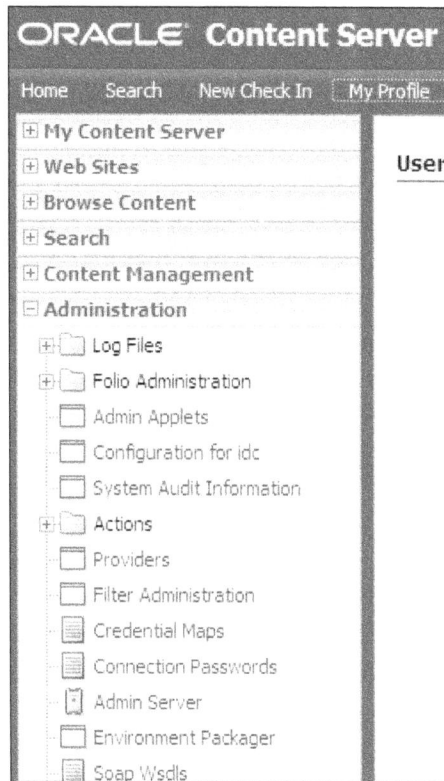

If your screen doesn't look like one shown on the screenshot, one of two things might've happened:

If you do see the trays on the left, but just don't see **Admistration** then you're not logging in as sysadmin. Close all of your browser windows and log in again to Content Server as sysadmin.

If you don't see any trays on the left of your screen, you might've changed your preferred screen layout in your personalization settings. Click on the **My Profile** link on the top (shown in the previous screenshot), and under the **User Personalization Settings** group, change the value in the **Layout** dropdown to **Trays**.

You're now looking at the main Content Server administration controls. Let's see how you can use them.

View or change configuration

Administration Controls define how things work in Content Server. Let's look at them one by one:

Admin Applets

Click on **Admin Applets** on the left. The Admin Applets Screen loads on your right, which can be seen in the next screenshot:

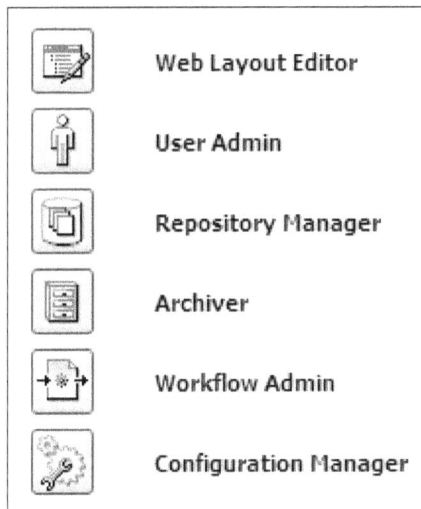

> If you get broken image icons instead, you may need to re-install the Java Plug-in in your browser. Just Google for "download java plug-in IE", if you're using Internet Explorer. Make sure you download an offline installation!
>
> If you're running a Virtual Machine (VM) that we built in *Chapter 1, Getting Up and Running*, drag the executable over to your VM and run it there, and then restart your browser.

Here's what Admin Applets can do for you. Let's start by looking at Web Layout Editor.

Web Layout Editor

Web Layout Editor lets you create the Library hierarchy, define reports, modify search result pages, and update the Portal Page.

What is the Portal Page? In Content Server it's a page you see when you're about to log into Content Server (as shown in the following screenshot):

Web Layout Editor lets you customize the Portal Page, add links to it, change graphics, and so on.

What's the Library hierarchy? It's the Library folders aligned at the left, and also a page that you access by clicking on the **Library** link on the portal page:

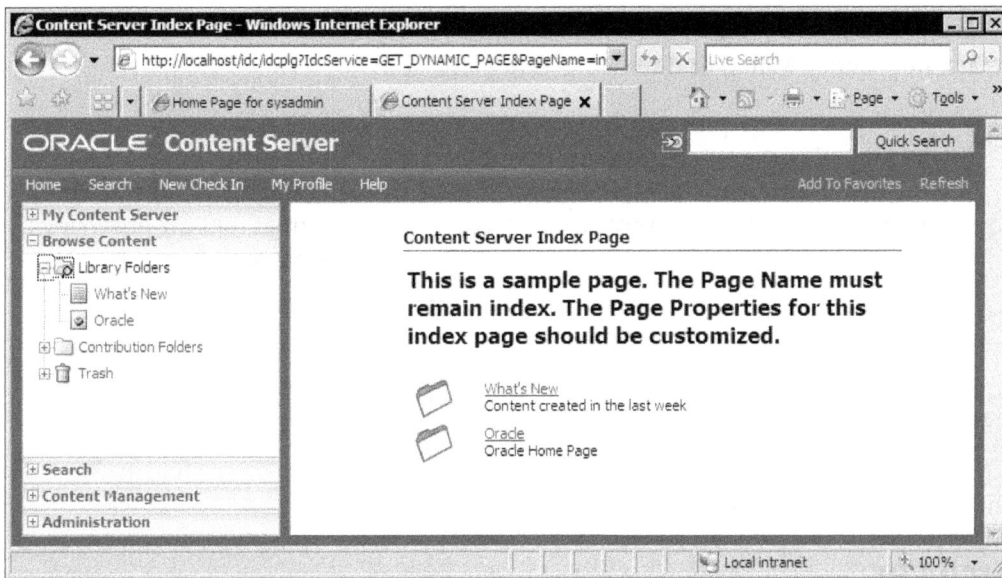

The Library hierarchy is purely virtual. It's up to the administrator to define folders and links and build them.

These are some of the most under-used and extremely powerful capabilities in Content Server. The Library hierarchy can be used to create fully dynamic groups of related content. Folders can be defined as search queries, so when new content is added that matches the criteria, it will automatically appear in the corresponding folders.

And if this is not enough, the library folder pages allow you to customize them with iDoc Script, Content Server's built-in scripting language. This means you can create dynamic descriptions, display query results, and build some very cool, very quick customizations that way.

Now let's take a look at the next applet, User Admin.

User Admin

This is where you add and remove users, and modify their access. But it's also where you define your security model. (See *Chapter 4*, *Understanding Security*, for detailed coverage of the Content Server Security Model.)

The next applet has several useful features.

Repository Manager

In fact, Repository Manager does three things for you:

- It allows you to query and edit your content. Think of it as an alternative to a Content Server web interface (in many cases it's more convenient than the regular interface). You can see all revisions instead of just the latest, filter your view, add and remove display columns. It's a great tool for browsing your repository and quick cleansing and matching tasks.

- It provides a central place to manage content subscriptions (e-mail notifications of content changes).

- It lets you configure, start, and stop the indexer (the engine that allows you to run Content Server searches and queries, and makes them run fast). This one is probably the most frequently used feature of Repository Manager.

The next applet is critically important.

Archiver

Archiver is the tool you can use to back up and restore repository content. You can also do a number of other useful things with Archiver, such as mass deletion of unused content and global updates of metadata values.

This is also the tool that allows server-to-server content replication (you will be learning more on Archiver in *Chapter 9, Migrating Configuration*).

Workflow Admin

This is probably the only admin applet that doesn't require any explanation. It's here to define and customize workflows. We have an entire chapter (*Chapter 5, Understanding Workflows*) dedicated for workflows and you'll be learning more about it over there.

Configuration Manager

I bet you'll be using this last applet most frequently. Any time you need to add a metadata field, hide an unused one, or add a content type, you'll be starting Configuration Manager. We'll be spending lots of time with it in the next chapter.

Now let's look at another set of Content Server controls with a similar name but very different purpose.

Admin Server

Admin Server is a separate web application that controls Content Server processes. It also helps you change its global configuration.

Why do you need such an app? Simple! One Admin Server can manage multiple Content Server instances. You can install additional instances on the same physical machine or manage instances running on other machines.

I recommend you put a lot of thought into creating additional Content Server instances. You don't want to manage too many—especially on the same physical server (for one thing, they will take a long time to start after reboot). You'll be facing issues with backup, updates, and administration.

To bring the Admin Server up, click on the **Admin Server** link under **Administration** on the left. It usually comes up in a new window (as shown in the following screenshot):

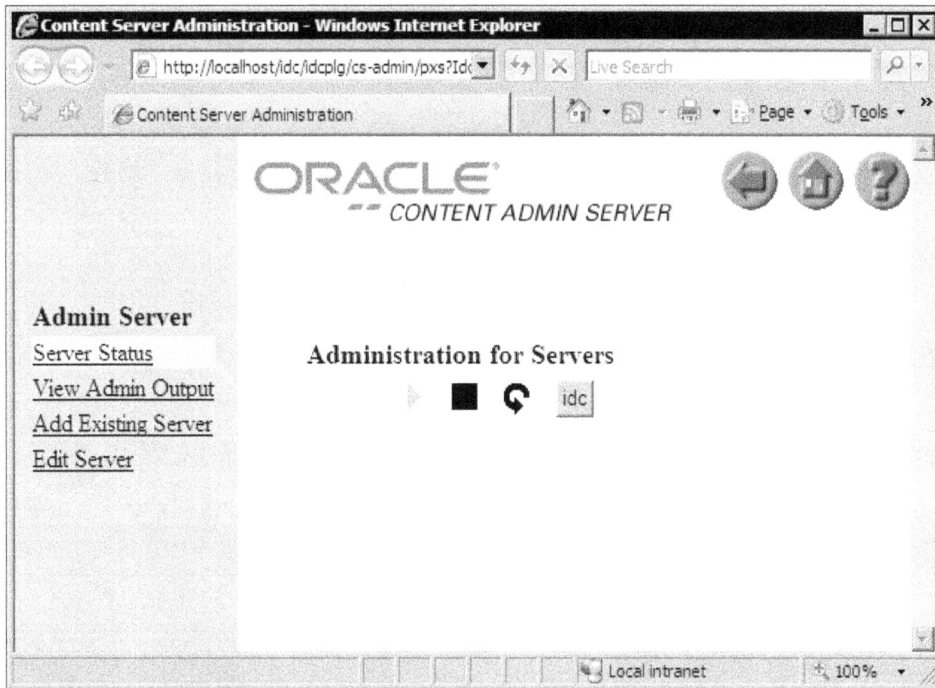

As you can see, there are buttons to start and stop Content Server. There will be one set of controls per Content Server instance (as shown in the following screenshot):

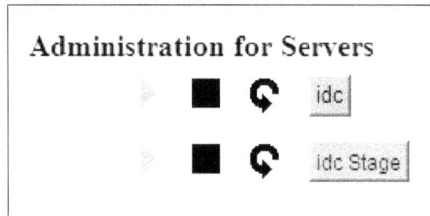

Here I've asked Admin Server to also manage another instance called **idc Stage**.

Now here's a little trick that will save you an hour of digging documentation. Remember I mentioned that Admin Server also lets you change Content Server settings? How would you get to those pages?

The answer is this: *The instance name is a button*. Click on it! So click on the **idc** button now. Voila! the **Content Admin Server** screen comes up (as shown in the following screenshot):

You will see a number of administration links on the left. Let's look at the ones you will be using most often:

General Configuration

The name speaks for itself. This is where you can change a few common configuration options. For instance, you can have Content Server automatically assign Content ID to new items you check in.

To enable this, just put a check next to **Automatically assign a content ID on check in.** You can also specify a prefix for the new content ID in the box below. For example, to have your content ID look like EC00023456, just type EC.

The most important part of this page is that **Additional Configuration Variables** section in the bottom. Why?

This is simply a text box with the Master Content Server configuration file loaded there. If there is anything you need to add or update in Content Server configuration, use this Window and hit **Save** when you're done.

Warning! It's easy to break things when you change configuration this way. Make backups or just copy entries and comment out the old ones by placing a hash symbol at the beginning of the line. For instance, to change the main port, do something like this:

```
#IntradocServerPort=4444
IntradocServerPort=4445
```

If the new setting doesn't work out then you have an easy way back.

The next link reads **Content Security**.

Content Security

This section gives you a few additional options to tweak access to content. For instance, you can allow the author of the content to delete their revisions, even if they don't have permission to delete content. The options are annotated and descriptions are pretty clear.

The next link may seem confusing.

Internet Configuration

This is where the mail server address goes. If you took a shortcut during installation and are now wondering why you aren't getting any e-mail notifications then this is where you check.

The next link brings up one of the key customization controls of the Content Server.

Component Manager

Component Manager is the number one place people go to when using Content Admin. This is where you install and uninstall, enable and disable custom components.

In Oracle UCM, the term "custom" is used very loosely. All UCM features such as Web Content Management, and all hot fixes, are implemented as custom components. Think of them as UCM extensions.

We will learn more about Component Manager in *Chapter 11*, *Web Content Management and Collaboration*.

And here's another link used for extending and integrating the Content Server, **View Provider**.

View Providers

View Providers allows you to configure Providers or "Connectors" that are there to allow Content Server to connect to external systems. We will be using providers to:

- Connect to the database (the provider named SystemDatabase is pre-configured for you at install time)
- Set up LDAP or Active Directory authentication
- Set up Replication—automated scheduled backup and restore for keeping a number of Content Server instances in sync

The last three links give you access to the key auditing and troubleshooting information. We will study them in the following section.

Server Output, Logs, and System Audit Information

Even though these links are available in Admin Server, they are *Operations* controls, not *Administration*. They are here to help you get audit and diagnostic information, not to change Server configuration. We will look at these in just a few moments.

And now let's continue exploring your main Content Server **Administration** tray. The next important link we need to look at is Folder Configuration.

Folder Configuration

Folder Configuration allows you to control configuration and behavior of **Virtual Folders**. As I mentioned in the previous chapter, virtual folders provide users with a convenient and familiar metaphor for storage and classification. Content Server folders may be browsed just like other, familiar systems.

Every content item may be associated with a virtual folder. Remember, the content is not physically stored in that folder. It's just linked to the folder so users can also find it that way, in addition to using the search feature. The **Folder Configuration** link is where you control the global parameters of folder structure hierarchies. It also allows you to back up, restore, and migrate your folder structures.

Click on **Folder Configuration** in the bottom of the Administration Tray (as shown in the following screenshot):

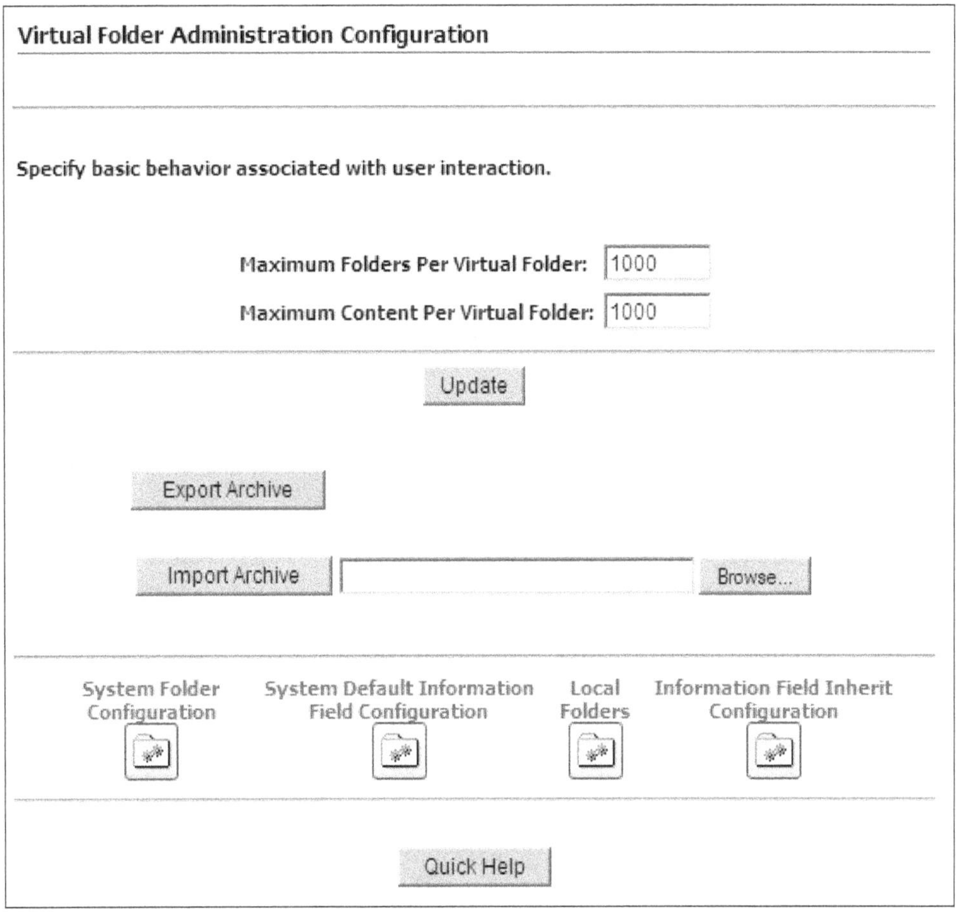

Virtual Folder Administration Configuration

Specify basic behavior associated with user interaction.

Maximum Folders Per Virtual Folder: 1000
Maximum Content Per Virtual Folder: 1000

Update

Export Archive

Import Archive _____ Browse...

System Folder Configuration | System Default Information Field Configuration | Local Folders | Information Field Inherit Configuration

Quick Help

One of the most useful features on this screen is the **Export** and **Import Archive** buttons. When you click on **Export Archive**, your entire folder structure (the folders you see under **Browse Content | Contribution Folders**) is exported into a single text file. You can then use it to re-create the same structure on another server or use it as a backup.

Note that this feature only exports the folders themselves, not the content. If you need to back up folders *and* their content, use the Folder Structure Archive Utility.

Other controls on this page are there to show and hide system folders, set up replication, and control folder metadata.

You will learn more about virtual folders (and other options on this page) in *Chapter 6, Understanding Virtual Folders and WebDAV* and *Chapter 10, Customizing Oracle UCM*.

And now let's see what's involved in Content Server operations. Here's what you need to know to keep it up and running.

Keep it up and running

Operations are all about keeping things up and running smoothly. If you're facing a content or functionality issue and need to diagnose it, then this is also the best place to start.

When things go wrong, the first thing you usually look at is the log files.

Log files

For rookies in the crowd: Content Server log file is a list of sequential entries where it takes a record of all significant activities it engages or is about to engage in.

Almost always, the log file contains more detail on error messages and you can look at a whole sequence of events; what Content Server was doing just before the error occurred.

Expand the **Log Files** folder under **Administration**. Click on **Content Server Logs** (as shown in the following screenshot):

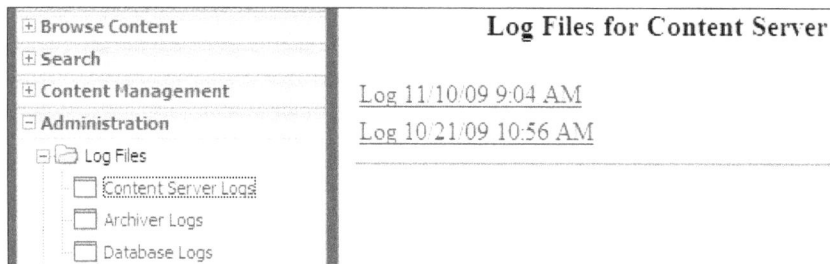

[![note icon] This screen is also available in Admin Server when you click on the instance name button (that is **idc**).]

Click on the link that leads to a log file for the data you need to explore. Log file messages are fairly clear and self-explanatory, but if you need more information, I'll be helping you get maximum value of Oracle help, documentation, and support in *Chapter 10*.

You can also zoom in and capture mountains of additional information, not shown in the log files with System Audit Information.

System Audit Information

Follow the link on the left, the second one below **Admin Applets**.

This is where you control what information gets printed on Content Server output. If you need to see exactly what's going on with a specific sub-system like mail or indexer then select that in the dropdown and click on **Update**.

The round information icon following **Tracing Section Information** brings up a screen with their detailed description.

Full verbose tracing, where each tracing section displays an even greater level of details, may also come handy:

> **Just remember to un-check the box after you are done with diagnostics.**
> Keeping verbose tracing checked affects performance and uses up a lot of disk space.

Placing a checkmark in the **Save** box will preserve your choices between Content Server restarts.

Once tracing sections are configured, the following screen will actually show you the info you requested. The screen is called View Server Output.

View Server Output

Click on the **View Server Output** link on the top left of the screen (as shown in the following screenshot):

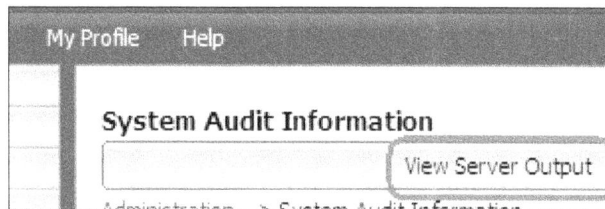

Server output is the most detailed, trace-level logging. If you were to start a Content Server process from a console window then this is exactly what you would see. As I mentioned, tracing provides you with the next level of details that you cannot get from the log files. You can also select what Content Server sections should be providing you with that level of info.

Use the **Clear** and **Refresh** buttons above to keep output to a manageable size.

The System Audit Information page also has a few vital indicators like memory and database connection information (you can also access this screen from Admin Server).

And the next link down under the **Administration** tray brings up Environment Packager.

Environment Packager

Environment Packager is a useful utility, which you use when contacting Oracle Support. It makes copies of your log files and your system configuration, and places then into one ZIP file. You can them e-mail it to Oracle Support or attach to your online inquiry. (I'll be helping you discover the treasure that lies hidden in Oracle Support later in *Chapter 10.*) In the next section we will see how to manage users.

Managing users

At last! We're about to see how you can let other people use the system.

It's also a good idea to create a non-admin user account for yourself and only use `sysadmin` for administration and operations.

So let's begin by adding a user.

Adding a user

Let's add a new user:

1. Go to **Admin Applets** and click on **User Admin**. The User Admin applet comes up (see screenshot below):

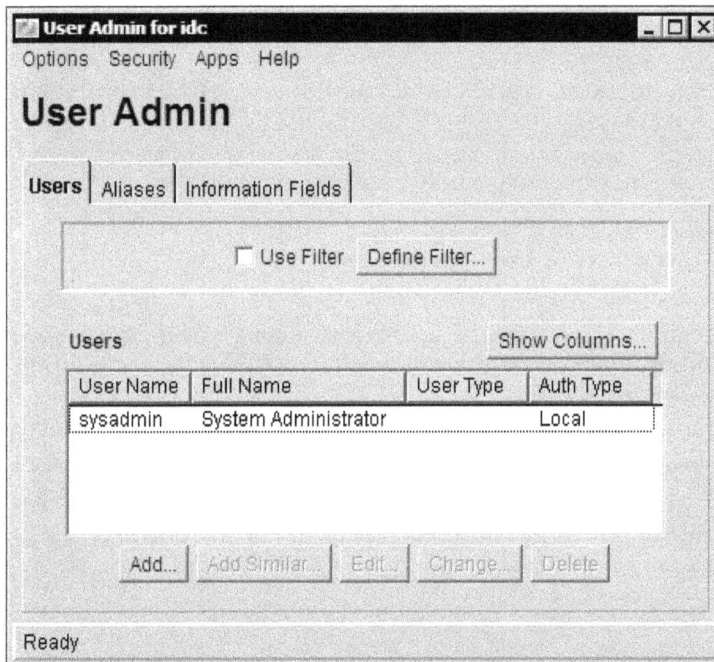

2. Click on the **Add** button.

3. Leave user type as **Local**. Click on **OK**.

4. Fill in user info. The first field, **Name**, is the actual user name the user will be using to log in (as shown in the following screenshot):

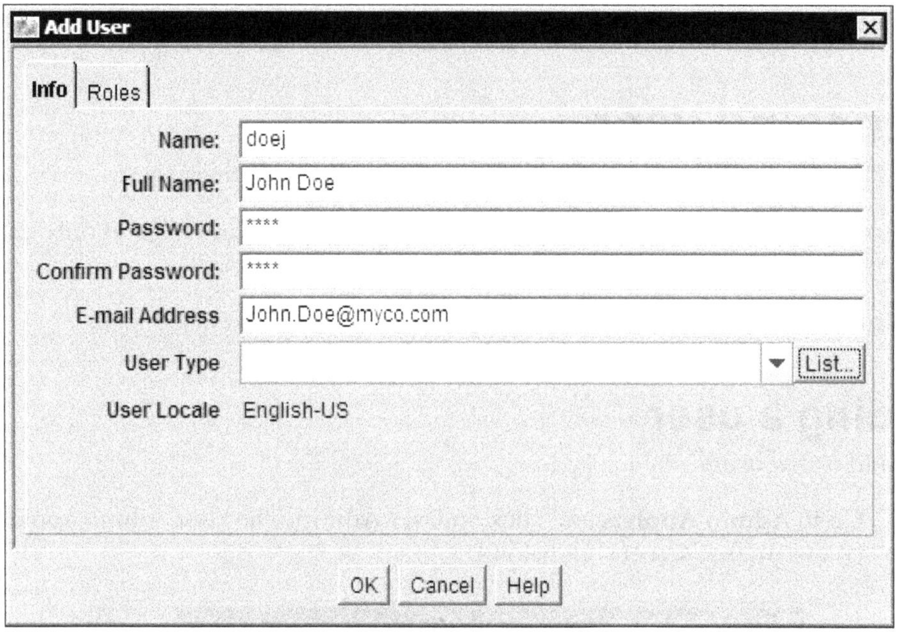

5. Go to the **Roles** tab and click on **Add Role**. Pick **Contributor**. Click on **OK** to close the dialog.

Congratulations! You now have a new user in the system.

What were those User Types all about?

In some deployment scenarios you can have one **Master** Content Server control a few dependent or **Proxied** Content Servers. When you have a Global user on the Master server they will also be able to log into dependent servers.

Local users can only log into the server where they were created. In a single server deployment Local and Global users behave the same way.

But what if you need to allow everyone from a department to access a certain block of content? Here's how you'd go about it.

Adding a group of users

In Content Server a group of users is called an **Alias** and here's how you create one:

1. Go to the **Aliases** tab on the User Admin Applet.
2. Click on **Add**.
3. Pick a name and description.
4. Pick users to be added.

You're done (see screenshot below):

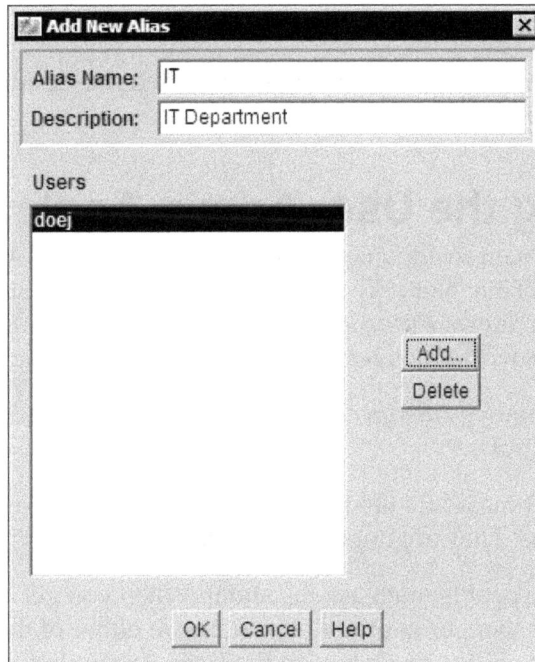

What if you already have your users authenticating to an LDAP or Active Directory? Does it mean they will have to log in again to the Content Server and use yet another user name and password?

Not necessary. The following section covers these issues in detail.

Integrating with external authentication providers

You can integrate Content Server with Windows Active Directory and other LDAP authentication providers, so the user doesn't need to authenticate again. The user's group membership within LDAP then determines his/her permissions in the Content Server.

To set up this integration, you will need to understand the Content Server security model. (I will be covering that in detail in *Chapter 4*.) The actual integration is covered in detail in the **Managing Security and User Access** guide, available from the Oracle UCM online documentation page.

There is one more useful thing I want you to know about user administration. Let me show you what's involved.

Customizing the User Admin Applet

Sometimes it's convenient to add custom columns to your User Admin Applet such as Department or Job Title. Not only will these fields make it easier for you and your sub-administrators to filter for people in a specific department, these values can also come really handy for workflow escalations and various personalization.

It's easy to add and remove custom columns. Just go to the **Information Fields** tab on the User Admin Applet.

Remember, those user metadata fields only live in User Admin and custom workflow applications. They are not content metadata fields.

Here's something else people often ask me about: When you get a fair number of users you either loose them or get tired of scrolling. If either of these occurs then either uncheck the **Use Filter** check box on the **Users** tab to show ALL the users, or check it and define the criteria to only show the users you really want to see.

Congratulations! You now understand how to manage users. Next, let me show you some ways to get content in.

More ways to get content in

In the previous chapter we were using a check-in form to bring content in. I mentioned that there are a few other ways to do it. Let's look at them really quickly.

Desktop integration

Oracle Desktop integration is an add-on component, available as part of Content Server Document Management. Once installed, it allows you to simply drag and drop documents into Content Server folders, just as if those were your local folders or your shared drive (as shown in the following screenshot):

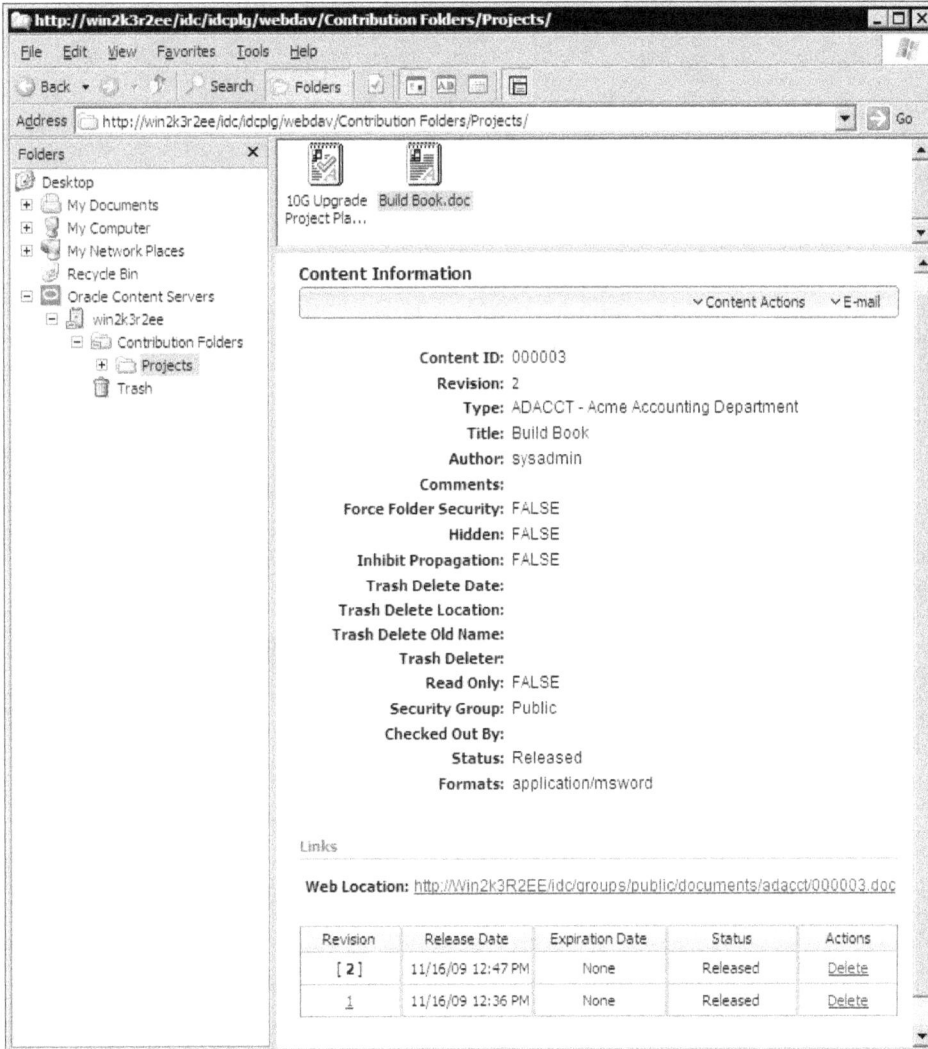

You can also check out and check in by right-clicking on a document.

If you have MS Office installed, Desktop Integration allows you to check content in and out from Outlook and other Office Applications.

I'll show you how to install Oracle Desktop Integration Suite in *Chapter 6*.

Another way to bring content in is the use of custom programming.

Custom programming

Content Server follows open industry standards. It has a number of Application Programming Interfaces (APIs). You can connect to it from a Java Component, ASP page, or using a Web Service.

Let's see how we can use Web Services to integrate the Content Server into our enterprise. Currently, the most popular communications protocol for Web Services is Simple Object Access Protocol (SOAP). It uses a common web protocol, HTTP, to exchange XML-based self-describing messages between a server and a variety of clients.

To use SOAP Web Services, you'll need a WSDL Generator Component. (If you download Oracle Universal Content Management Document Management bundle, you can use Component Manager to install it.)

WSDL Generator includes samples on how to automate Content Server operations virtually from any programming language. Here's how a remote check-in might look:

First, we need to know the URL of our Content Server and user credentials (see screenshot below):

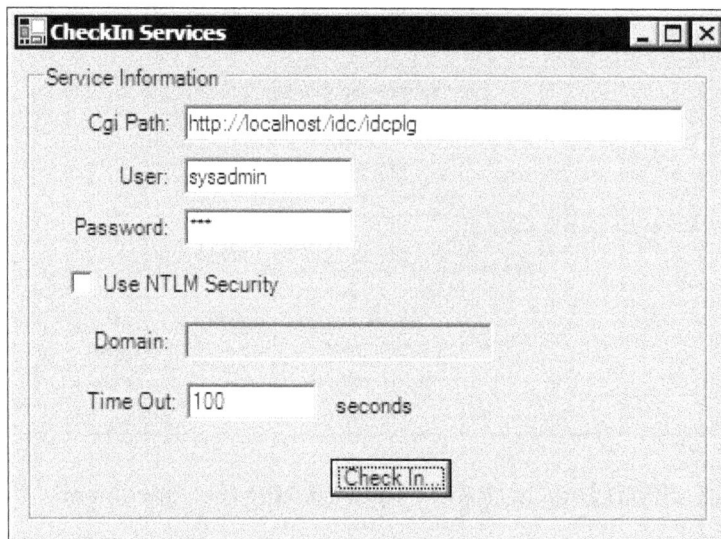

Then we specify metadata values and the file we're about to check in (as shown in the following screenshot):

Voila! The file was successfully checked in using a SOAP Web Service! (check out the following screenshot):

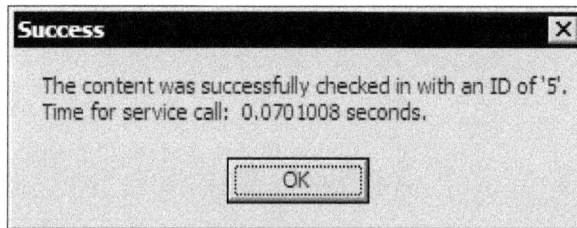

That's it. Were almost done with this section. There's just one more useful tip I want to give you here. It is related to Content Server configuration.

How to auto-generate content IDs

Many times, it's a lot easier and more convenient to have Content Server generate Content IDs for you. They must be globally unique and you may not want to bother your users with extra error messages.

I hope you remember how to enable auto-generation; check the **Automatically assign a content ID on check in** box on the **General Configuration** page in Admin Server. We covered it earlier in this chapter.

Summary

You've just seen all of the Content Server's major controls. You know how to manage users and where to get detailed error information for troubleshooting.

In the next chapter we will take a detailed look at the metadata. We will learn how to find information quickly and efficiently, and how to customize your check-in form.

3
Metadata

Welcome back! You're almost done building the foundation of your Content Server expertise. In fact, you're just two chapters away — this one and the next one, on security. You will then have a full and clear picture of what Oracle UCM is all about and how you can get the most value out of it.

We will look at the types of metadata available in the system and how to put them to good use. You will learn to find information quickly, and how to customize your Content Server screens without programming. More specifically, you will learn:

- How to use standard and custom metadata — a major ingredient among UCM's critical success factors that can spell both "success" and "disaster" in your organization

- How to quickly customize Check In, Content Info, and Search screens without coding, and how to work dependent choice lists (allowing you to complete even advanced customizations without writing a single line of code)

- How Content Server stores metadata in the database — a bit of insider knowledge that will make many of your complex development, data migration, and code generation tasks a piece of cake

That's right. This will be another easy chapter. Let's begin by looking in the metadata.

Exploring metadata

In case you forgot, *metadata fields* are there to describe the actual data such as the file name, shooting date, and camera name for a digital picture.

After we installed Content Server in Chapter 2, I mentioned that there're two types of metadata fields: Standard and Extended or Custom. Let's take a closer look at what they can do for us.

Standard metadata

Standard metadata is essential for the system to function. These are fields like content ID, revision ID, check-in date, and author. Let's take a quick look at all of them so you have a full picture.

Lab 2: Exploring standard metadata

Click on the **Quick Search** button on the top right. Yes, leave the search box blank. If you do that, you'll get all content in the repository.

In the last column on the **Search Results** page click on the **i** icon on any of the result rows. That brings up a **Content Info** screen.

From this screen there is no way to tell which fields are Standard and which are Extended. So how do you tell?

Explore the database

That's right. A Content Server uses a relational database, like Oracle or SQL Server to store its metadata, so let's look there.

If you followed my instructions in *Chapter 2* and used SQL Server 2005 as your database, then open SQL Server Management Studio, and if not then bring up your SQL tool of choice.

Check the list of columns in the table called `Revisions` (as shown in the following screenshot):

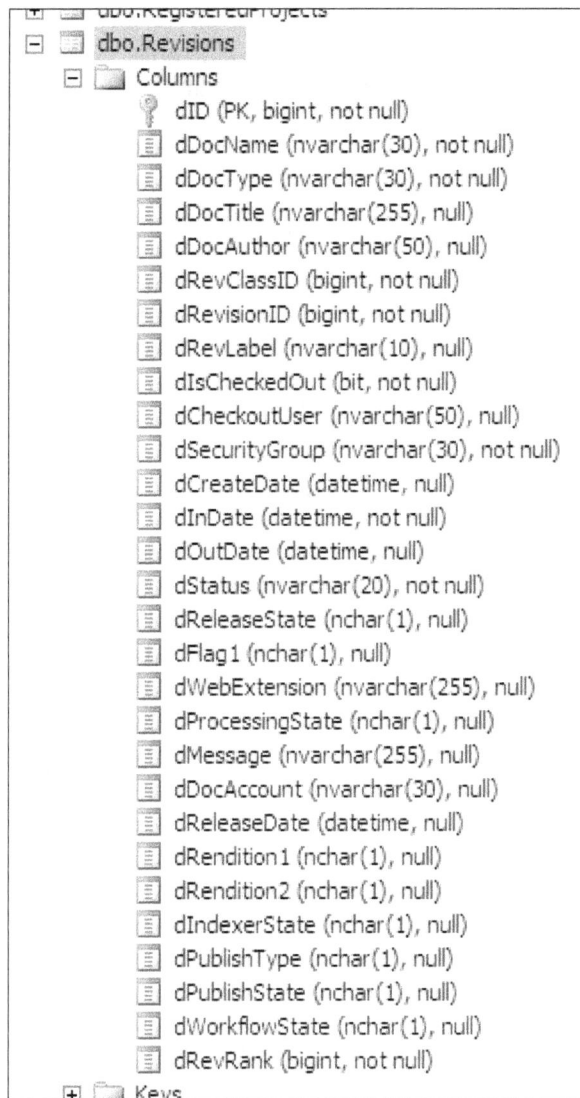

```
      dbo.RegisteredProjects
  ⊟    dbo.Revisions
    ⊟  📁 Columns
         🔑 dID (PK, bigint, not null)
         📄 dDocName (nvarchar(30), not null)
         📄 dDocType (nvarchar(30), not null)
         📄 dDocTitle (nvarchar(255), null)
         📄 dDocAuthor (nvarchar(50), null)
         📄 dRevClassID (bigint, not null)
         📄 dRevisionID (bigint, not null)
         📄 dRevLabel (nvarchar(10), null)
         📄 dIsCheckedOut (bit, not null)
         📄 dCheckoutUser (nvarchar(50), null)
         📄 dSecurityGroup (nvarchar(30), not null)
         📄 dCreateDate (datetime, null)
         📄 dInDate (datetime, not null)
         📄 dOutDate (datetime, null)
         📄 dStatus (nvarchar(20), not null)
         📄 dReleaseState (nchar(1), null)
         📄 dFlag1 (nchar(1), null)
         📄 dWebExtension (nvarchar(255), null)
         📄 dProcessingState (nchar(1), null)
         📄 dMessage (nvarchar(255), null)
         📄 dDocAccount (nvarchar(30), null)
         📄 dReleaseDate (datetime, null)
         📄 dRendition1 (nchar(1), null)
         📄 dRendition2 (nchar(1), null)
         📄 dIndexerState (nchar(1), null)
         📄 dPublishType (nchar(1), null)
         📄 dPublishState (nchar(1), null)
         📄 dWorkflowState (nchar(1), null)
         📄 dRevRank (bigint, not null)
    ⊞  📁 Keys
```

Most of the column names in `Revisions` are the standard metadata fields.

Here's a list of the fields you will be using most often:

- **dID**: ID of the document revision. This number is globally unique. If you have a project plan with three revisions—each of the three will have unique dID and all of them will have the same Content ID.

- **dDocName**: this is the actual Content ID.

- **dDocType**: content type of the document.

> dDocName or Content ID is the unique identifier for a content revision set. dID is the unique identifier of each individual content revision within a set.
>
> Being able to identify a content revision set is very useful, as it shows and tracks (makes auditable) the changes of content items over time.
>
> Being able to identify each individual revision with dID is also very useful, so we can work with specific content revisions. This is one of the great advantages of the Content Server over other systems, which only store the changes between revisions. Full revision sets as well as individual revisions are managed objects and each one can be accessed by its own unique URL.

Now run this SQL statement:

```
select * from Revisions;
```

This shows the actual documents in the system and their *values* for standard meta fields (as shown in the following screenshot):

	dID	dDocName	dDocType	dDocTitle	dDocAuthor	dRevClassID	dRevisionID	dRevLabel	dI
▶	1	test	ADACCT	Title	sysadmin	1	1	1	Fa
	2	000002	ADACCT	10G Upgrade Pr...	sysadmin	2	1	1	Tr
	3	000003	ADACCT	Build Book	sysadmin	3	1	1	Fa
	4	000003	ADACCT	Build Book	sysadmin	3	2	2	Fa
	5	WSDL_Test	ADENG	Test Project Plan	doej	4	1	1	Fa

Table - dbo.Revisions / Summary

And now let's look at the all-important Content Types.

Content Types

Content Type is a special kind of meta field. That's all. UCM puts a special emphasis on it as this is the value that differentiates a project plan from a web page and a team photo from a vendor invoice.

You may even choose to change the way your check-in and content info form looks —based on the type of the document.

Let's look how UCM handles Content Types.

Lab 3: Exploring content types

In Content Server go to **Administration | Admin Applets**.

Launch the Configuration Manager.

Select **Options | Content Types...** (as shown in the following screenshot):

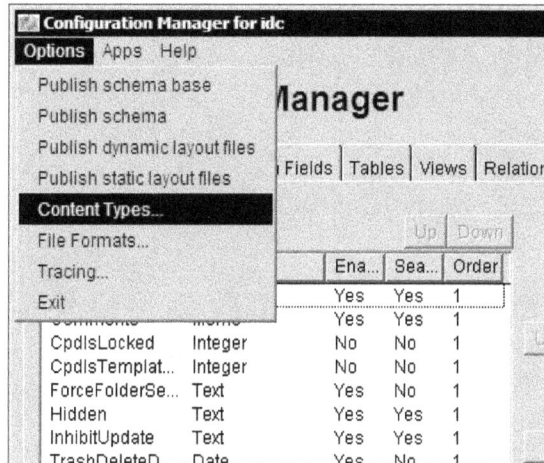

The **Content Types** dialog opens. As you see, out of the box, Content Server has seven types—one for each imaginary department. This is a good way of segregating content. You can also go by the actual type of content. For instance, you can have one Content Type for Invoice and one for Project Plan.

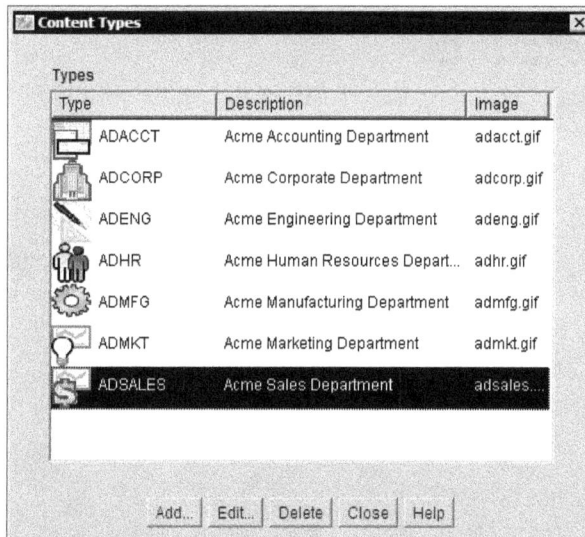

They will also have different meta fields. For instance, an Invoice will have a Contract Number and a Total Amount. A Project Plan will have a project name and manager's name. Now let me show you how to add content types.

How to add a Content Type

It's easy to add a new Content Type. Just click on **Add...**, fill in the type name and the description. You can also select an icon for the new type.

What if you need to upload a new icon? Just make it into an 8-bit GIF file, 30x37 px, 96 dpi and upload it to:

```
C:\oracle\ucm\server\weblayout\images\docgifs
```

If your install path is different or you're not running on Windows then make appropriate corrections.

How to edit or delete a Content Type

The only thing to know about editing is that you can not really change the type name. All you can update is the icon or description.

If you're ready to delete a type then make sure there is no content in the repository that's using it. Either update it all or delete.

How would you go about doing a mass-update? I'll show you one of the ways in Chapter 10 on using Archiver.

And now let's proceed to Custom Metadata.

Custom metadata

This is what the most of the metadata is. All new fields you will be creating will also be Custom metadata. Let's take look.

Lab 4: Exploring custom metadata

Once again, there is no way you can tell Custom metadata from Standard metadata—just by looking at the Content Information screen. Just as we did before—let's look at its database.

Custom metadata in the database

Go to your favorite database tool and check the list of columns in the table called DocMeta (as shown in the following screenshot):

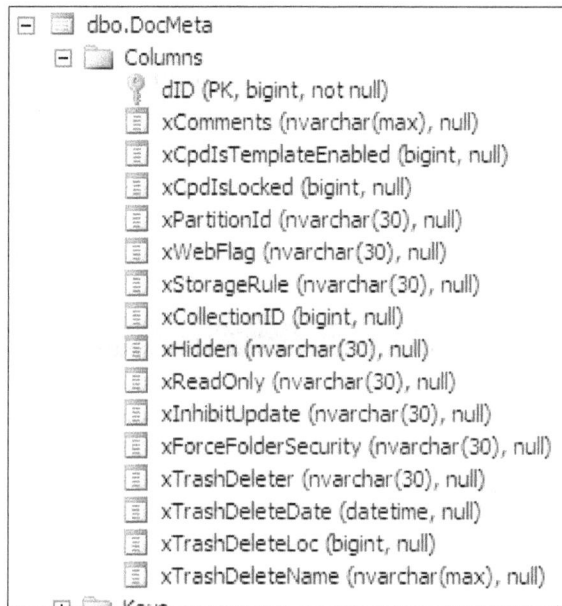

```
□ 🔳 dbo.DocMeta
    □ 📁 Columns
         🔑 dID (PK, bigint, not null)
         📄 xComments (nvarchar(max), null)
         📄 xCpdIsTemplateEnabled (bigint, null)
         📄 xCpdIsLocked (bigint, null)
         📄 xPartitionId (nvarchar(30), null)
         📄 xWebFlag (nvarchar(30), null)
         📄 xStorageRule (nvarchar(30), null)
         📄 xCollectionID (bigint, null)
         📄 xHidden (nvarchar(30), null)
         📄 xReadOnly (nvarchar(30), null)
         📄 xInhibitUpdate (nvarchar(30), null)
         📄 xForceFolderSecurity (nvarchar(30), null)
         📄 xTrashDeleter (nvarchar(30), null)
         📄 xTrashDeleteDate (datetime, null)
         📄 xTrashDeleteLoc (bigint, null)
         📄 xTrashDeleteName (nvarchar(max), null)
    □ 📁 Keys
```

The column names in DocMeta are the *custom* metadata fields.

> Notice that Custom or Extended fields have an "x" prefix, not a "d" prefix, like Standard fields.

Here's a list of the fields you will be using most often:

- **dID**: Unique ID of the document revision. Note that this field was also used in the Revisions table. This is how you can link standard and extended metadata of one content item.

- **xComments**: The Comments text box from your check-in form.

- **xCollectionID**: Unique numeric ID or a virtual folder where the item is residing. If an item is not assigned to any folder, its xCollectionID is zero.

Now run select * from DocMeta; and see the values for Custom meta fields for items in your repository.

And here's how to add new fields.

How to add new fields

It's easy to add a new metadata fields. Let me walk you though. Let's begin with a simple text field.

Text fields

1. Bring up Configuration Manager Administrative Applet. (Expand the **Administration** Tray and follow the **Admin Applets** link to bring up a page with Admin Applets. See *Chapter 3* if you need a refresher.)

2. Click on **Add**.

3. Give it a name and change field properties as you see fit (as shown in the following screenshot):

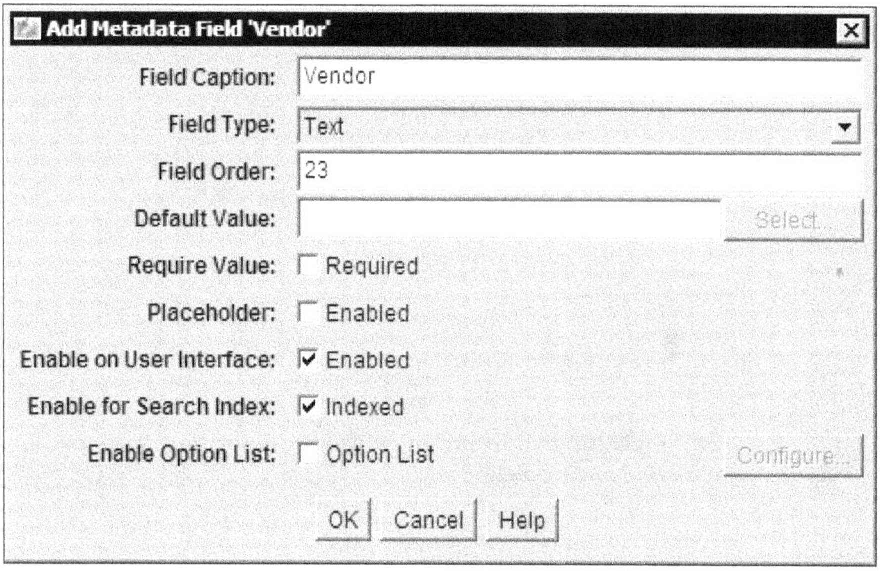

Click on **Update Database Design** to commit your changes.

How to make sure your recent changes reflect on the Check In form:

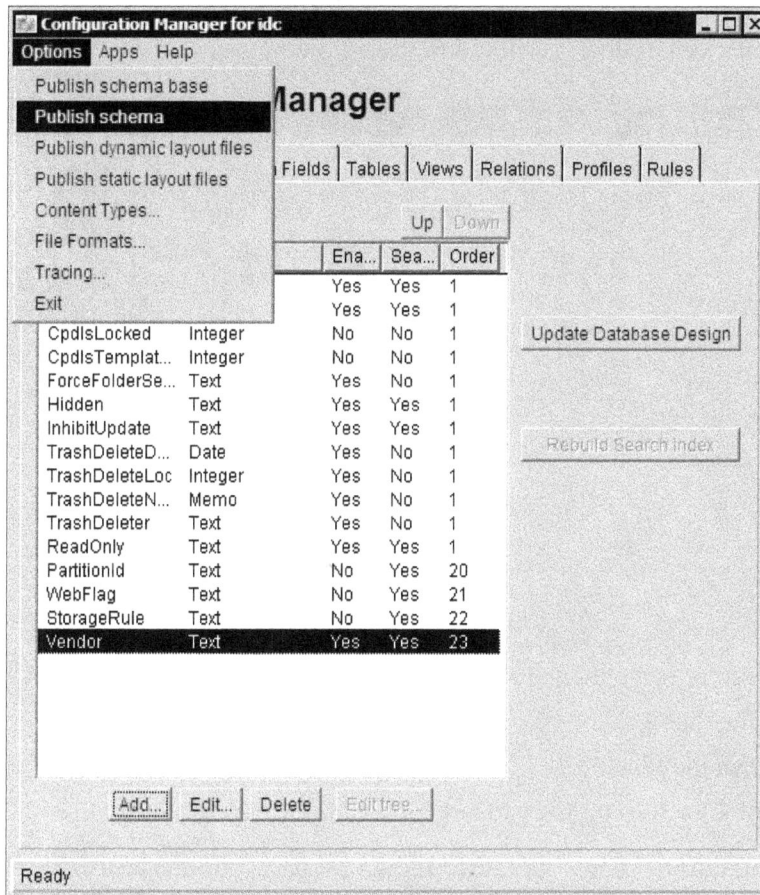

	Ena...	Sea...	Order
	Yes	Yes	1
	Yes	Yes	1
CpdIsLocked — Integer	No	No	1
CpdIsTemplat... — Integer	No	No	1
ForceFolderSe... — Text	Yes	No	1
Hidden — Text	Yes	Yes	1
InhibitUpdate — Text	Yes	Yes	1
TrashDeleteD... — Date	Yes	No	1
TrashDeleteLoc — Integer	Yes	No	1
TrashDeleteN... — Memo	Yes	No	1
TrashDeleter — Text	Yes	No	1
ReadOnly — Text	Yes	Yes	1
PartitionId — Text	No	Yes	20
WebFlag — Text	No	Yes	21
StorageRule — Text	No	Yes	22
Vendor — Text	Yes	Yes	23

> Every time you change meta fields, make sure you publish the schema by selecting **Publish Schema** from the **Options** menu in Configuration Manager (as shown in the previous screenshot).

And now let me show you how to add option lists.

Option lists

What if you want to add a drop-down box that displays a list of values to pick from? Here's how you do it. Let's add a dropdown to our newly created text field:

1. Bring up Configuration Manager and click on **Edit**.

2. Check the **Option List** box. Click on **Configure to open the Configure Option List dialog** (as shown in the following screenshot):

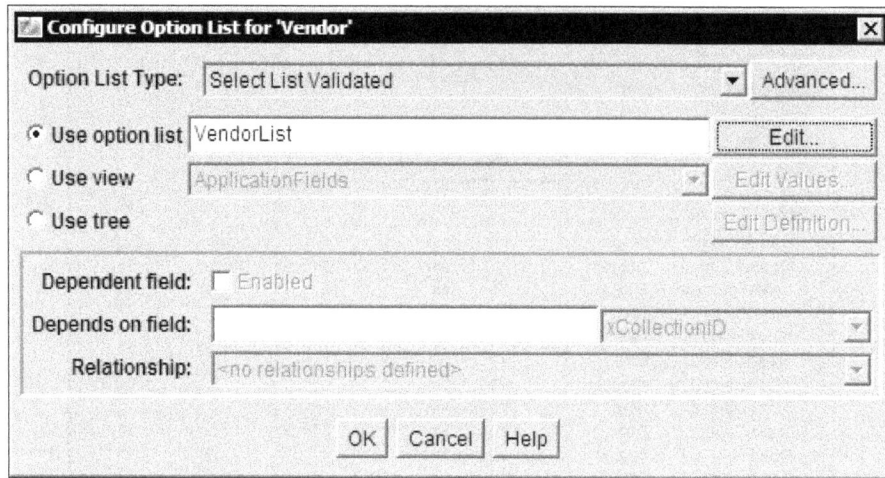

3. Click on **Edit**.
4. Type in or paste the values.
5. **OK** the dialogs.
6. Publish the schema.

Click on **New Check In** on the top left.

Voila! The Vendor field now has a dropdown (as shown in the following screenshot):

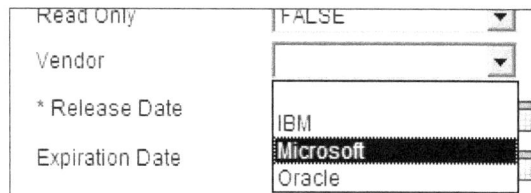

And what if you need user's to pick a contract for a specific vendor? How can you make a list of contracts refresh every time you pick a new vendor? Let's see this in the following section.

How to add fields that depend on each other

This is a little tricky. Not hard, but it takes a few minutes of preparation. Let me walk you through it. You'll like the result!

We have a Vendors list. Let's add a list of their contract engagements. Oracle UCM calls it **Dependent Choice Lists**. You can make any number of lists depend on each other. As soon as we get these two connected, you'll see how to add more.

First, we need to create database tables to store the values for both vendors and contracts. It's actually very simple. Begin with creating the database tables.

Creating database tables

To create the database tables carry out the following steps:

1. Bring up Configuration Manager.
2. Go to the **Tables** tab and click on **Create Table**.
3. Give the table name and description (as shown in the following screenshot):

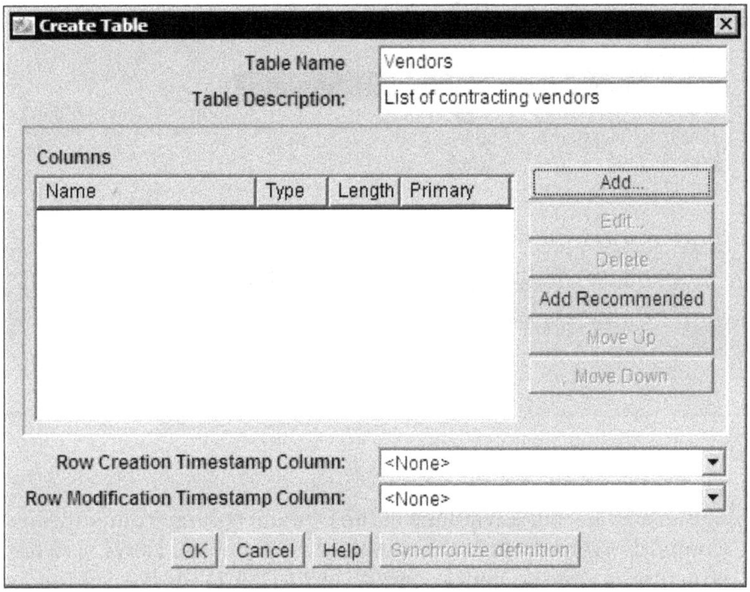

4. Add these two columns:

   ```
   Id, int, primary key
   Name, varchar 100
   ```

5. Now click on **Add Recommended**. This adds timestamp fields, needed for replication.

6. Click on **OK** to save the changes.

Create another table for Contracts:

1. Call it `VendorContracts`.

2. Add the following columns:

   `id, int, Primary key`

   `Vendor Id, int` (this will be a link to the Vendors table, a foreign key)

   `Description, varchar 100`

3. Click on **Add Recommended** and then on **OK** to close the dialog and create your table (as shown in the following screenshot):

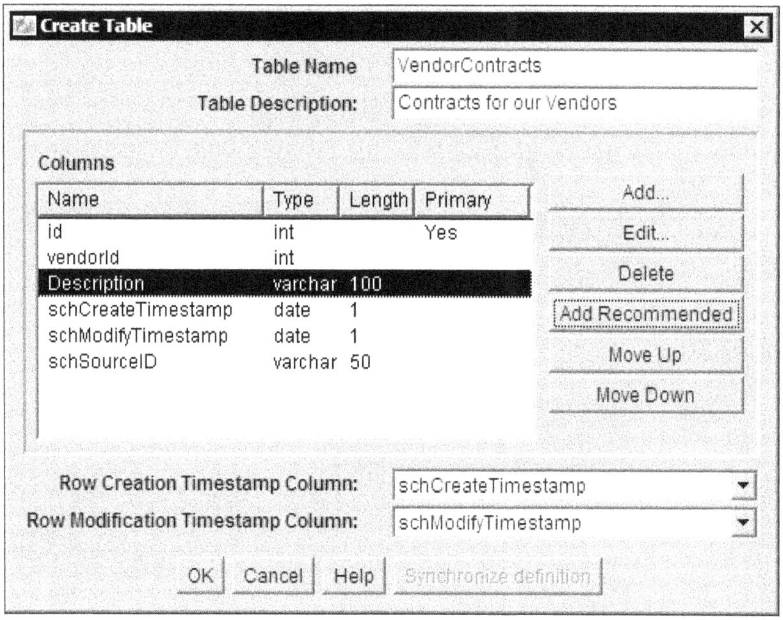

> This is another big advantage of the Content Server. Your super-user Content Server admin is able to safely create tables, views, and database structures for the content server WITHOUT A DBA! It is safe and easy for them to do so, and the interface helps to protect users from making dangerous mistakes.

We're done creating tables! Now you need to link them. How? By creating Views.

Creating Views

1. In Configuration Manager select the **Views** tab and click on the **Add** button to open the Add View dialog (as shown in the following screenshot):

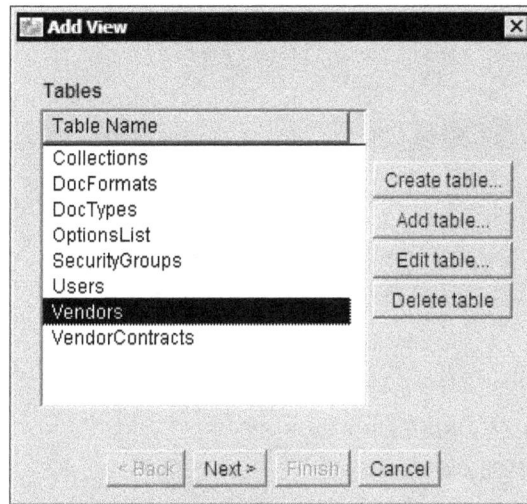

2. Select the **Vendors** table and click on **Next**.

3. Place checkmarks against **id** and **Name** so you can use them for your metadata values. Then click on **Finish** to proceed (see the following screenshot):

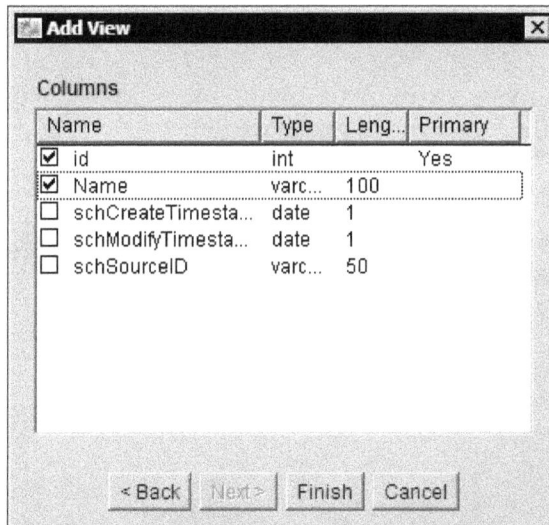

4. Name it **VendorsView** and add a description.

5. Pick **id** as **Internal Column** and **Name** as **Visible Column**. This way you will be storing Vendor ID in the database as a metadata value while your users will see vendor name.

6. **OK** the dialog. Your view is now created (as shown in the following screenshot):

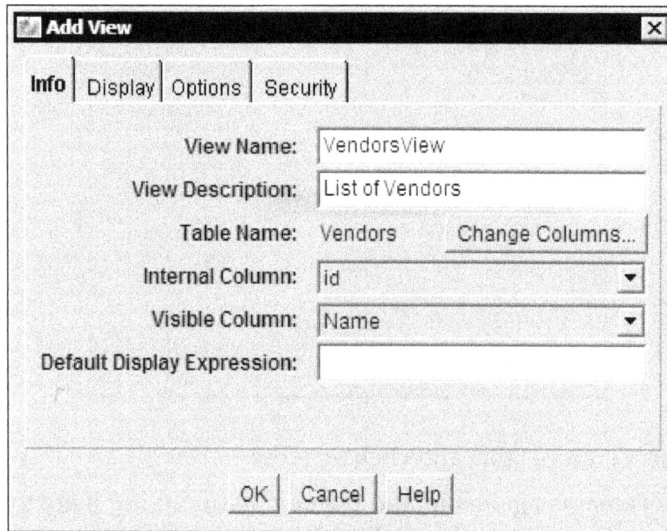

7. Repeat steps one to four to create another view for the `Contracts` table. Call it `VendorContractsView`. Make sure you make all three columns visible—`id`, `vendorId`, and `Description`.

Congratulations! Your views are now created. You're almost ready to put your dependent fields on the form. The last preparation is defining the relationships.

Defining relationships

This one will only take a few seconds. In Configuration Manager, go to the **Relationships** tab and click on **Add**.

Give it a name and pick **Parent** and **Child** views and fields (as shown in the following screenshot):

Now you're ready to create drop-down fields. I'll also show you another neat, brand-new way of doing it with Content Server 10G R3 — **tree views**.

Populating option lists

Wait! What good will these fields do to us if they have no values to display? Let's put the values in real quick.

My personal favorite is the **batch edit** feature. It allows you to put in hundreds of values at once, even paste from Excel. Here's how you do it.

In Configuration Manager select the view where you need to add or edit values. Click on **Edit Values...** on the bottom right (as shown in the following screenshot):

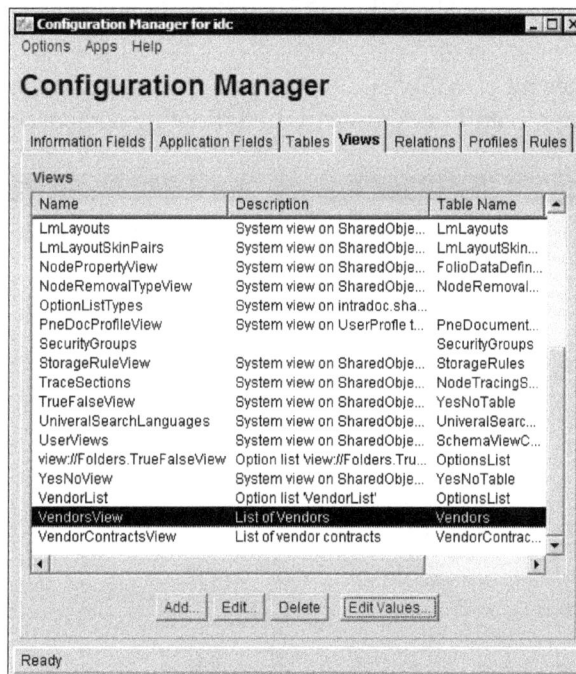

Click on **Edit Batch** on the bottom right. A simple text box comes up (as shown in the following screenshot):

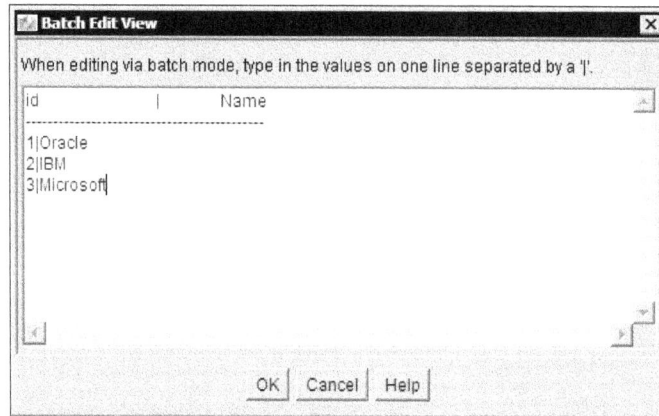

```
┌─────────────────────────────────────────────────────────────┐
│ ▓ Batch Edit View                                        [×] │
├─────────────────────────────────────────────────────────────┤
│ When editing via batch mode, type in the values on one line separated by a '|'. │
│ ┌─────────────────────────────────────────────────────────┐ │
│ │id               |      Name                            ▲│ │
│ │--------------------------------------------             │ │
│ │1|Oracle                                                 │ │
│ │2|IBM                                                    │ │
│ │3|Microsoft|                                             │ │
│ │                                                         │ │
│ │                                                         │ │
│ │                                                        ▼│ │
│ │◄                                                      ► │ │
│ └─────────────────────────────────────────────────────────┘ │
│                    OK    Cancel   Help                       │
└─────────────────────────────────────────────────────────────┘
```

Just type in or paste your values. They need to be separated by a pipe character, the one above the back slash on most keyboards. It's that simple. If you need to put Oracle with ID of 1 then simply type:

1 | Oracle

The header row shows you an example. Just paste your value below it and **OK** the dialogs. Ready?

Now put in the values for VendorContractsView. You can add spaces and tabs if you like so it's easier to edit (as shown in the following screenshot):

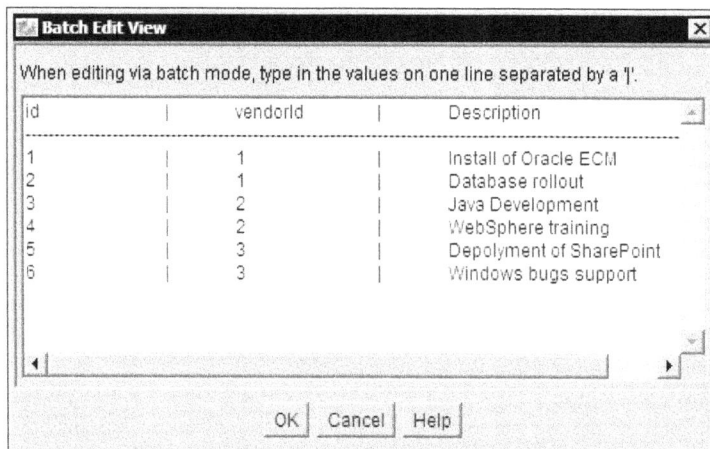

```
┌─────────────────────────────────────────────────────────────┐
│ ▓ Batch Edit View                                        [×] │
├─────────────────────────────────────────────────────────────┤
│ When editing via batch mode, type in the values on one line separated by a '|'. │
│ ┌─────────────────────────────────────────────────────────┐ │
│ │id          |    vendorId     |    Description          ▲│ │
│ │--------------------------------------------             │ │
│ │1           |    1            |    Install of Oracle ECM │ │
│ │2           |    1            |    Database rollout       │ │
│ │3           |    2            |    Java Development       │ │
│ │4           |    2            |    WebSphere training     │ │
│ │5           |    3            |    Depolyment of SharePoint│ │
│ │6           |    3            |    Windows bugs support   │ │
│ │                                                         │ │
│ │                                                        ▼│ │
│ │◄                                                      ► │ │
│ └─────────────────────────────────────────────────────────┘ │
│                    OK    Cancel   Help                       │
└─────────────────────────────────────────────────────────────┘
```

Done! Let's put the fields on the form now. Seriously!

Putting the fields on the form

We already have a **Vendor** field. Let's just edit it so it uses the **VendorsView**:

1. In Configuration Manager go to **Information Fields** and select **Vendor**.
2. Click on **Edit**.
3. Check the **Enable Option List** box and click on the **Configure** button next to it.
4. Select **Use View** and pick **VendorsView**.
5. **OK** the dialogs to complete the edit.

Now let's add a field for vendor contracts.

1. In configuration Manager, click on **Add**. Type **Contract** for the field name.
2. Check the **Enable Option List** box and click on the **Configure** button next to it.
3. Select **Use view** and pick **VendorContractsView**.
4. In the bottom portion of the form check the **Dependent field** box.
5. Pick **xVendor** for **Depends on field**.
6. Pick **Vendors_Contracts** for the relationship (as shown in the following screenshot):

7. You're done! **OK** the dialogs to complete.

Update Database Design. Publish the schema. Bring up your check-in form. Notice how the options in your **Contract** field change when you change the selection in the **Vendor** box (as shown in the following screenshot):

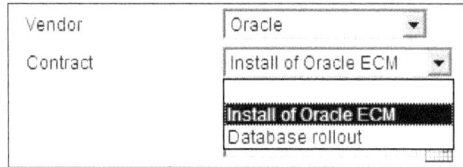

And here's how to handle multiple selections.

Multiple selections

Sometimes you need to select more than one value. For instance, you may engage Oracle on more than one project. So how would you enable that?

Really simple! Just edit the **Contracts** field in Configuration Manager and change the **Option List Type** to **Multiselect List**. That's it! Just publish the schema when you're done (see the following screenshot):

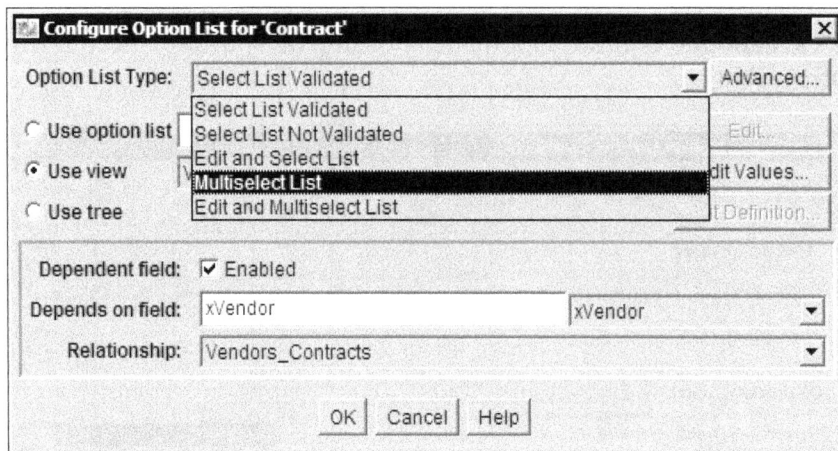

Every time you make a selection from a contract list, a new value is added to the right. The red X next to a value allows users to delete it (see the following screenshot):

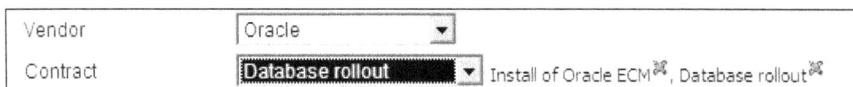

And I left the best for the last. Check out how you can create tree views.

Tree views

It's the cool new addition in 10*g* R3. Instead of two fields for vendors and contracts you can have only one, and still allow multiple selections:

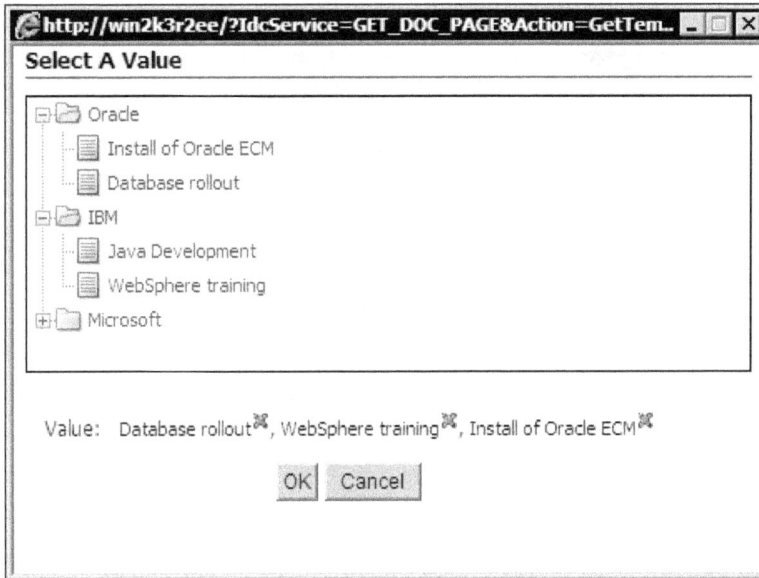

How to enable that?

Just pick **Use Tree** on the **Configure Option List** dialog and click on **Edit Definition**.

All you need to do is pick your first-level view, a relationship, and a second-level view. That's it! And yes, you can still have **Option List Type** set to **Multiselect List**.

Perfect! We have defined new metadata fields. Now what?

Well, first of all, you will see them on the Check In screen. Once you check in a new item you will see your new fields and values on the Content Info screen. And you can also use your new fields to find your content.

In the following section I'll show you how to find content quickly.

How to find content quickly

You already know about the Quick Search box on the top right, and you might've noticed that you can type both content ID and title. What if you need to run a more complex query? What if you need to find all invoices for Oracle Consulting dated after July 1st? Let's use advanced search.

Advanced search

There are two types of advanced search you can perform. The basic is Expanded Form. Click on **Search** on the top left of the screen. The **Expanded Form** comes up (as shown in the following screenshot):

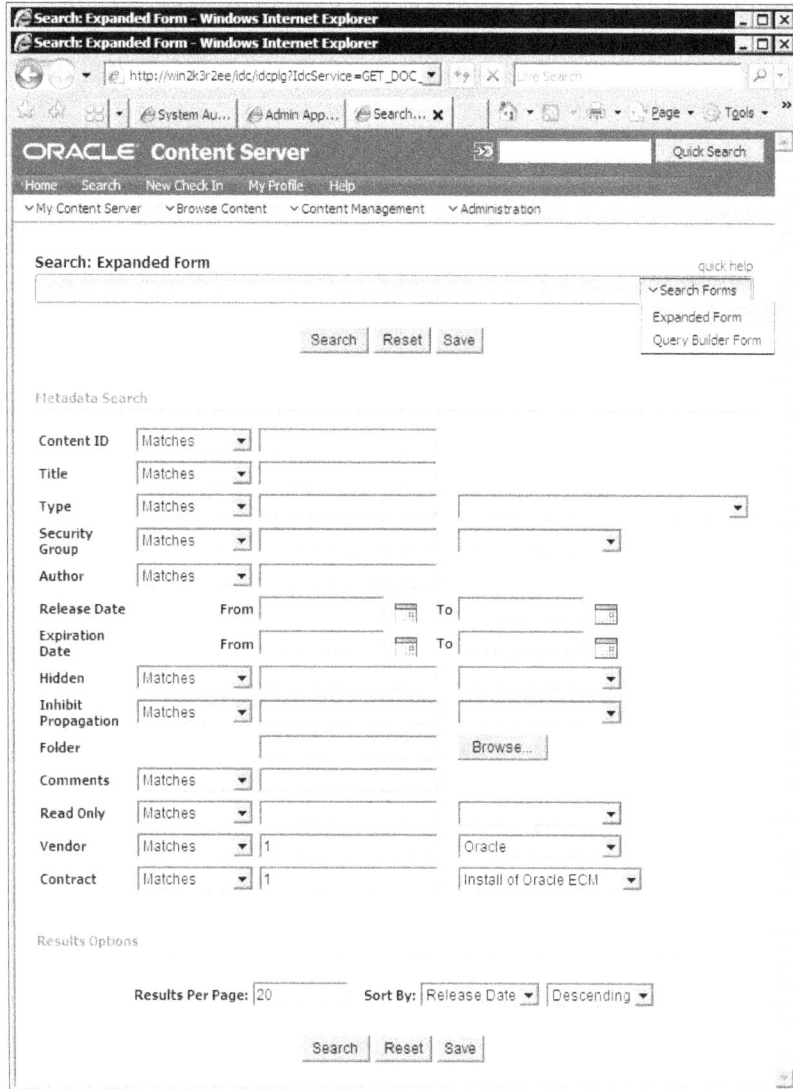

Notice that the Vendor and Contract fields that we added in the previous section are also included in the form. Values for the Contract field change every time you change Vendor!

Lab 6: Finding content

Now change the **Search Forms** dropdown on the top right to **Query Builder Form**
Click on **Show Advanced Options** (as shown in the following screenshot):

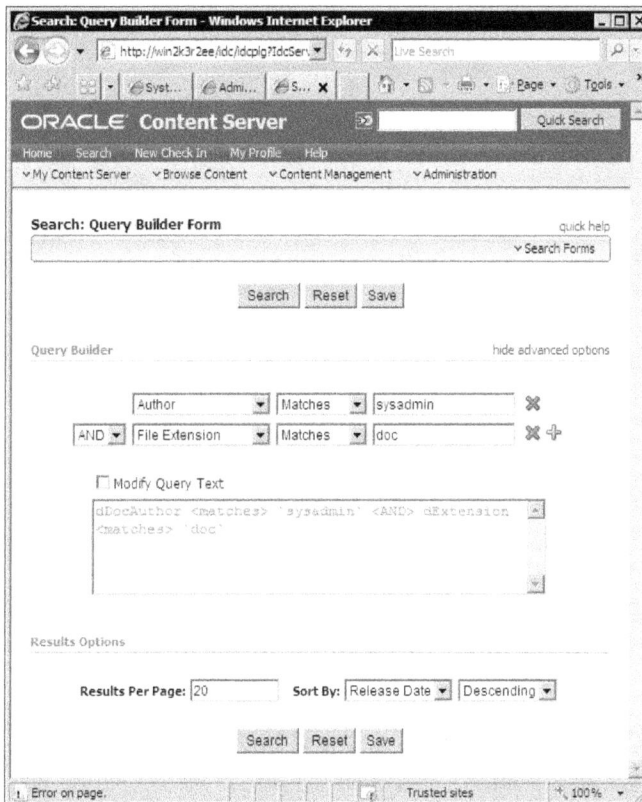

Notice the query expressions getting built in the text box below. I'm sure you
recognize the internal field names we've seen earlier in this chapter. They were
the field names in the database!

Perform a few searches. See how query expressions get built. You'll be using them
later. Content Server query expressions are very powerful. They are used in many
other places from workflows to web development.

Notice that there are several different ways to search the Content Server. There's
a quick search box on the top right, there's the Expanded Search Form, and there's
the Query Builder. Here are a few tips that will help you get things done faster:

- If you need to find an item by a part of its content ID or title then use the
  Quick Search Box.

- If you need to search within the item's content (full text search) or you need to specify values for one or more metadata fields, use the Expanded Search Form.

- If you need to type a query expression then use the Query Builder.

Can't see the fields you've just created in the Expanded Form? Make sure you mark it as **Indexed** in the Configuration Manager when you create or update it (see the following screenshot):

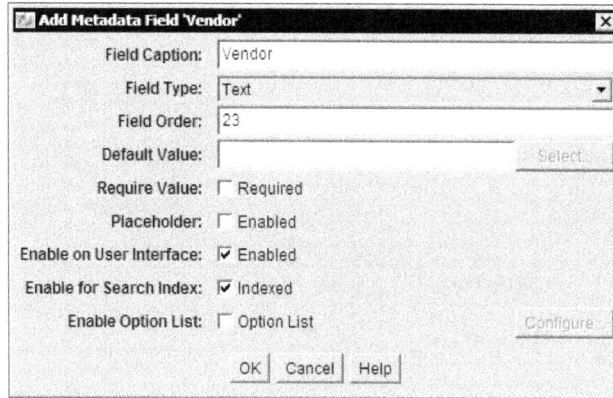

And here's how to make your search results look exactly as you want them. Let's look at how to customize search results.

Customizing search results

There're several ways to customize search results. The easiest one is to use **Change View | Customize** on the search results screen (as shown in the following screenshot):

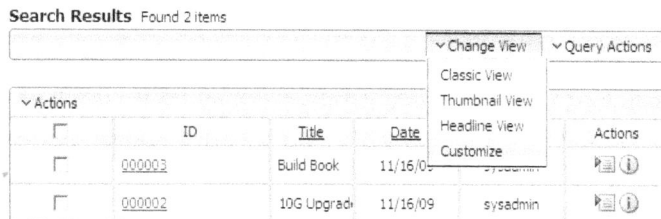

This is great but what about the check-in form? Isn't it critical that users only see the relevant fields, so they don't feel frustrated and overwhelmed, and end up putting garbage in the fields?

Its sure is critical, so let's see what's involved in customizing the check-in and content info forms.

Customizing the check-in and content info forms

I saved the best for the last, didn't I? So how do you only show the fields that you really want to show? And how do you move them around on the form so they make the most sense?

There are two ways. Let's see them one by one.

How to hide unused fields all the time

Content Server has a tool for controlling how meta fields appear on the check-in form, content info, search, and so on. It calls **Rules**.

Go to the **Rules** tab on Configuration Manager, and click on **Add** to open the Add New Rule dialog (as shown in the following screenshot):

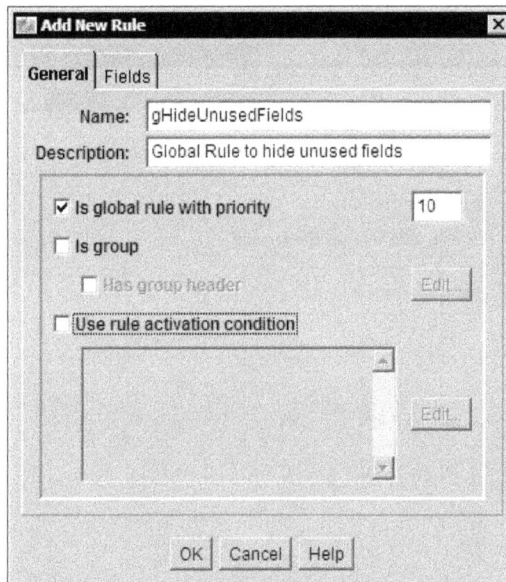

1. Mark the rule as Global.
2. Give it a name. I recommend that you prefix global rules with "g" or "Global_".

3. Flip to the **Fields** tab. This is where the magic starts happening!

4. Click on **Add**.

5. Let's say, we wanted to hide **Trash Delete Date**. Pick that in the **Field Name** dropdown (as shown in the following screenshot):

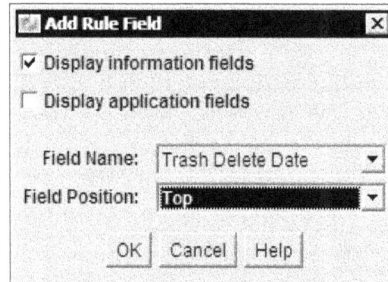

> You can also move fields around on the form. This is what the **Field Position** dropdown is for.

6. Define what you want the field to look or behave like (see the following screenshot):

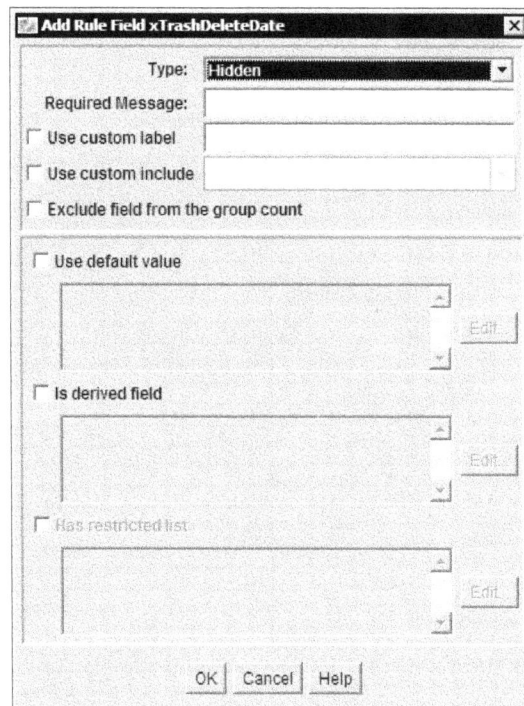

The dialog **Add Rule Field** gives you a lot of control. Here're a few things you can do with it:

- You can simply hide the field by picking **Hidden** from the **Type** dropdown at the top.
- You can make it required by picking **Required** from it.
- You can change the label for the field by specifying a custom label.
- You can specify a default value that will be pre-populated in the field.
- You can derive the value from another field.
- You can restrict the values the user can type in or select.

You can add as many fields to the rule as you like. In the screenshot below I marked all Trash Delete fields as **hidden**:

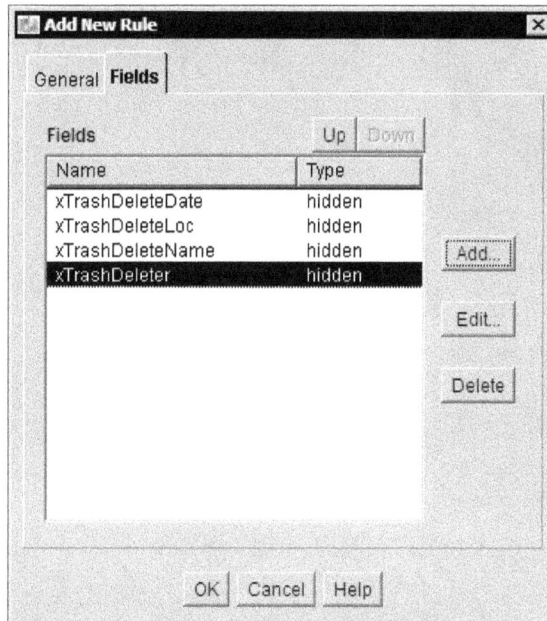

Click on **OK** and publish your schema. Then bring up a Check In form to see your changes.

The rule we created is a global one, with no activation conditions. The fields will be hidden on the search and content info screens.

What if we only want to hide the field on a Check In form, but show on a Content Info screen? Here's how to show fields based on condition.

How to show fields based on condition

Let me walk you through the steps to set it up:

1. Edit the rule and check **Use rule activation condition** (as shown in the following screenshot):

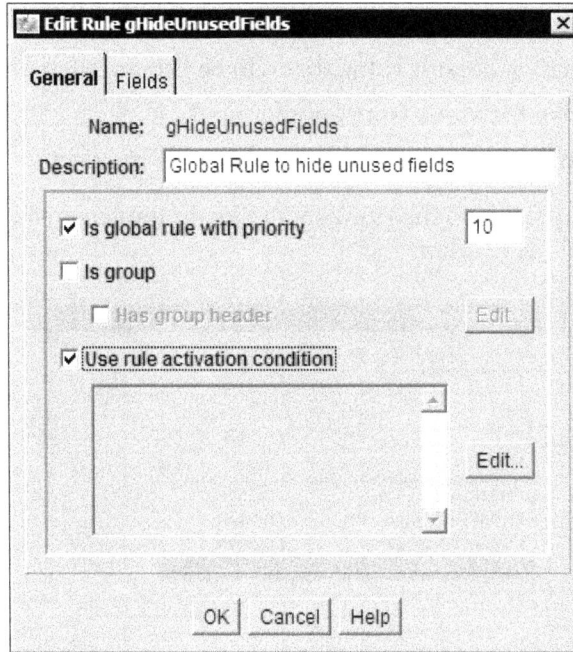

2. Click on **Edit**.
3. In the **Edit Activation Condition** dialog click on **Add...**. Name your condition something like "Check in Only".
4. Pick **Use action | Check In New** (as shown in the following screenshot):

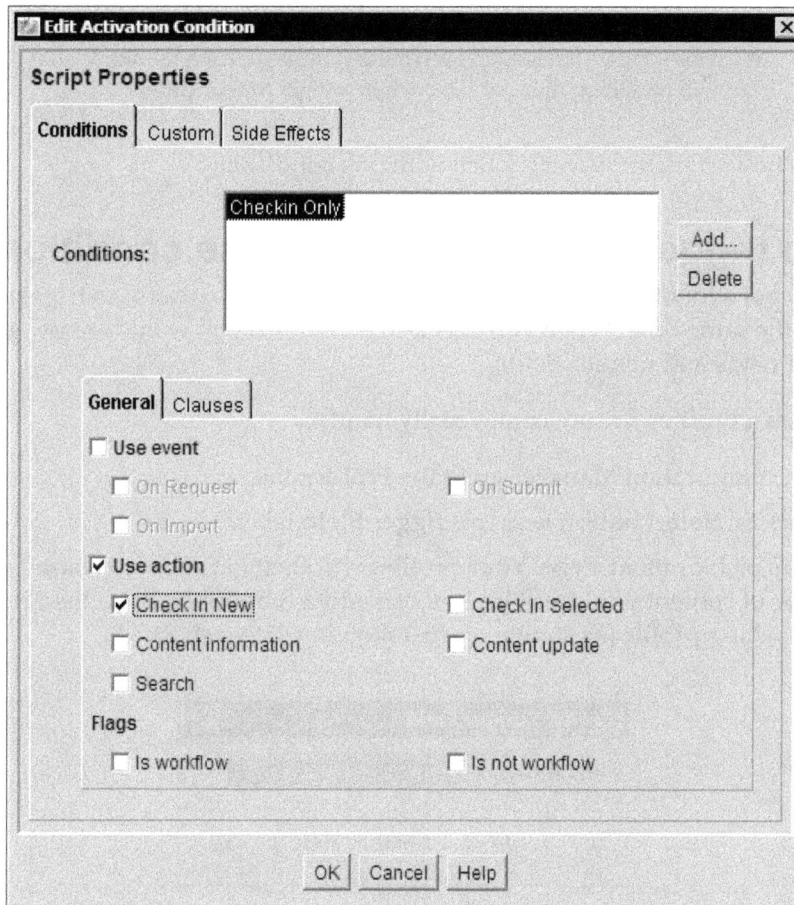

OK to close the dialogs. Publish the schema and test your changes.

> Did you notice the script that now appears in the Rule Activation
> Condition box (as shown in the following screenshot)?

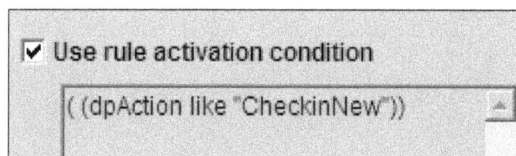

> It's iDoc script, Oracle UCM scripting language. It's a lot like Visual Basic. We will be seeing more of iDoc when we get to workflows.

And here's how to trigger several rules with one condition.

How to trigger several rules with one condition

It's hard to put a lot of fields in one rule. Sometimes it's also useful to trigger a set of rules at the same time. When you check-in an invoice you want to show general accounting fields and invoice fields.

This is when a **Profiles** feature comes really handy.

1. In Configuration Manager go to the **Profiles** tab.

2. Click on **Select** button next to **Trigger Field** label.

3. Let's pick Content Type. Your profiles will then get activated based on the type of content you check in. You can add a brand-new meta field just for switching profile (as shown in the following screenshot):

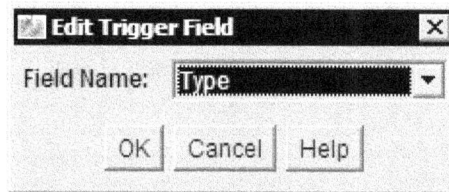

4. Click on **Add** at the bottom of the dialog to add a new profile.

5. Let's call it **MarketingDocuments**. You can then specify the properties of the profile and add rules to it (as shown in the following screenshot):

6. **OK** the dialogs and publish your schema.

Once the profile is created in the system, you'll notice that the **Search** and **New Check In** buttons at the top now have dropdowns next to them (as shown in the following screenshot):

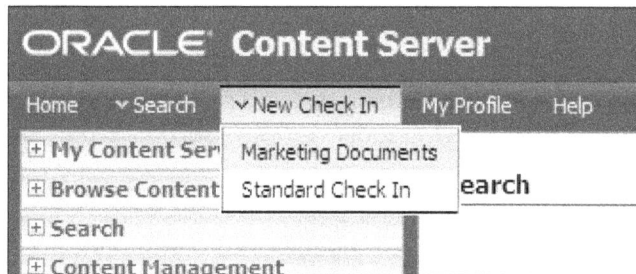

If you try loading the check-in form for Marketing Documents, you will see exactly the same form as if you picked Standard Check In. Why?

Because the only rule that profile now has happens to be a *global* rule. This means, it's always on. NO matter WHAT profile you select.

If you edit this rule and uncheck the **Is Global Rule** box (and publish the schema) then your hidden fields will begin to show on a Standard Check In form. But they will continue to be hidden on the Marketing Documents. The Profile system works!

Now I'm going to ask you for a little favor. Pause for a second and think of the power of profiles and rules. See how very complex business logic can be used to control the display of the check-in, search and the content info forms, and how you can use them to engineer a smooth, logical, and pleasant user experience.

The purpose of profiles is to display to the user only what he or she needs to see to correctly contribute and classify their content.

Other systems define rigid metadata lists required for separate libraries or collections. Oracle UCM has the most flexibility by allowing any metadata field to be used and re-used in many different scenarios. You don't have to create many variations of the same field (one for each collection), just to make sure it shows and displays where you want it.

The designers of the UCM know that users HATE filling out long forms, especially ones filled with extraneous and empty fields. Profiles and rules are truly the way to dynamically display relevant information at the time when the user needs it.

And there's more to this story! Let's take a look at the future of metadata.

The future of metadata

Metadata may be the single most important feature of Oracle UCM. Imagine trying to find a scanned copy of a vendor invoice if you had no metadata, no title, description, date of the invoice, vendor name, or contract number. Imagine going through thousands of digital images wasting many hours just to find the one you need. You now have the power to take your project and your organization to the next level by bringing just the info your business needs — exactly when it's needed. And you have a complete picture of what tools you can use.

But what if you'd like to tap the brain power of your entire organization and have your users shape and redefine your metadata over time? I'm sure you've heard of the Web 2.0 tools such as Tag Clouds and Folksonomies that let you build on and benefit from the collective intelligence.

Even if this is not the direction you're taking right now, this trend is simply too important to ignore, and you owe it to yourself to keep current. There are thousands of online resources and books on this subject. The best introduction that I've been recommending to my friends for a while is a book by Billy Cripe and others, called *Reshaping Your Business with Web 2.0: Using New Social Technologies to Lead Business Transformation*. If you don't yet consider yourself an ace of Web 2.0 then grab a copy of this book and see for yourself what you've been missing out on.

This's it for this chapter. All I have left is a brief summary.

Summary

You now know where Content Server stores all metadata values, how to add, edit, and delete fields. You know how to display them on the forms just the way you need them to show. You also know how to hide the fields you don't want at the moment, and how to show and rearrange them when you need them back.

And you know how to do all this without writing a single line of code!

In the next chapter we will complete your foundation of Oracle UCM expertise. We will look at the controversial and confusing subject, Content Server Security. But don't worry. Over the years, I came up with a special way of explaining security. It will be easy for you.

4
Understanding Security

A few years ago I was spending days in the meeting room with a couple of very bright students and two talented developers who were new to Stellent. We were there for nearly a week trying to make security work for that organization and it wasn't a pleasant experience!

A lot of people are confused and even scared when it comes to Content Server security. You might be too. I've seen committees and organizations spending months at a time trying to understand it.

What's going on?

In March of 2009 I uploaded a video tutorial on YouTube (www.youtube.com/stellentexperts) where I tried a totally different approach at explaining Content Server security. Hundreds of people have watched it since and I'm proud to tell you that it made it crystal clear, logical, and easy to understand.

The new approach made all the difference!

Let's use it here to make Content Server security clear and easy for you. Here's what you will learn in this chapter:

- A simple trick to quickly understand the Security Model — the surest path to get it right the first time and avoid costly redesigns! And another damaging UCM myth shattered, Groups, Roles, and Accounts can be easy to use — if you, as Administrator, know what you're doing!

- Understand the components of Content Server security — how they work together to give you the power and flexibility you need for addressing today's tough business problems.

- Things you need to know when planning your security model that will steer you clear of common pitfalls, and save you from weeks and months of nasty cleansing and matching.

- How to use the Content Server role-based security — the foundation of almost any other security model and many other important UCM controls such as workflow and virtual folders.

- How to use the account-based security component to add the flexibility you require for addressing the needs of hierarchies, web and shared environments.

Ready? Let's get into it and let me show you the security model.

Security model made easy

First of all, let me mention that by saying **Security Model** I mean primarily its **authorization** component. It's the one that defines what users can do and what content they can access. There's also the **authentication** piece that determines who the user really is, and there's **auditing**, that keeps track of what people do. We've seen the use of the Content Server log files and the use of providers to connect the Content Server to LDAP for authentication in *Chapter 2, Major Controls*, so let's focus on authorization.

We will start by placing "red flags" around common confusion points.

Why does it seems confusing

Most of us are used to Windows and UNIX security systems, user groups, file and folder permissions, and so on. We're comfortable with these and are expecting Oracle UCM to work the same way. But it doesn't! What you need is a paradigm shift.

A paradigm shift

We've seen that Content Server is like a database, not like a directory structure. There is no hierarchy, so you cannot just go to a folder and say that John can access this folder but Mary cannot. We can't even say that the folders and content items would inherit permissions from their parent.

If all you have is one big database table then you have to assign permissions at the row level; that is, at the level of individual content items.

And if you have a million records, you're not going to assign permissions to each individual record. So how does Stellent do it?

It groups together records with similar security.

For example, if you have records belonging to different departments then you can group them by department. On a website you can group them by section of the site.

Now here's a second reason for people being confused about the UCM security model. It's the use of multiple dimensions.

Multiple dimensions

If you follow documentation you'll be learning many ways to control content item security one after another. Soon enough, you'll be hopelessly confused.

It's like a backhoe hat has five different sets of handles for moving it left to right, up or down, one for grabbing and releasing the soil, one for moving its base up and down. And yes there's another pair for moving the platform!

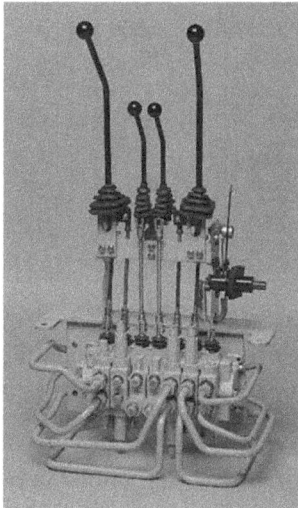

So new operator's first month on the job will be nothing except for swearing and the noise of an erratically moving mechanic shovel, crashing into trees and closely parked cars!

OK, OK. There's a better way to learn them. Let's look at the main components of UCM security.

Components of UCM security

There are two components, that get used most of the time — the role-based and account-based authorization. If you install additional components such as Web Content Management, Collaboration Manager, or Records Management, you will end up with additional locks. So how do you manage all of them without getting confused?

Here's the way I found to work really well. Once you understand it, you will never be confused again.

Imagine the door in your house or apartment with several locks on it. Let's say, it has three locks. If you open one lock, lock number 1, but locks number 2 and 3 are still engaged, the door is still locked.

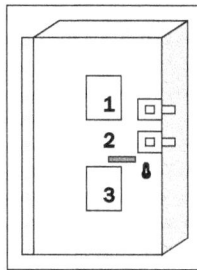

Let's say, the role-based authorization is your lock number one, and account-based authorization is the lock number two. If John's role gives him access to a content item, but his account prevents it then lock #1 will be open and lock #2 closed. It's that easy.

Never again will you have to consider interactions between components of the UCM security model. There is none! Just check your locks one by one. If all of them are open then John has access.

Now it's time to look at individual components. Shall we? Let's start with the role-based component.

Understanding the role-based component

Earlier in this chapter I mentioned that setting permissions on each individual content item is not practical and that UCM groups together content with the same security. How does it do that?

Security groups

A **Security Group** is a group of content items that have the same level of security.

There is a standard metadata field called **Security Group**, dSecurityGroup.

In a sample organization that has accounting, sales, and manufacturing — you may split content into three security groups, one for accounting, one for sales, and one for manufacturing. Content in sales will have dSecurityGroup=sales.

Out of the box, there're two security groups — **Public** and **Secure** (as shown in the following screenshot). You can create additional security groups as you see fit; I'll show you how to do this later in this chapter.

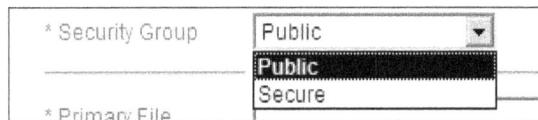

So now that you've seen how the content is grouped together by security, let's see how user access is controlled. Let's start by examining user roles.

User roles

What are the **Roles**? In short, access to groups of content is controlled through the *user role membership*. What do I mean by role membership?

Let's say, we have a local accounting manager who has full control over documents in accounting, and clerks, who can only modify and create content but not delete. Let's also assume that the manager can go to user administration to add new people in accounting and give them permissions.

Let's complete this picture by adding auditors who can read content in accounting but not create, modify, or delete. They shouldn't grant permissions either.

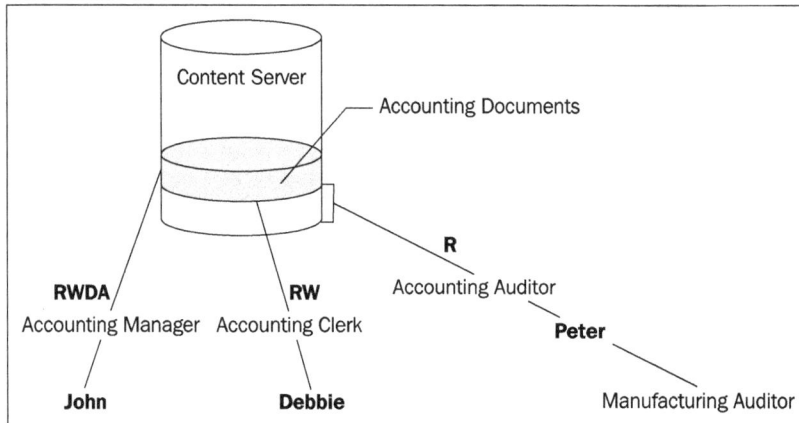

When a manager adds a new clerk to accounting, wouldn't it be easier just to say that "Debbie is an Accounting Clerk" rather than specify that she has read and write access to accounting documents?

Also if Peter is an internal auditor and he also needs access to documents in Manufacturing, all you need to do is to add him to another role. Now Peter has read access to both Accounting and Manufacturing and is set to perform his auditing task.

That's great, but how are we going to do this? How are we going to specify that the Manager Role has full access and Auditor is read only?

The answer to this question is **Permissions**.

Permissions

Permissions define what user roles can do on content groups. This is the easiest piece of the entire role-based security system. Check out the following screenshot:

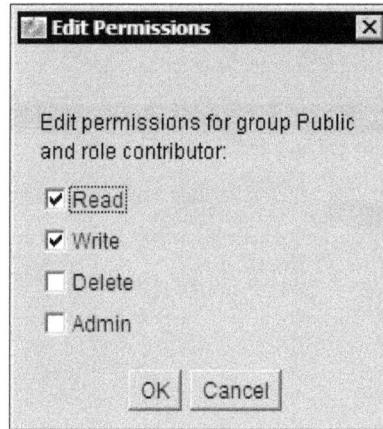

Just check the boxes against permissions that you want to assign to your role. **Admin** permission lets you give access to this security group to other users. This is how **sub-administrators** get created.

And now that the picture is complete, let's see role-based security in action.

Lab 9: Working with content groups and user roles

1. Bring up User Admin.

2. Click on **Security | Permissions by Group...** (as shown in the following screenshot):

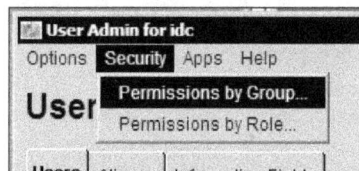

3. The **Permissions by Group** dialog comes up. Select **Public** (as shown in the following screenshot):

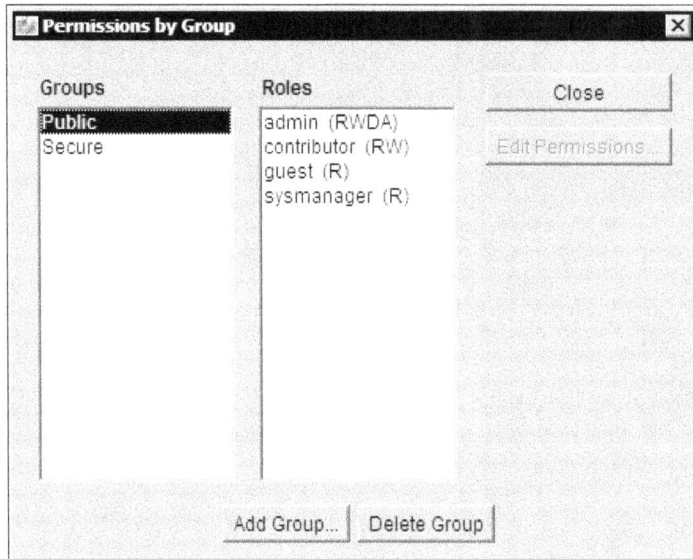

4. Notice that the list of user roles is displayed on the right, with their corresponding permissions specified in brackets. For example, the **contributor** role has read and write access to the **Public** security group.

5. Click on **Add Group...** button at the bottom of the dialog.

6. Add a group called **accounting** (as shown in the following screenshot):

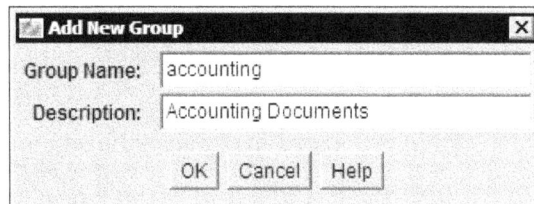

7. Add another group called **manufacturing**.

8. Close the dialogs to return to User Admin.

9. Now select **Security | Permissions by Role**.

10. Click on the **Add New Role** button and add a role called **Accounting Manager**.

11. Select it and select **accounting** security group (as shown in the
    following screenshot):

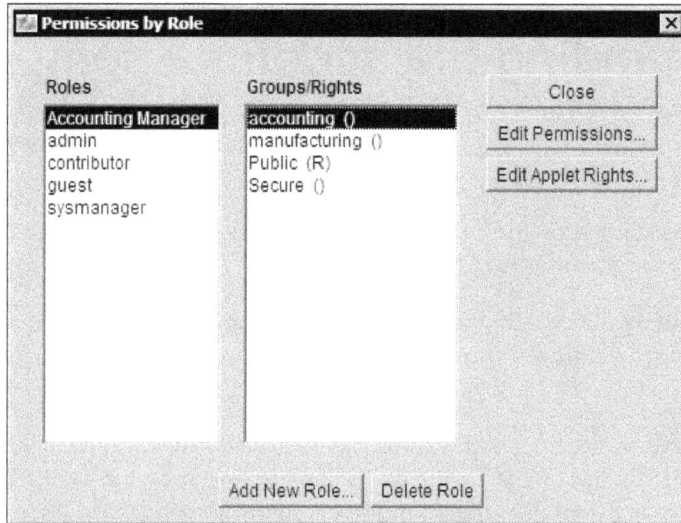

12. Click on the **Edit Permissions...** button on the right. Click on **Admin**.
    Notice that other lower-level permissions also get checked.

13. Add **Accounting Clerk** and **Auditor** roles.

14. Give **Auditor** read access to both **accounting** and **manufacturing** security
    groups (as shown in the following screenshot):

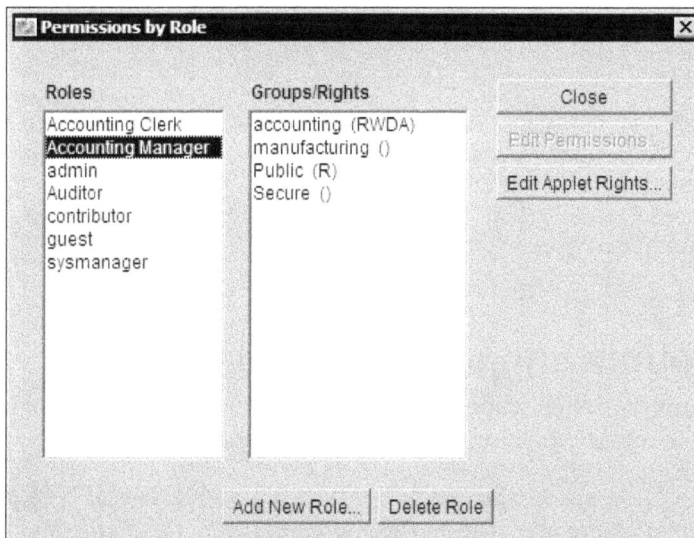

Note that **Accounting Manager** and **Accounting Clerk** can only access documents in accounting.

Understanding the accounts component

Let's say, you only want accounting clerks to work with the *current year's* data and have *read-only access to historic content*. If you try to do this with role-based security the picture will get really ugly.

Now if you split your accounting into payable and receivable, it will get even messier. What are we going to do about it?

Role-based security that we just looked at is lock number one on the door. Sometimes you'd want a more detailed control than it can give you. We need more locks on that door!

If Debbie is in Accounts Receivable and tries to access any content in Accounting then our lock #1, the role-based security, will be open. But we need lock #2 to be closed when she accidentally tries to modify a historic record or a document in Accounts Payable.

Let's see how adding lock #2 helps us solve this problem.

How accounts are different

Accounts, our lock #2, are completely different from our lock #1 — role-based security. As we've just seen, the role-based component can really use some help when it comes to *supporting hierarchies* and this is exactly where accounts excel.

> I've seen how the actual use of the word "*Account*" can be very confusing. When they say "account", most people think of the *User Account*, the record in the system that gives them access. I found that when you call Accounts in Content Server "*Content Accounts*" at least, for a month or two, it may prove really clear things up.

How accounts support hierarchies

Content Account is another standard metadata field, dDocAccount. It's also there to group together content with similar security. But here's the big difference:

Unlike dSecurityGroup, dDocAccount support hierarchies based on a prefix rule. For example, if you have access to ca/on then you'll also have access to:

- `ca/on/montreal`
- `ca/on/toronto`
- `ca/on/ottawa` and also
- `ca/ontario_business`, please note that slashes are optional!

Slashes make values in dDocAccount easier to read, but you can use any other character to separate levels of access.

Now you know how to solve the problem I mentioned earlier in this section. Let's define the following Content Accounts for our sample company:

- `accounting/payable/current` — current active documents in Accounts Payable. Clerks will have read and write access here.
- `accounting/payable/past` — past, archived documents in Payable. Only a manager will be able to modify them but the clerks are Read Only.
- `accounting/receivable/current` — current active documents in Accounts Receivable.
- `accounting/receivable/past` — past documents in Receivable that only a manager can modify.

And here's how we are going to specify access:

- A head of accounting will have access to `accounting`.
- A manager of Accounts Payable will have access to `accounting/payable`.
- A clerk in Receivable will only have full access to `accounting/receivable/current`.

Before we go on, let me give you a word of caution:

The maximum length of dDocAccount *is limited to* 35 *characters.*

Now let's see how to differentiate read-only from full access to a content account.

How permissions are specified

This the easy part. User's permissions to access specific content accounts are specified directly on the Edit User screen. If John is the head of Accounts Payable, he will have `accounting/payable` in the list of Content Accounts he can access.

Let's put it all together:

Lab 10: Working with content accounts

First, we need to make sure that Content Accounts are enabled on the system.

> By default, Accounts are disabled. To find out see if the Accounts tab is present when you edit a user in User Admin. If the tab is not there then you'll need to enable accounts before you can use them.
>
> The following screenshot shows the Edit User dialog when Accounts are enabled and the Accounts tab is present:

Edit User Peter

Info | Roles | Accounts

Name: Peter
Full Name: Peter
Password: *****
Confirm Password: *****
E-mail Address: peter@myco.com
User Type:
User Locale: English-US

OK Cancel Help

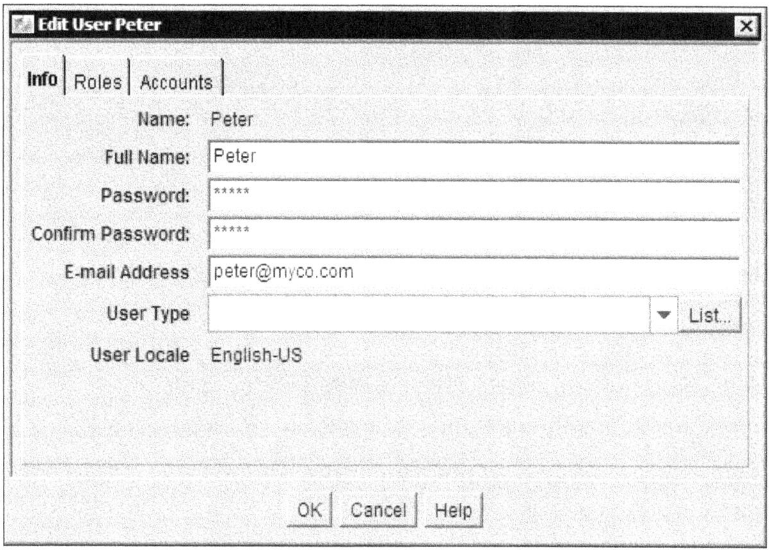

How to enable accounts

Here's how to do it:

1. Bring up Admin Server. (See *Chapter 2* if you need a refresher.)
2. Click on the Content Server instance where you need to enable accounts.
3. Go to **General Configuration** (as shown in the following screenshot):

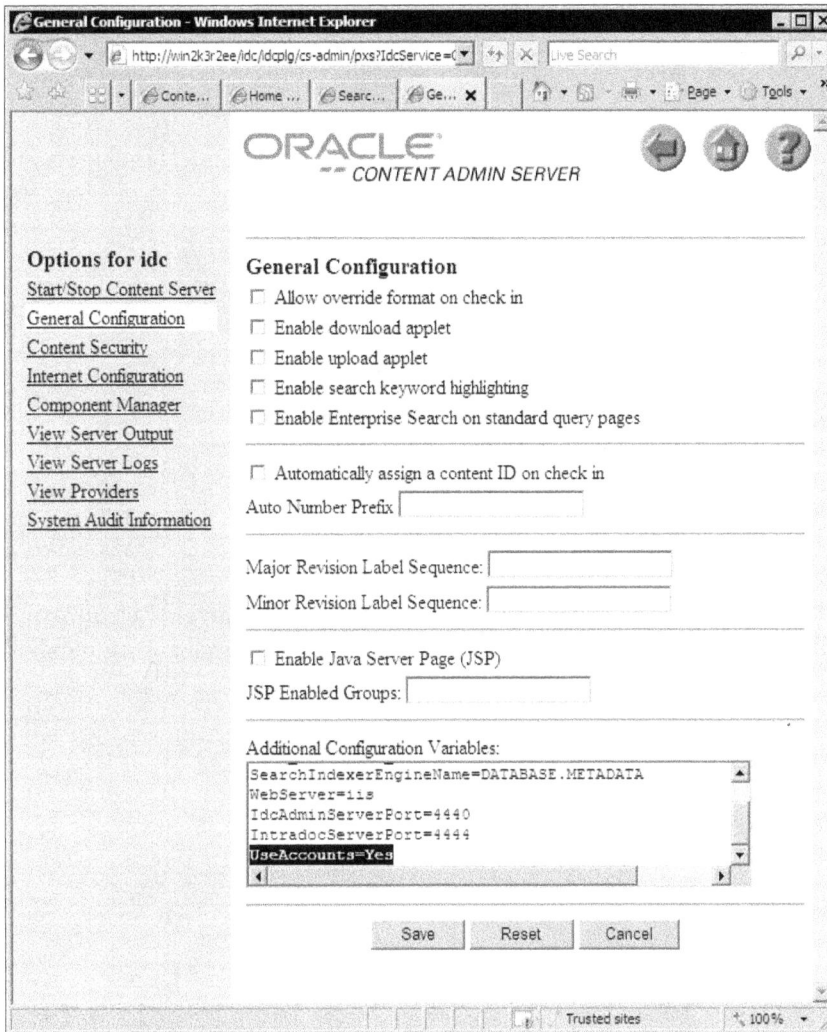

4. Scroll to the **Additional Configuration Variables** text box at the bottom of the page.

5. Append the following at the end: **UseAccounts=Yes**.

6. Restart Content Server.

Accounts are now enabled. You'll need to close and re-open the User Admin application to see the changes.

And there's one more step that you need to do if you need a list of values to show in a dropdown next to the account field. In the following section we'll see how to create pre-defined accounts.

How to create pre-defined accounts

Let's go ahead and create the four content accounts we looked at earlier in this section:

1. In User Admin go to **Security | Predefined Accounts...** (as shown in the following screenshot).

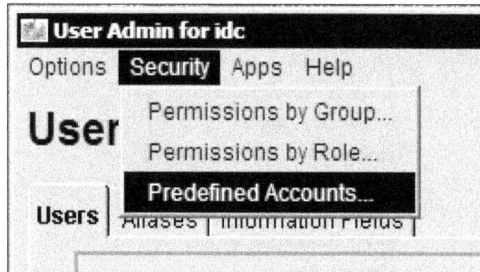

2. Click on the **Add** button.

3. Add the following accounts: **accounting/payable/current**, **accounting/payable/past**, **accounting/receivable/current**, and **accounting/receivable/past** (as shown in the following screenshot).

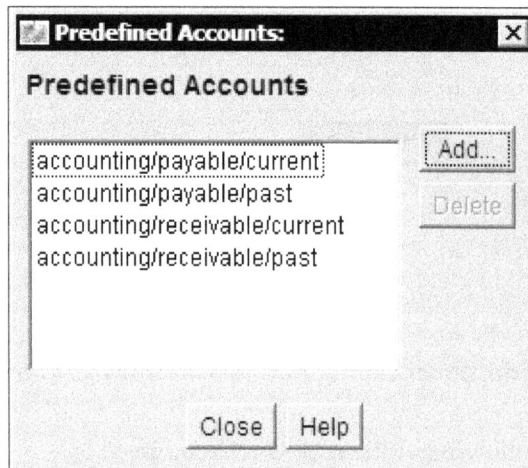

OK. We now have the accounts defined, but we're not done yet. The next section shows you how to give users access to content accounts.

How to give users access to content accounts

Here's how to put it all together, it's actually very simple:

1. Create a new user, just like you did in *Chapter 2*. Switch to the **Accounts** tab as shown in the following screenshot:

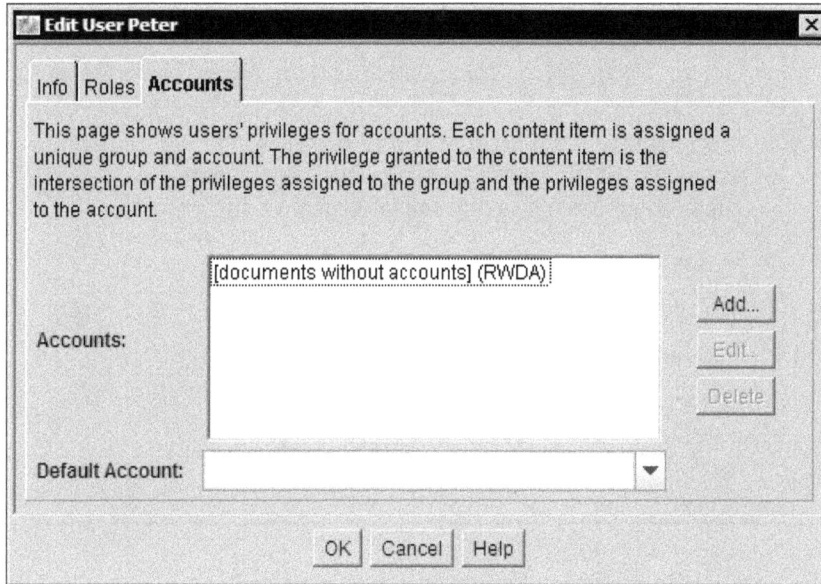

> Did you notice the two special accounts — the **[documents without accounts]** and the **[all accounts]**? They give you a chance to grant your admin users access to all content regardless of its account, and to control access to content where no account value is specified.
>
> When creating users with iDoc Script these will become #none and #all correspondingly.
>
> And when you need to select all content items that have no value set in the account field, use the following query:
>
> ```
> dDocAccount <matches> ''
> ```

2. Click on **Add**. The **Add New Account** dialog displays. You can now pick from a list of pre-defined accounts or type it in (as shown in the following screenshot):

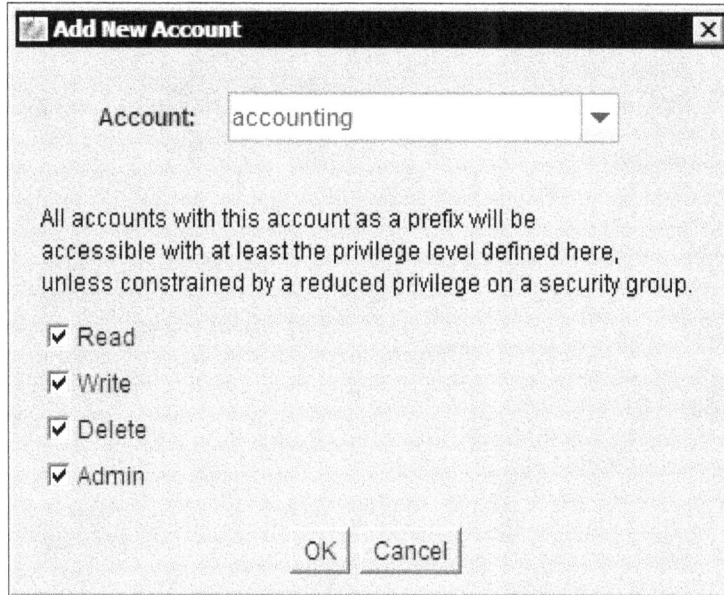

3. Uncheck **Write** to reduce Peter's access to read-only.

All done! Now bring up your check-in form (as shown in the following screenshot).

Notice how your newly created Security Groups and Content Accounts are displayed in the drop-down boxes.

And here are a few important last minute comments on planning your security model.

Planning your security model

A security model, just like a metadata model, has long-ranging implications. It's much easier to spend a few more days planning when you still have no content in the system than trying to migrate your content into a new model later.

This said, it's still better to go ahead with your best guess than get stuck in a planning stage forever! And yes, you can change your security model at any time— I'll show you how to mass-update your content in *Chapter 9, Migrating Configuration*.

The best way to get started is by reviewing the things that affect security.

Things that affect security

When using multiple security components together such as role-based, account-based, Web Content Management, and others you may decide to place more emphasis on one of the "locks" and keep others relatively open. For instance, when you rely on accounts to control your access to content hierarchies, you may decide to place most of your content into the Public security group.

Also, when planning a security model, you might find it easier to start with broad strokes, such as defining your content categories, the degree of control you require over them, and your use case model.

We will look at these in a bit more detail in the following sections.

Content categories

Content categories are main "buckets" of content that you want to keep separately, like departments in your company or sub-sites in a large website.

You may consider using security groups to split content into these but you can also keep your lock #1 wide open and use accounts to control them.

The next aspect to look at is the degree of control.

Degree of control

These are additional degrees of control you might need over your broad content categories. For example, you may need to implement hierarchies and folder structures with different levels of access or you may need to separate public, private, and top secret content.

Your use cases

In many cases, a good use case model can be very helpful when it comes to security. For once, it identifies the types of users you have. You'll immediately see what your Head of Accounting needs to do, what the Manager of Receivable can, and how his system interactions are different from those of an Auditor.

Other UCM products you might be using

This book focuses on Oracle Content Server and Web Content Management. If you use or are planning to use other products such as Collaboration Manager or Universal Records Management, these products will affect your security. Why?

Each of them adds another "lock on the door" to your security model. You then have an option of keeping these new locks wide open and using the role-based and account-based security or adding the new locks to the mix.

Just remember to keep the locks separate. Each of them has its own use.

Summary

In this chapter you learned how to use Oracle UCM Security. You've learned why so many people get confused by it, and a simple and effective strategy to keep things clear.

You now know its major components, Role-based and Account-based security, and how they complement each other to help you meet your needs.

In the next chapter you'll learn about Content Server workflows, and how to harness their powers to automate approval processes.

5
Understanding Workflows

Welcome! In the previous chapter we finished laying the foundation of our Oracle Content Server expertise. Now let's build on it, to give you the tools you'll need in daily operations and administration. This chapter will fill you in on Content Server workflows.

Workflows are one of the most used and useful features of UCM. They give you the power to quickly set up reviews and approvals for documents, web pages, product documentation, "stage gates" for project management artifacts, "virtual voting" on government legislation, gathering digital signatures, and SOX compliance reviews.

This chapter covers things you'd be doing most of the time as well as other important things you ought to know about workflows. More specifically you will learn:

- How to set up and change Content Server workflows—allowing you to get up to speed really fast, walking you step by step through an automation of a real-world approval process.

- Hidden (and frequently overlooked) facts about content life cycle that will help you locate and reclaim your disappeared content items.

- Tools you need for advanced workflow design such as workflow templates, jumps, sub-workflows, and scripting—that let you harness the true power of Content Server workflows.

- How to group approvers and even select them dynamically based on the business rules—maybe the last bit of advice you will need to automate that complex business process you were looking at.

- Different types of workflows you have to choose from and how to pick the best one for your task at hand.

How to set up and change workflows

First thing's first. Let's start by looking at the tools that you will be using to set up and configure your workflows.

Discover the Workflow Admin application

Go to **Administration | Admin Applets** and launch **Workflow Admin**. The Workflow Admin application comes up (as shown in the following screenshot):

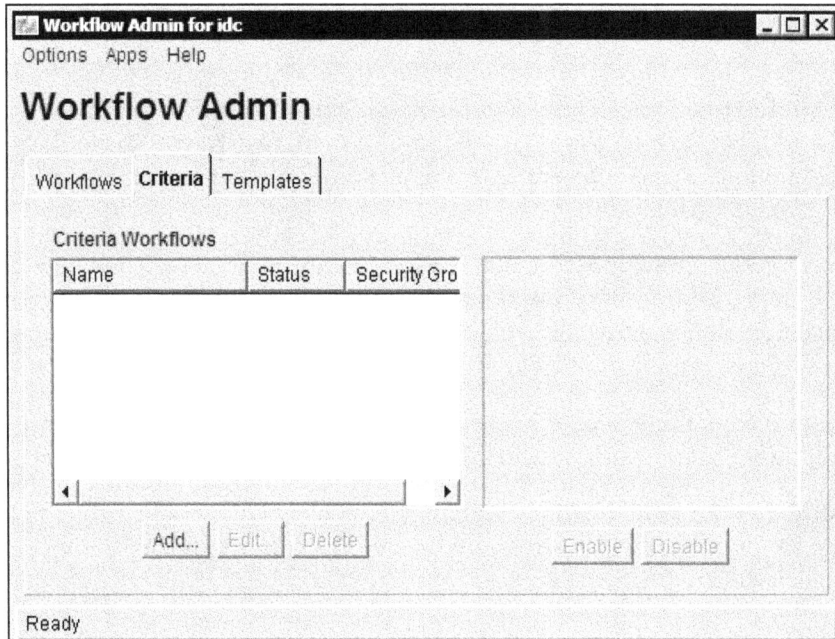

There are three tabs:

- **Workflows**: This tab is used for administering Basic or Manual Workflows. We will be covering them later in this chapter.

- **Criteria**: This tab deals with Automatic or **Criteria Workflows** — the type we will be using most often.

- **Templates**: This is the place where you can pre-assemble **Workflow Templates** — reusable pieces that you can use to create new basic workflows.

Let's create a simple automatic workflow. I call it *automatic* because content enters the workflow *automatically* when it is modified or created.

> If you will be using e-mail notifications then be sure to
> check your **Internet Configuration** screen in Admin Server.
> See *Chapter 2, Major Controls,* if you need a refresher on how
> to launch the Admin Server interface.

I'll walk you through the steps in using automatic workflows.

Lab 7: Using automatic workflows

Here's the process for creating a criteria workflow:

Creating a criteria workflow

Follow these steps:

1. Go to the **Criteria** tab and click on **Add**. The **New Criteria Workflow** dialog comes up (as shown in the following screenshot):

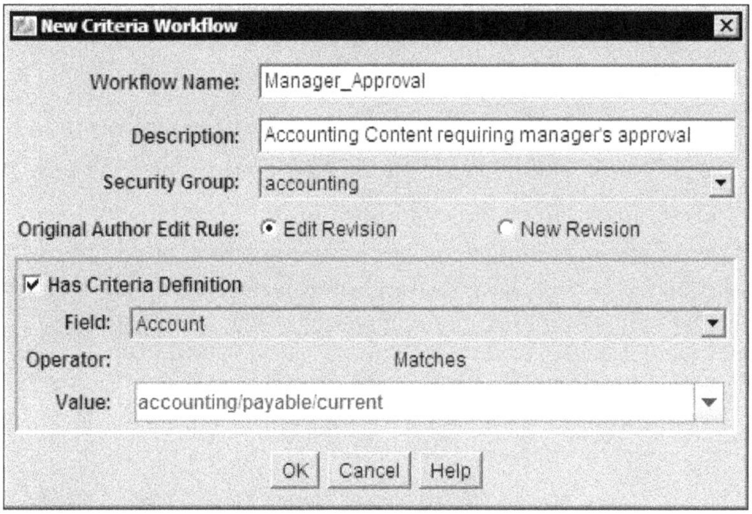

2. Fill in **Workflow Name** and **Description**.

3. Pick the **Security Group**. Only items with the same security group as the workflow can enter it. Let's use the security group we've created in the previous chapter. Select **accounting**.

4. We're creating a Criteria Workflow, so let's check the **Has Criteria Definition** box.

5. Now you can specify criteria that content must match to enter the workflow. For the sake of this lab, let's pick **Account** for the **Field**, and **accounting/payable/current** for the **Value**.

Please note that a content item must match at least two conditions to enter the workflow: it must belong to the same security group as the workflow, and it must match the criteria of the workflow.

As soon as a new content item is created with Security Group of `accounting` and Content Account value is set to **accounting/payable/current**, it will enter our workflow.

> It will not enter the workflow if its metadata is simply updated to these values. It takes a new check-in for an item to enter a criteria workflow.
>
> If you need it to enter a workflow after a metadata update then consider custom components available from the Fishbowl Solutions (`www.fishbowlsolutions.com`).

You can use any metadata field and value pair as criteria for entering the workflow. But you can only have one condition. What if that's not enough?

If you need to perform additional checks before you can accept the item in a workflow then keep your criteria really open, and do your checks in the workflow itself. I'll show you how, later in this chapter.

The diagram next illustrates how a content item flows through a criteria workflow. You may find it useful to refer back to it as you follow the steps in this lab.

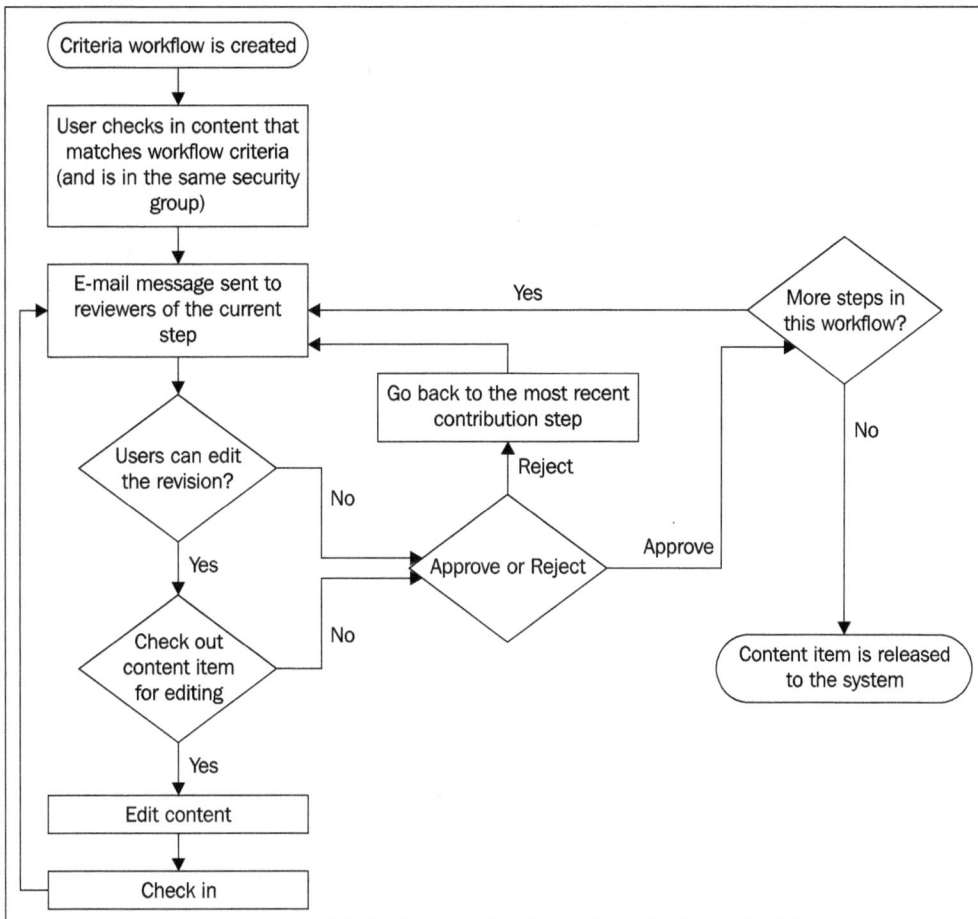

OK. We have a workflow created but there're two problems with it: it has no steps in it and it is disabled. Let's begin by seeing how to add workflow steps.

Adding workflow steps

Here's how you add workflow steps:

1. Click on the **Add** button in the **Steps** section on the right (as shown in the following screenshot):

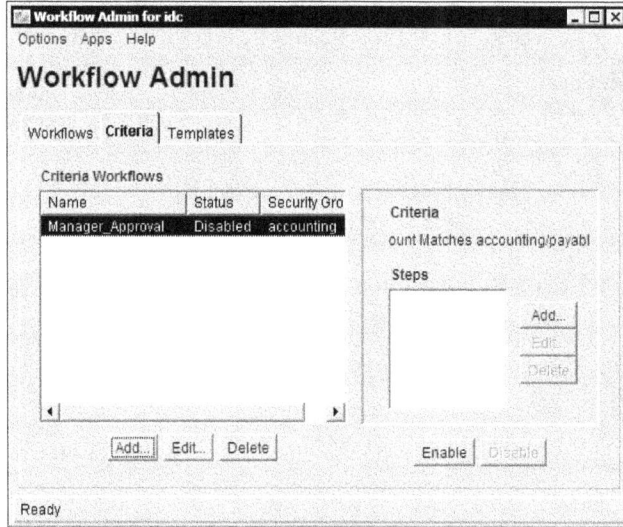

2. The **Add New Step** dialog opens. Fill in the step name and description (as shown in the following screenshot):

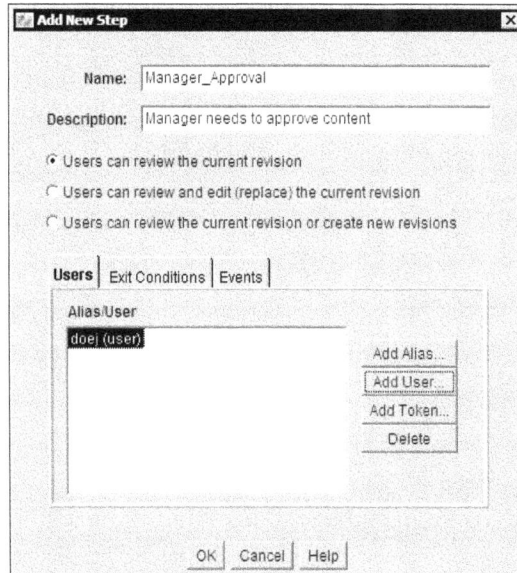

3. Click on the **Add User** button on the right and select approvers for this step. Also add yourself to the list of approvers so you can test the workflow.

4. Switch to the **Exit Conditions** tab (as shown in the following screenshot):

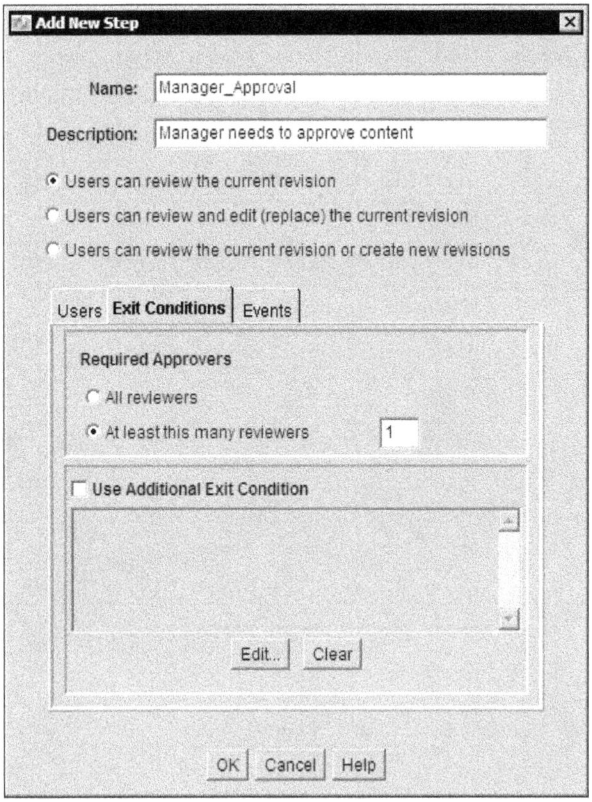

5. You can change the number of approvers required to move the item to the next step. You can make all approvers required to advance a step or just any one as shown on the screenshot.

6. And if you put zero in the text box, no approvers will be required at all. They will still receive notification, but the item will go immediately to the next step. And when the current step is the last the workflow will end and the new revision will be released into the system. What do I mean by that? Until workflow is complete, revisions that are currently in a workflow will not come up in searchers and will not show on the Web. You will still see them in the content info screen but that's it.

7. OK the dialog. You now have a workflow with one step. Let's test it.

But first, you need to enable the workflow.

Enable the workflow

This is the easiest step of all:

1. Click on the **Enable** button on the bottom right. Say **Yes** on a confirmation dialog. The workflow is now enabled.

2. Bring up your Check In form and check in a small document with **Security Group** set to **accounting** and **Account** of **accounting/payable/current** (as shown in the following screenshot):

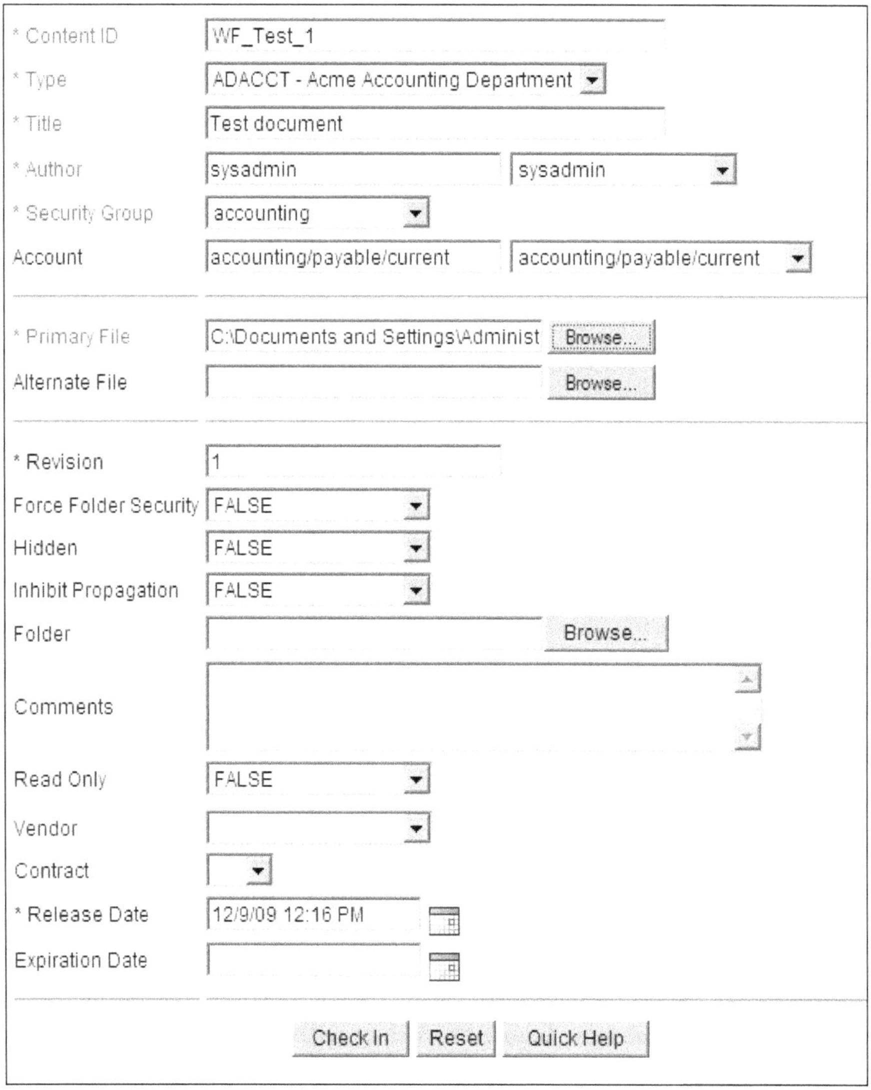

* Content ID	WF_Test_1
* Type	ADACCT - Acme Accounting Department ▼
* Title	Test document
* Author	sysadmin / sysadmin ▼
* Security Group	accounting ▼
Account	accounting/payable/current / accounting/payable/current ▼
* Primary File	C:\Documents and Settings\Administ Browse...
Alternate File	Browse...
* Revision	1
Force Folder Security	FALSE ▼
Hidden	FALSE ▼
Inhibit Propagation	FALSE ▼
Folder	Browse...
Comments	
Read Only	FALSE ▼
Vendor	▼
Contract	▼
* Release Date	12/9/09 12:16 PM
Expiration Date	

Check In   Reset   Quick Help

The **Check in Confirmation** dialog is displayed as shown in the following screenshot:

Check In Confirmation for 'Workflow Test 1'

Content ID : WF_Test_1   [Content Info]
Title: Workflow Test 1
Checked in by: sysadmin

You may check in a **new** document with similar attributes

Check In Similar

1. Click on the **Content Info** link.

2. Notice how the **Workflow** field shows the name of the workflow and the item's status is set to **Review** (as shown in the following screenshot):

Security Group: accounting
Account: accounting/payable/current
Checked Out By:
Status: Review
Formats: application/msword
Workflow: Manager Approval

3. If e-mail notifications are configured, your approver will receive an e-mail, inviting them to review an item (as shown in the following screenshot):

ORACLE **Workflow Review Notification**

You have been assigned to the following workflow step:

Message: Content item 'WF_Test_1' is ready for workflow step 'Manager_Approval'
Workflow Name: Manager_Approval
Workflow Step: Manager_Approval
Content Item: Workflow Test 1 (WF_Test_1)

[Review workflow item]

4. Click on the **Quick Search** button on the top right. Notice that your item does *not* show in the search results!

5. Expand the **Content Management** tray on the left and click on the **Active Workflows** link. The **All Active Workflows** screen displays as shown in the following screenshot:

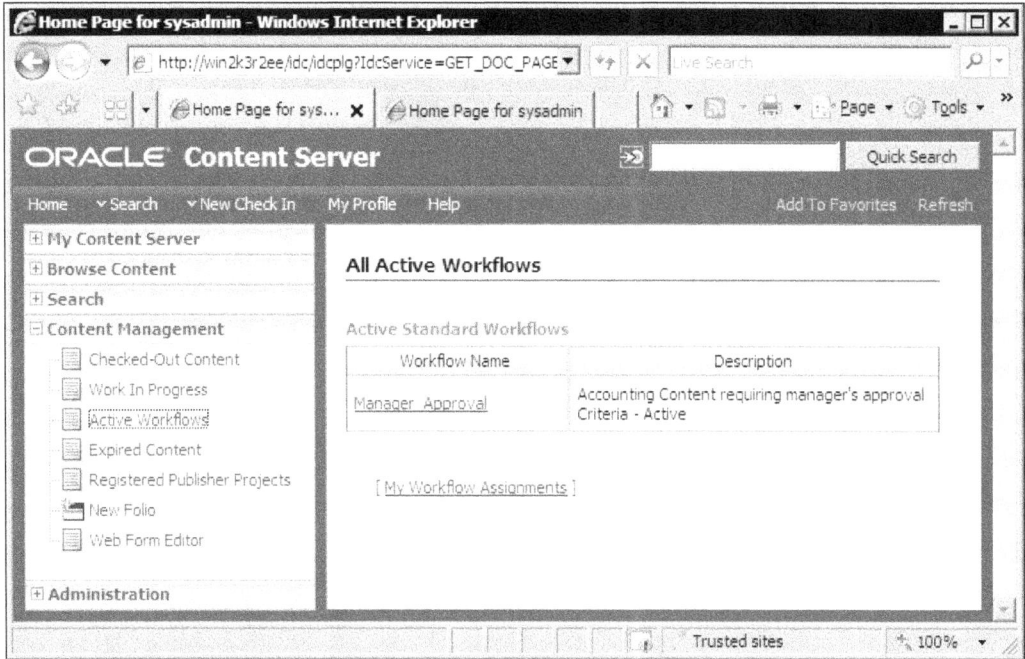

6. Click on **Manager_Approval**. Content items in the workflow will be displayed (as shown in the following screenshot):

7. You can now approve content by clicking on the **Workflow Actions** icon. A link under the item's content ID brings up the content item itself so you can preview the changes.

8. Select **Workflow Review**; it's the first item on the list. The **Workflow Review** screen comes up (as shown in the following screenshot):

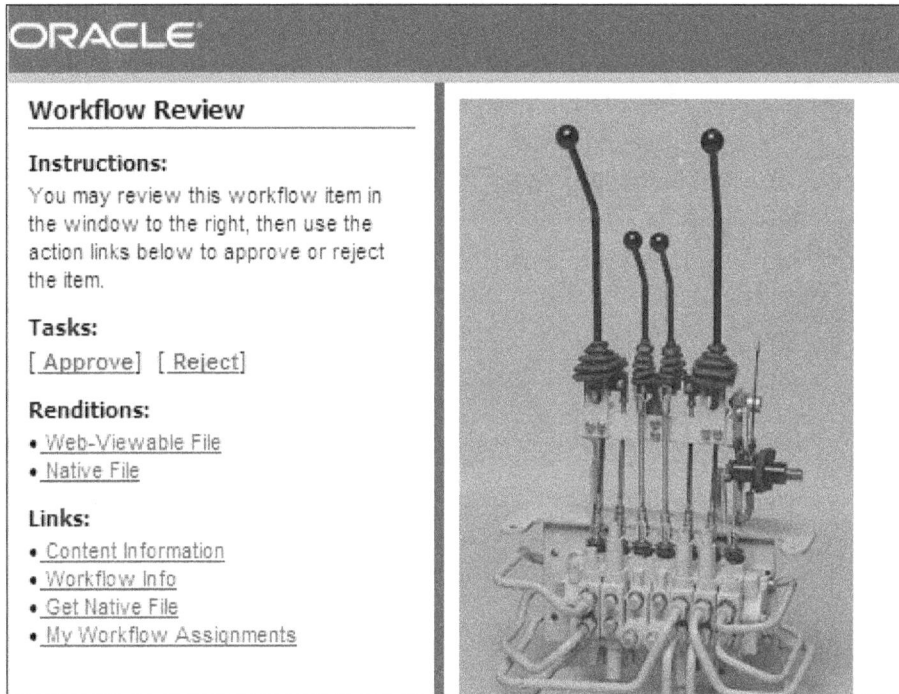

The right pane shows a web-viewable version of the file when available. The **Workflow Review** screen is another way to approve or reject an item in a workflow.

When rejected, content goes back to the previous step in a workflow. In our case, it will go back to the *Contribution* step, which is the stage of its original check in. You can then make the changes and check in to re-submit the item for approval. Or you can delete its current revision to cancel the change.

This is it! You're now all set to set up and use a simple workflow. Why don't you add another step to our test **Manager_Approval** workflow and check in another item?

> You will need to disable the workflow before you can make any changes.
>
> When you disable a workflow all content items that were going through it will be released. Be sure that you are OK with that consequence before making a changes to a workflow, which might be handling live content.

- Try approving an item on the first step and rejecting it on the next one. Watch it coming back to the first step.

- Observe how e-mail notifications change, reflecting the current step the item is in. Click on the link in e-mail notifications. See how it brings you to the **Workflow Review** screen.

- Get the item fully approved. Do a quick search. Watch the item being indexed and added to the search results.

And here's yet another way your approvers can access their pending items. Check out the **My Workflow Assignments** page (as shown in the following screenshot):

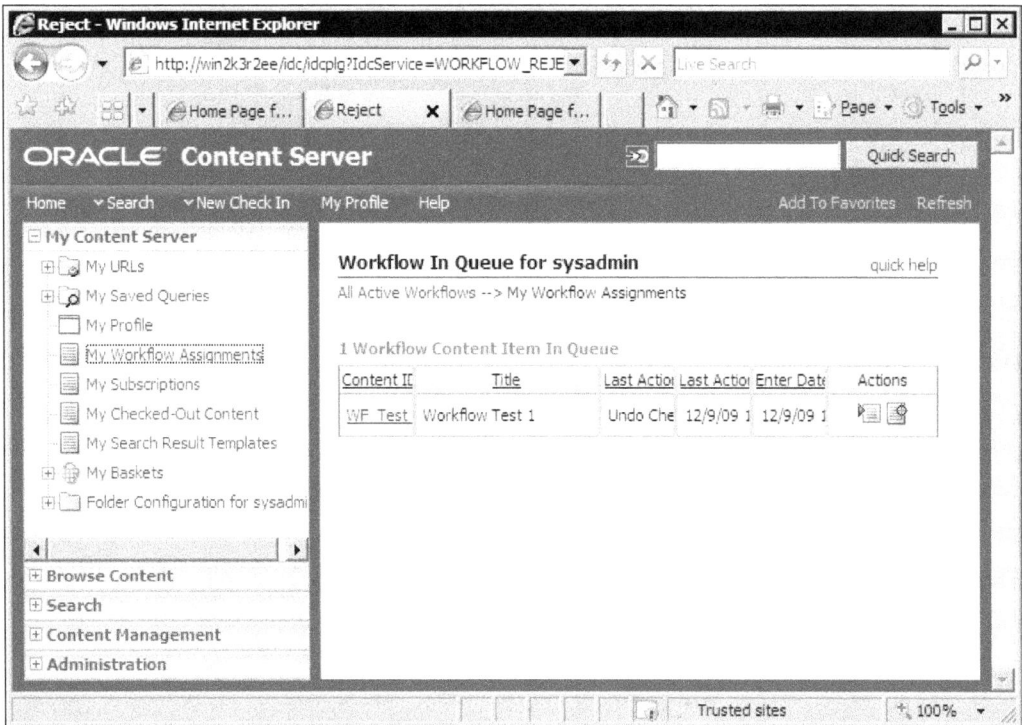

Congratulations! I hope you're getting a feel of what a simple workflow can do. Now let's get something quick but important out of the way.

Understanding the content life cycle

Is there a quick way to tell what's going on with a content item? Do you have to search all over the system to see where it might be?

Nope. It's much easier than this. All you need to do is bring up a **Content Info** screen. Have you noticed a **Status** field towards the bottom? This is the field that shows you exactly what's happening with the item (see the following screenshot):

```
         Contract:
   Security Group: accounting
          Account: accounting/payable/current
   Checked Out By:
           Status: Review
          Formats: application/msword
         Workflow: Manager Approval
```

Here're a few common states an item goes through and corresponding values you'll see in the **Status** field:

- **Review**: The item is in the workflow.
- **Edit**: The item is in the contribution stage. It has probably been rejected from the first step of the workflow.
- **Pending**: The item was included in a *basic* workflow along with the other items. It was approved and is waiting while the rest of the items go through the workflow.
- **Done**: Workflow is complete.
- **GenWWW**: Conversion is in progress. For instance, when you use the PDF converter to generate a PDF version after check in.
- **Released**: All done. The item is available and will appear in searches.

And now let's see another important use of the **Status** field in the next section.

Indexer glitches

Sometimes it might seem that a content item has disappeared on you! You know it was fully approved or there might even be no workflow configured for it. Yet the link to that item doesn't work or the content doesn't display on a web page. What happened?

The item may not be indexed yet. When you check in large number of documents, it may take a while for all that new content to get indexed and being showing up in searches. Or it may "get stuck" in an indexing stage and need to be reindexed.

The good news is that you can easily view all of that "hidden" content on the **Work In Progress page**. (Expand the **Content Management** tray to get to it, as shown in the following screenshot.) If content is there, you can use this page to resubmit it to the indexer:

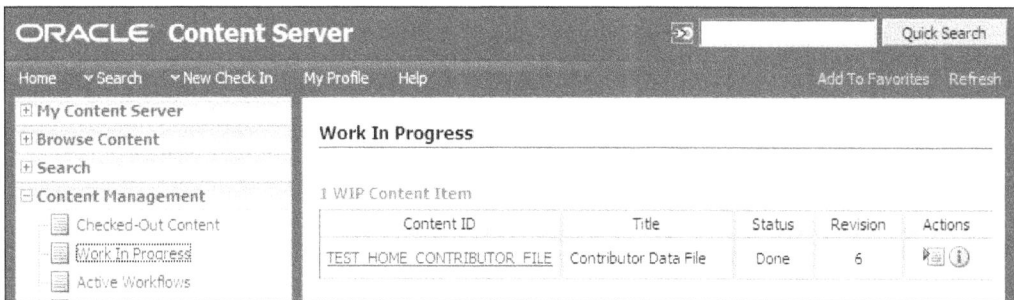

While one or two odd glitches may not be concerning, if you start getting those often then it may be the time to rebuild your search index. How?

Use the **Indexer** tab of the **Repository Manager Applet**. Be sure to check documentation before rebuilding a large index or doing it on a live production system, otherwise you may cause some downtime.

Wow! We're learning some advanced stuff here and this is just the beginning. Let's explore some more.

More things you can do with Content Server workflows

Now that you've built your first workflow, let's dig a little deeper and see what else can you do with Content Server workflows. I'll show you how to add groups of users as approvers, how to create jumps, use scripting, and perform other really powerful things. Let's begin by looking at the top three things.

The top three things

As we've just seen, the most common things you can do are these:

1. **Get content approved**: This is the most obvious use of the workflow we've just seen.

2. **Get people notified**: Remember when we were adding workflow steps there was a number of required approvers on the **Exit Conditions** tab in the **Add New Step** dialog. If we set that to zero we accomplish one important thing: Approvers will get notified, but no action is required of them. It's a great way to "subscribe" a select group of people to an event of your choice.

3. **Perform custom actions**: And if that's not enough you can easily add custom scripts to any step of a workflow. You can change metadata, release items, and send them to other workflows. You can even invoke your custom Java code.

And here's another really powerful thing you can do with custom workflow actions. You can integrate with other systems and move from the local workflow to process orchestration. You can use a Content Server workflow to trigger external processes.

UCM 10gR3 has an Oracle BPEL integration built in. This means that a UCM workflow can be initiated by (or can itself initiate) a BPEL workflow that spans many systems, not just the UCM. This makes ERP systems such as Siebel, PeopleSoft, SAP, and Oracle e-Business Suite easily accessible to the UCM, and content inside the UCM can be easily made available to these systems.

So let's look at the jumps and scripting.

Jumps and scripting

Here's how to add scripting to a workflow:

1. In **Workflow Admin** select a step of a workflow we've just created. Click on the **Edit** button on the right.

2. The **Edit Step** dialog comes up. Go to the **Events** tab (as shown in the following screenshot):

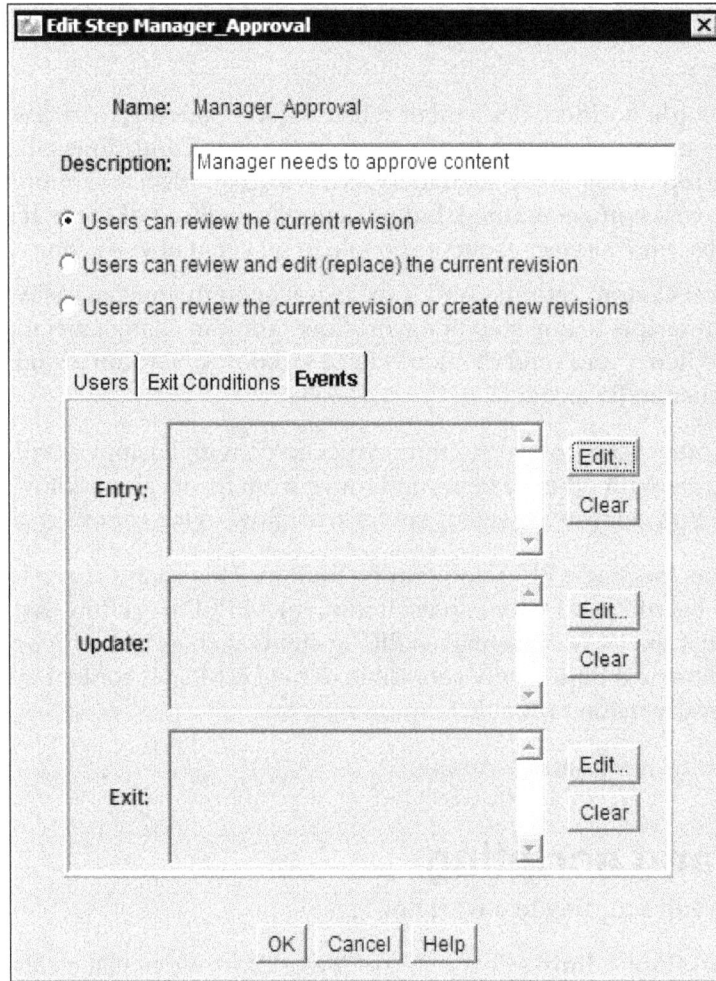

```
Edit Step Manager_Approval                                    ✕

          Name:   Manager_Approval

    Description:  │Manager needs to approve content

    ⦿ Users can review the current revision
    ○ Users can review and edit (replace) the current revision
    ○ Users can review the current revision or create new revisions

    │ Users │ Exit Conditions │ Events │
    ┌─────────────────────────────────────────────────────────┐
    │                        ┌──────────────────────┐  ┌────────┐
    │            Entry:      │                      │  │ Edit.. │
    │                        │                      │  └────────┘
    │                        │                      │  ┌────────┐
    │                        └──────────────────────┘  │ Clear  │
    │                                                   └────────┘
    │                        ┌──────────────────────┐  ┌────────┐
    │           Update:      │                      │  │ Edit.. │
    │                        │                      │  └────────┘
    │                        │                      │  ┌────────┐
    │                        └──────────────────────┘  │ Clear  │
    │                                                   └────────┘
    │                        ┌──────────────────────┐  ┌────────┐
    │            Exit:       │                      │  │ Edit.. │
    │                        │                      │  └────────┘
    │                        │                      │  ┌────────┐
    │                        └──────────────────────┘  │ Clear  │
    │                                                   └────────┘
    └─────────────────────────────────────────────────────────┘

                    ┌────┐  ┌────────┐  ┌──────┐
                    │ OK │  │ Cancel │  │ Help │
                    └────┘  └────────┘  └──────┘
```

There are three events that you can add custom handlers for:

- **Entry**: This event triggers when an item arrives at the step.
- **Update**: This happens when an item or its metadata is updated. It's also initiated every hour by a timer event, **Workflow Update Cycle**. Use it for sending reminders to approvers or escalating the item to an alternative person after your approval period has expired.

- **Exit**: This event is triggered when an item has been approved and is about to exit the step. If you have defined **Additional Exit Conditions** on the **Exit Conditions** tab then those will be satisfied before this event fires.

The following diagram illustrates the sequence of states and corresponding events that are fired when a content item arrives at a workflow step:

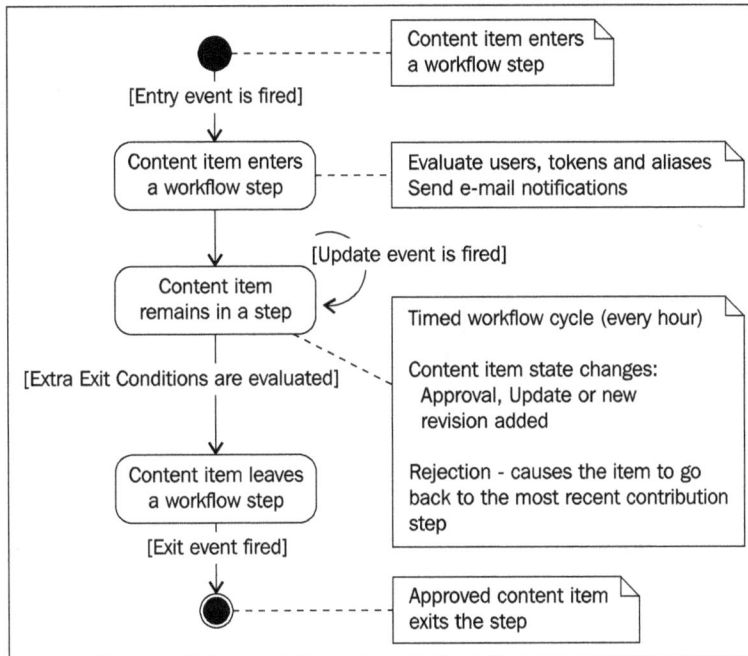

Great! But how do we can actually add the jumps and custom scripts to a workflow step?

How to add a jump to a workflow step

Let's add an exception where content submitted by `sysadmin` will bypass our Manager Approval workflow. We will use a **jump**—a construct that causes an item to skip the normal workflow sequence and follow an alternative path. Here's how to do it:

1. Add a jump to an **Entry** event of our very first step. On the **Events** tab of the **Edit Step** dialog, click on the **Edit** button—the one next to the **Entry** event.

2. The **Edit Script** dialog displays (as shown in the following screenshot):

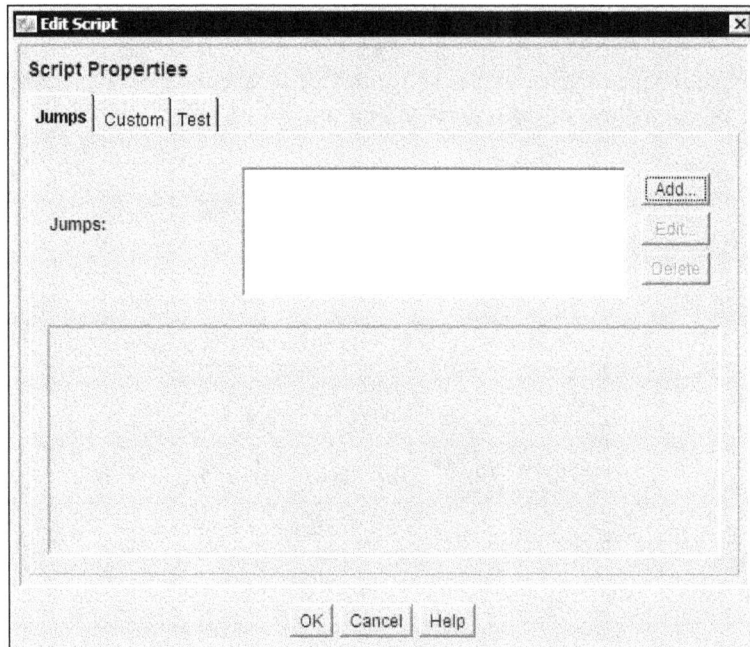

3. Click on the **Add** button. The **Add Jump** dialog comes up (as shown in the following screenshot):

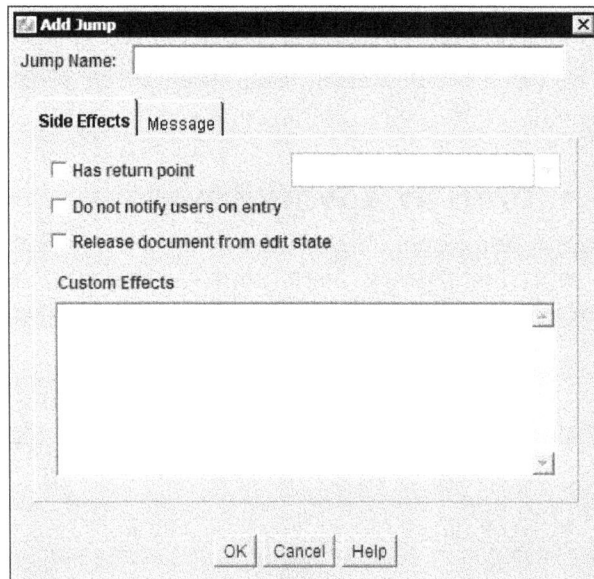

4. Let's call the jump **Sysadmin WF bypass**. You don't need to change anything else at this point. Click on **OK** to get back to the **Edit Script** dialog.

5. In the **Field** drop-down box pick **Author**.

6. Click on the **Select...** button next to the **Value** box. Pick **sysadmin** (if you have trouble locating **sysadmin** in the list of users, make sure that the **filter** check-box is un-checked).

7. Click the **Add** button below the **Value** field. Make sure that your clause appears in the **Script Clauses** box below.

8. In the **Target Step** dropdown pick **Next Step**. Once you have done so the value will change to its script equivalent, **@wfCurrentStep(1)**.

9. If you have more than one step in the workflow, change **1** to the number of steps you have. This will make sure that you jump past the last step and exit the workflow. Here's how the completed dialog will look (as shown in the following screenshot):

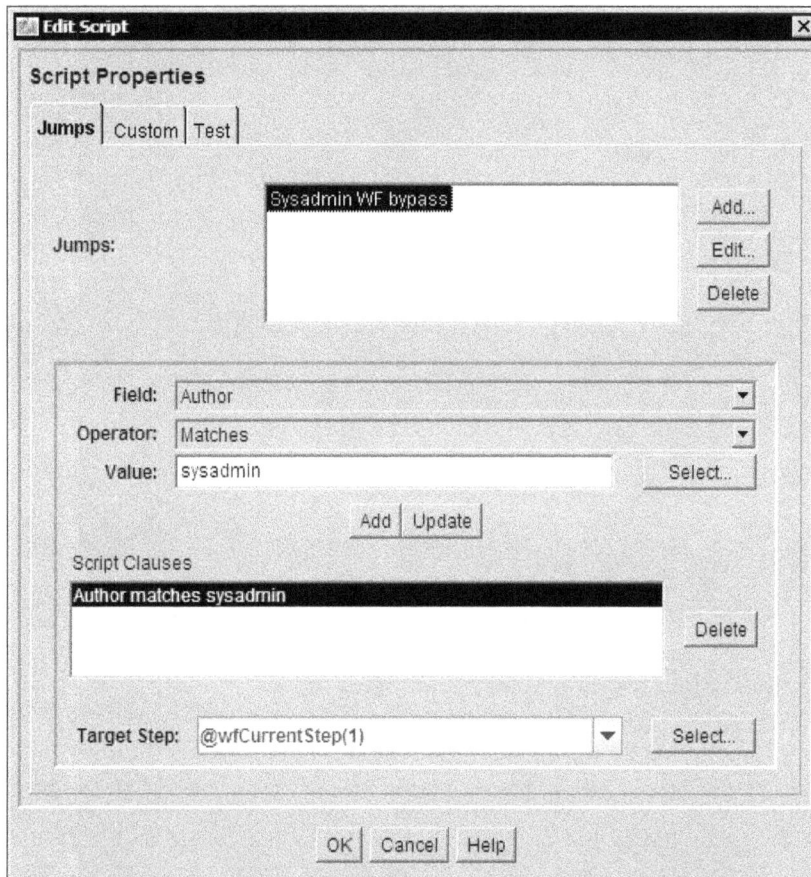

10. Click on **OK** to close. You're now back to the **Events** tab on the **Edit Step** dialog. Notice a few lines of script being added to the box next to the **Entry** event (as shown in the following screenshot):

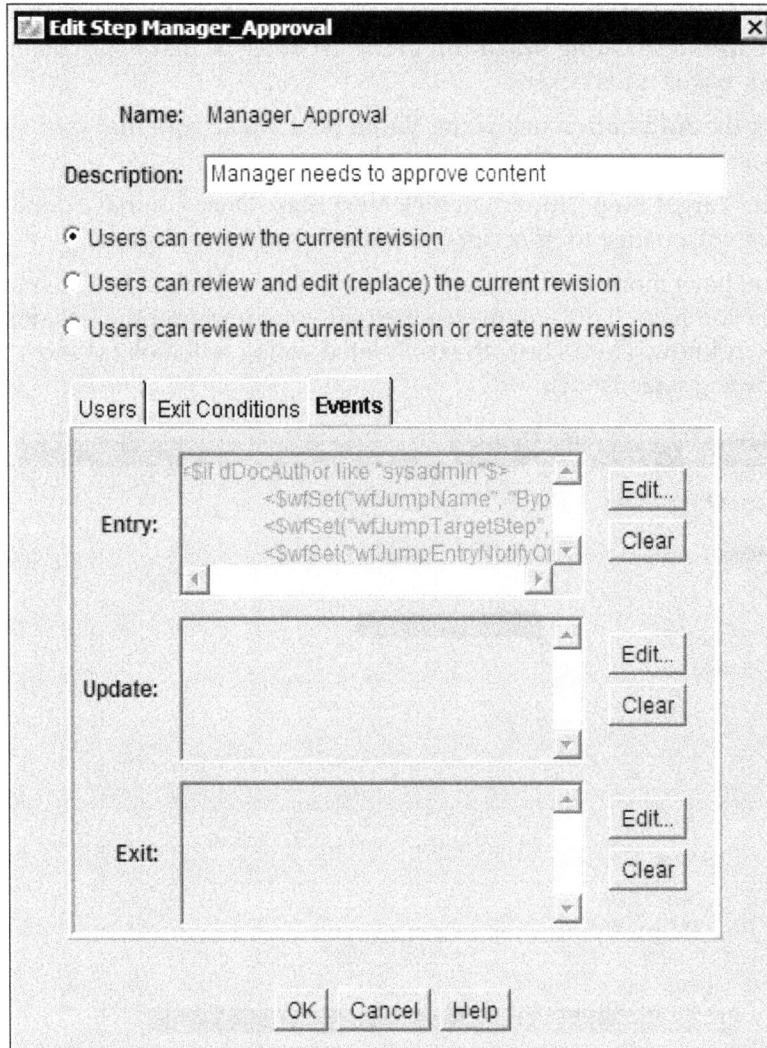

11. **OK** the dialog. It's time to test your changes.

12. Check in a new document. Make sure you set the **Author** field to **sysadmin**. Set your **Security Group** to **accounting**, and **Account** to **accounting/payable/ current**. If you don't, the item will not enter our workflow in the first place (as shown in the following screenshot):

* Content ID	WF_Test_5	
* Type	ADACCT - Acme Accounting Department ▼	
* Title	Bypass test	
* Author	sysadmin	sysadmin ▼
* Security Group	accounting ▼	
Account	accounting/payable/current	accounting/payable/current ▼

13. Complete your check-in and follow the link to go to the Content Info page. See the status of the item. It should be set to **Released**. That's right. The item got right out of the workflow.

Check in a new document again, but use some other author. Notice how your item will enter the workflow and stay there. As you've seen, the dialog we used for creating a jump is simply a code generator. It created a few lines of script we needed to add the handler for the Entry event.

Click on the **Edit** button next to that code and pick **Edit Current** to study it. You can find all the script function definitions in *iDoc Reference Guide*.

Perfect! And we're still not done.

What if you have a few common steps that you'd like to reuse in a bunch of workflows? Would you just have to manually recreate them? Nope. There are several solutions that allow you to reuse parts of the workflow. The one I find to be most useful is sub workflows.

Sub workflows

Sub workflows are reusable blocks of steps that you can then jump into from a number of other workflows. It's easy to create a sub workflow, just keep the **Has Criteria Definition** box un-checked when you create a regular criteria workflow (as shown in the following screenshot):

This is it…

And if this is not enough, let's look at the workflows that can hold multiple items at once. Let's look at the Manual or Basic workflows.

Basic workflows

The reason they're called "Basic" or "Manual" is because this type of a workflow doesn't trigger automatically. It has to be started by hand, by an administrator, or a power user.

> The User's role must have a right to run the Workflow Admin application. Go to **Security | Permissions By Role | Edit Applet Rights** in the **User Admin** applet to make sure.

Basic Workflows have a big advantage, they can hold more than one content item and get them approved together. You can even create new item placeholders and get them elaborated as part of the workflow.

How do you create a Basic Workflow? Let me show you in the following section.

Lab 8: Using manual workflows

Follow these steps:

1. Bring up Workflow Admin and go to the **Workflows** tab (as shown in the following screenshot):

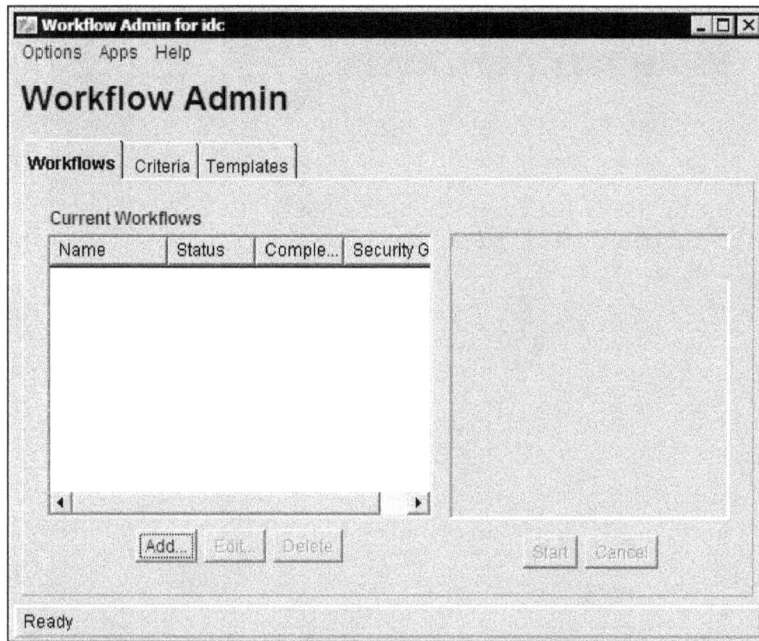

2. Click on the **Add...** button and create new workflow.
3. Select content items that you're going to run through the approval process.
4. Select one or more contributors. The first step of a basic workflow is always a contribution step. Contributors will be invited to check-out and check back in the items in the workflow.
5. Create one or more approval steps just as we did in *Lab 7*.

6. Your basic workflow is now ready to start (as shown in the following screenshot):

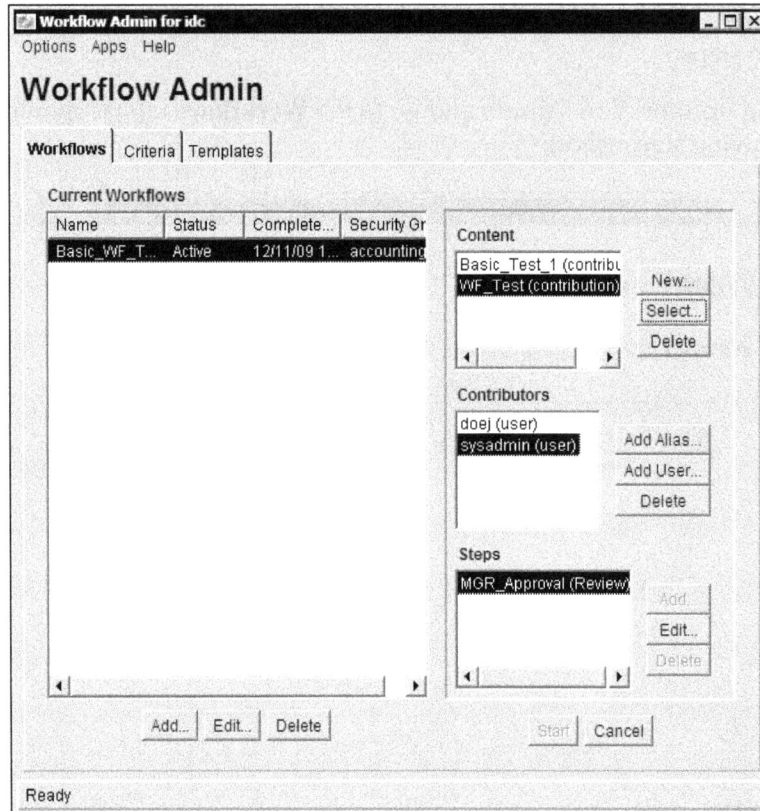

7. Start it by clicking on the **Start** button at the bottom right.

8. Log in as one of the contributors and go to **My Workflow Assignments**. Use the **Actions** column on your right to complete your workflow assignment.

Congratulations! You've just created and tested a basic workflow.

But what if you have to send additional items through a very similar basic workflow? Do you have to keep on recreating workflow steps every time? Of course not! Use Templates. Here's how to create templates.

Basic workflow templates

In Workflow Admin switch to the **Templates** tab. Give the new template a name and description. Now you can add and configure workflow steps just as you would in a "normal" basic workflow (as shown in the following screenshot):

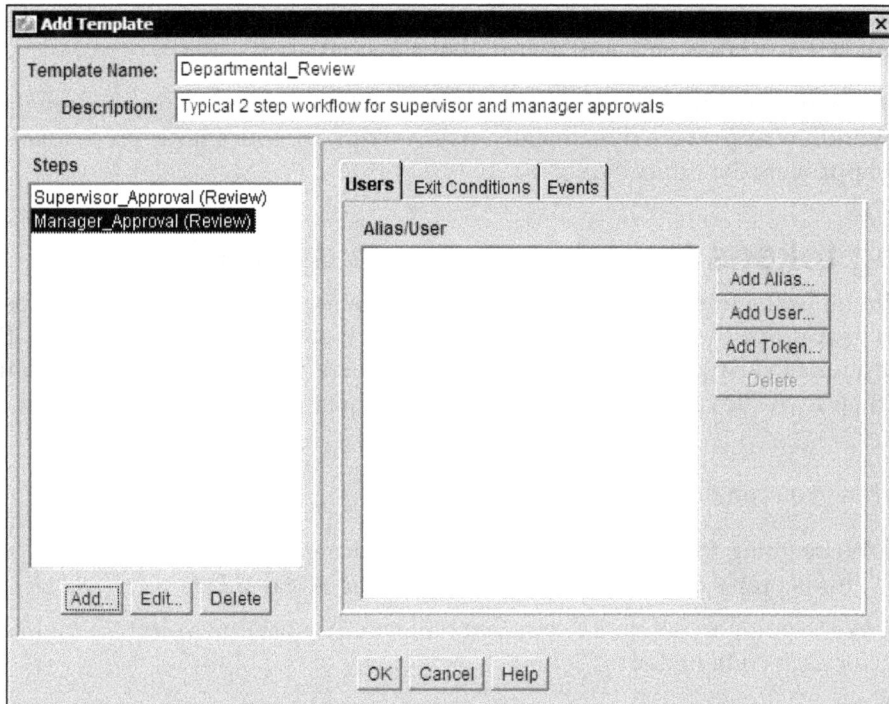

Once you have the template defined, you can use it for creating new basic workflows. Just check the **Use Template** checkbox on the **Add New Workflow** dialog.

Can you put yourself in the picture? See how much time the templates would save you?

And here's an even bigger time saver. Let me show you how to group approvers.

How to group approvers

I bet you've asked this question a few times while reading this chapter. How would you add a group of users as contributors or approvers? You've also seen **Add Alias** and **Add Token** buttons. So here's how to use aliases to group approvers.

Using aliases to group approvers

As you remember from the previous chapter, an *Alias* is group of users. It's easy to create aliases with the User Admin applet. This is it! Now you can use **Add Alias** button on workflow steps and workflow template dialogs to add a group of users.

Everyone in the group will receive notifications. And if just one approver is required to complete a workflow step any user in that alias can do it.

If you think that was useful then check out the next section. I'll show you how to select workflow approvers dynamically, using script. So here's how to use tokens to pick approvers dynamically.

Using tokens to pick approvers dynamically

What if you host a number of websites for your clients, and you need your website owners to approve their content? I know you can create one workflow per site. But is there a way to just use one workflow? What if you allow your users to dynamically create their own sites and one workflow per site is just not the choice you want to make?

Here's how you can do it:

1. We're going to create groups of approvers for each site using aliases. This is pretty obvious but the next step holds the real key:
2. We're going to define a **token** that will let our workflow select the right alias for each content item.

Let's define our aliases first.

Here's a little trick we're going to use. Let's assume that we have a meta field called xWebsites that holds the name of the website, that a content item belongs to.

> We'll be looking at the Web Content Management in *Chapter 11, Web Content Management and Collaboration*. If you don't have the Site Studio component installed in your Content Server, you will most likely not have a field called xWebsites defined yet. Just go ahead and create it yourself, so you can follow the steps next.

We're going to use the actual values of this field as the names of the aliases.

1. Bring up the **User Admin** applet. Go to the **Aliases** tab and click on the **New** button below.

2. Let's create an alias (group of users) called **marketing_intranet** (as shown in the following screenshot):

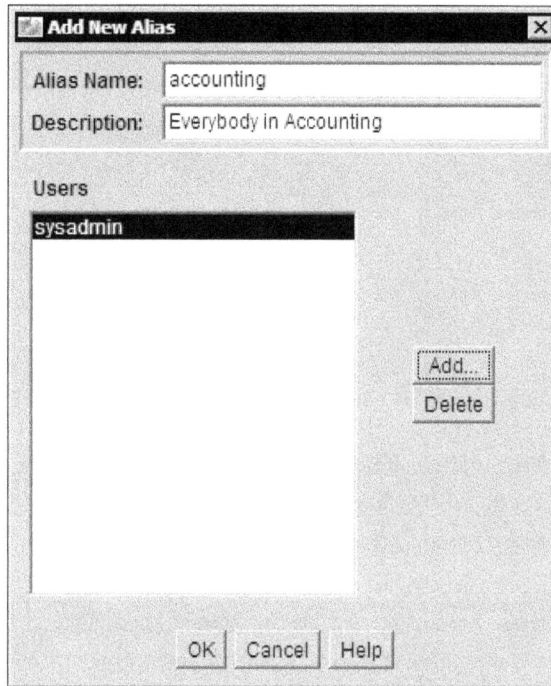

3. Go ahead and create aliases to other websites such as **marketing_extranet** and **corporate_www**.

Perfect. We're done creating aliases. Now it's the time to leverage the power of tokens:

1. Bring up Workflow Admin. Select **Options | Tokens** from the menu.

2. The **Workflow Tokens** dialog comes up. Click on the **Add** button at the bottom.

3. The **Add Token** dialog opens. Let's call it **Web_Sites** (as shown in the following screenshot):

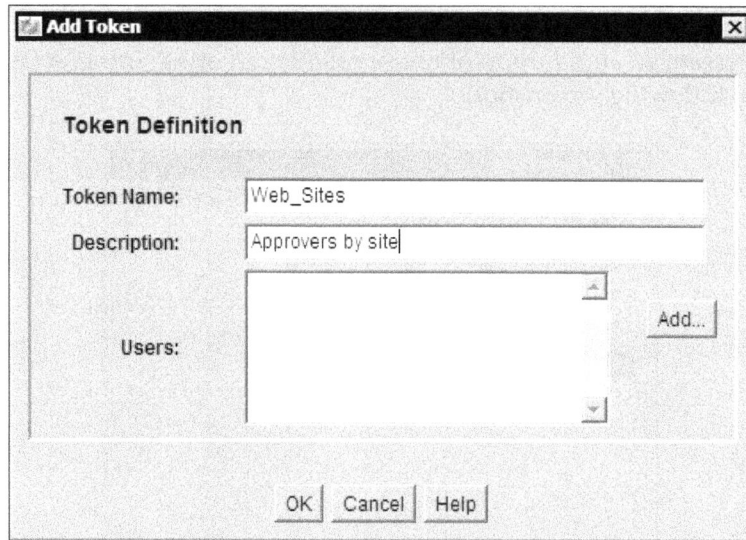

4. Click on the **Add** button. The **Add Token User** dialog comes up (as shown in the following screenshot).

5. Pick **Alias** for the **Type** and **xWebsites** for the **Name**.

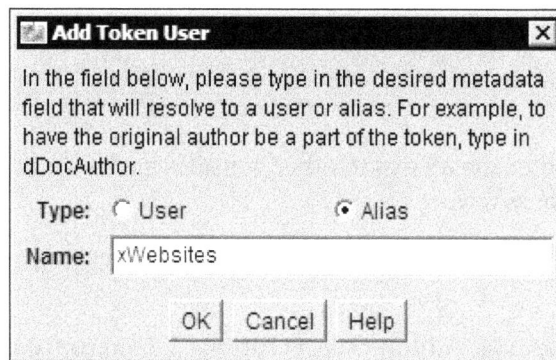

6. **OK** the dialogs to save changes.

We're all done! You can now add your newly created token to workflows. How does it work?

Actually it is simple. If we check in a content item with xWebsites set to marketing_
intranet, the token will get evaluated to marketing_intranet. Now the token was
created for an alias so it will resolve to an alias of marketing_intranet. This is it.

Now we have a dynamic way to pick a group of approvers based on the metadata
values. Nice!

And we're done with another chapter! Just one more tip before you flip the page. I've
shown you almost every tool and technique you will ever need while using Content
Server workflows, but you may still find it helpful to review the detailed *Workflow
Implementation Guide*, that you can find on the UCM documentation page.

Summary

Phew! It was a long chapter. But once again, we've learned almost all there is to
know about the Content Server workflows.

You now know how to create a workflow. You've seen the different types of
workflows and you've created one of each. You've seen how to use scripting to
customize them, how to create reusable pieces, and how to group approvers.

The next chapter will be an easy one. We will look at virtual folders and I'll show
you how to use Windows Explorer and MS Office applications to contribute content.

6
Understanding Virtual Folders and WebDAV

In the previous chapter we picked up almost all there is to know about Content Server Workflows. I hope I got you excited about how simple and powerful they are.

In this chapter I'll explain how to build and administer hierarchical folder structures. Here's what you'll learn in this chapter:

- What virtual folders really are
- How content items are linked to a folder
- Major controls you use in Content Server User Interface when you're working with folders
- How to use folders to manage metadata
- How to set up and use Windows Desktop Integration Suite

Wow! Isn't that a lot of material to learn in 30 minutes? I thought so too when I first had to use Virtual Folders a few years ago. But what made it easy for me to understand is the fact that there are just two simple concepts behind the way Folders work. Once you understand them it's an easy ride from there.

The key to understanding virtual folders

The key to understanding virtual folders is simply this: UCM Virtual Folders are just another way of displaying collections of content items that "go together". They look and feel like folders on a Windows system, but really they are "virtual". This makes them as easy to use as your plain old Windows filesystem folders, but it also makes them much more powerful and exciting.

New upcoming UCM v.11*g* is packed with major upgrades to desktop integration suite and virtual folders, that make them even better. Once it is released, I'll be demonstrating those to my newsletter subscribers, so be sure to claim your free subscription. You will find the link and the instructions in *Appendix A*.

So here are the two, more specific facts to keep in mind, while reading this chapter:

- Folders are standalone virtual structures. Content items are not physically stored in them. Every content item has a metadata field (xCollectionId) to store a numeric folder ID that links an item to a folder.

- Every folder has its own set of metadata fields. They're applied to new content items and folders created in that folder.

That's it. You have the key now. And here's the rest of the knowledge you'll need to use Folders. Let's begin by exploring virtual folders.

Exploring virtual folders

In this section we'll explore the major controls for using and configuring Folders, see some non-intuitive features to beware of, and check out the global configuration settings. But first of all, in case you didn't already, let's see what the Folders user interface looks like.

So let's begin with the major controls.

Understanding major controls

Log in to Content Server. Expand the **Browse Content** tray on the left (as shown in the following screenshot):

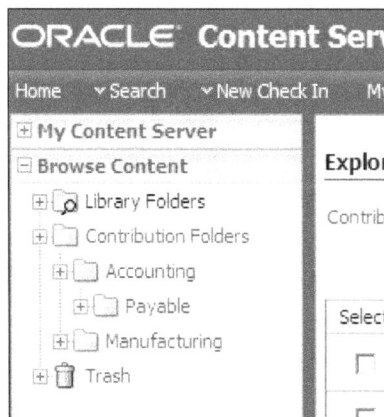

All of your active folders will reside underneath **Contribution Folders**. If you delete a folder, its content will go into **Trash**. When you select a folder its content displays on the right pane (as shown in the following screenshot):

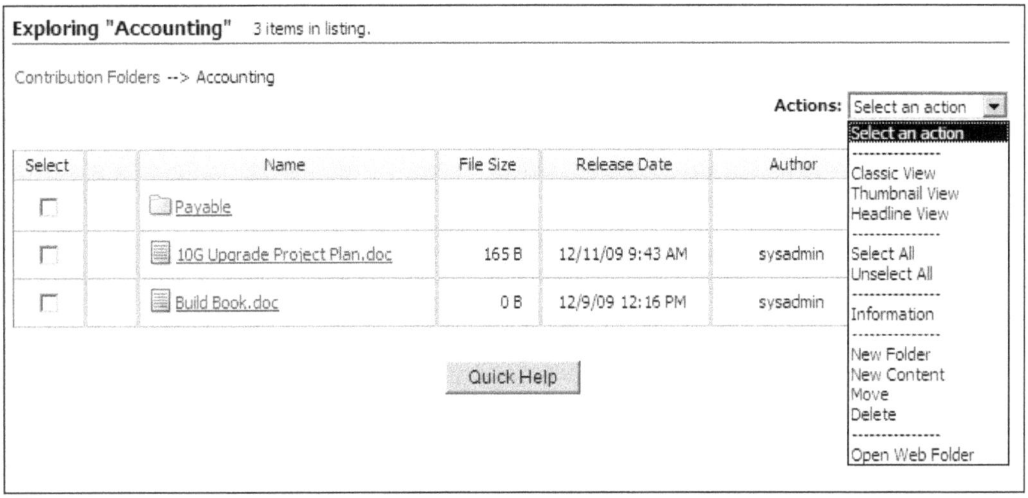

As you see, **Accounting** has two content items and one subfolder. I've expanded the menu on the top right. It works the same way as the menu on the Content Info page. You can update folder information, move, delete, and create subfolders.

Subfolders and content items in the folder all have their own context menus just like they do in search results screen (as shown in the following screenshot):

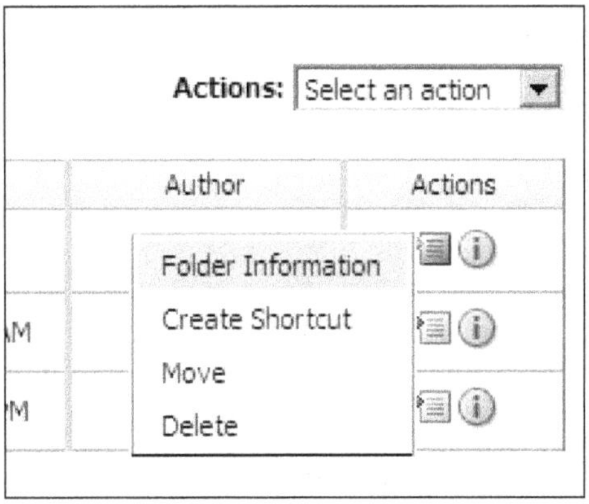

As I mentioned earlier, each folder has its own set of metadata. Here's how to bring it up. On the folder page select **Information** or **Folder Information** on its context menu. The **Hierarchical Folder Information** screen comes up (as shown in the following screenshot):

```
Hierarchical Folder Information
                                                    Actions: [ Select an action ▼ ]

                        Virtual Folder Name: Accounting
                                      Owner: sysadmin
                                      ☐  Prompts for metadata (using WEI)


                                      Folder Information
                               Title:
                               Type:
                     Security Group: accounting
                            Account: accounting/payable/current
                             Author:
                       Release Date:
                    Expiration Date:
               Force Folder Security: FALSE
                             Hidden: FALSE
                 Inhibit Propagation: FALSE
                             Folder:
                           Comments:
                          Read Only: FALSE
                   Trash Delete Date:
               Trash Delete Location:
               Trash Delete Old Name:
                       Trash Deleter:
                             Vendor:
                           Contract:

                              [ Quick Help ]
```

Doesn't it look just like a Content Info page? When you check in a new item in the folder these are the values that will be prefilled in the Check In form. And you can update folder metadata fields just like you would on a content item.

So far it all looks pretty simple and logical. But theres are a couple of the "odd bits" I don't want you to trip over.

Beware of "non-intuitive" behavior

Here're a couple of things that are not immediately obvious from the first glance. The first one is the understanding of how inheritance works.

How inheritance works

When you create a subfolder or a new content item in a folder, they inherit the parent's metadata values. That's clear. But it actually ends there. The items are on their own after that. If you update the values on the parent it stays on the parent. Child folders and content items will NOT reflect an update.

Another "quirk" to beware of is the fact that the item's metadata is NOT affected when you move it to another folder. It won't inherit that folder's values unless you explicitly push the values down.

And here's how to do it by using the Propogate feature.

Using the Propagate feature

This is what pushes the metadata values down onto the subfolders and content items that reside in the folder. Just select **Propagate** from the menu on the top right on the folder information page (as shown in the following screenshot):

But don't be surprised if it does nothing! That's right. Before you can use the Propagate feature, you need to specify what metadata fields are OK to push down.

Here's how you do it:

Expand the **Administration** tray. Expand **Folder Configuration** and click on **Information Field Inherit Configuration**. Here's what the **Information Field Inherit Configuration** screen looks like:

Information Field Inherit Configuration

Select information fields that are to be propagated to content.

- ☐ Title
- ☐ Author
- ☐ Type
- ☐ Security Group
- ☐ Account
- ☐ Release Date
- ☐ Expiration Date
- ☐ Force Folder Security
- ☐ Hidden
- ☐ Inhibit Propagation
- ☐ Folder
- ☐ Comments
- ☐ Read Only
- ☐ Partition ID
- ☐ Web Flag
- ☐ Storage Rule
- ☐ Vendor
- ☐ Contract

Update   Reset

Quick Help

Just place check marks against the fields you'd like to push down when you use the propagate feature, and click on **Update**. You're done. Now you can propagate the metadata values.

> And yes, you can "lock" the folder's metadata values so it can't be overwritten by propagating form its parent. Set the folder's **Inhibit Propagation** metadata value to `True`.

Great! We now know how folders handle metadata.

Understanding folder security

Again, there are two constructs at play here:

- Each virtual folder has an owner. It's a user who can change that folder's metadata and delete the folder. However, the folder owner doesn't have any additional privileges over the content items that reside in the folder.
- Users can only see the folder if they have at least Read permission to its Security Group, or if the folder has no security group assigned.

If you're not the owner of a specific folder, you must have Delete permission to its security group to update its metadata or delete the folder.

However, before you can delete a folder, you'll need to delete or move its entire content first. And again, content items in a folder may have different values for Security Group and Account than the folder itself.

We're almost done. All that's left to look at is some settings.

Important global settings

Actually, there's just one page I want you to peek at. It's the **System Defaults** page. Expand **Folder Configuration** under the **Administration** tray. Click on the **System Default Information Fields** link (as shown in the following screenshot):

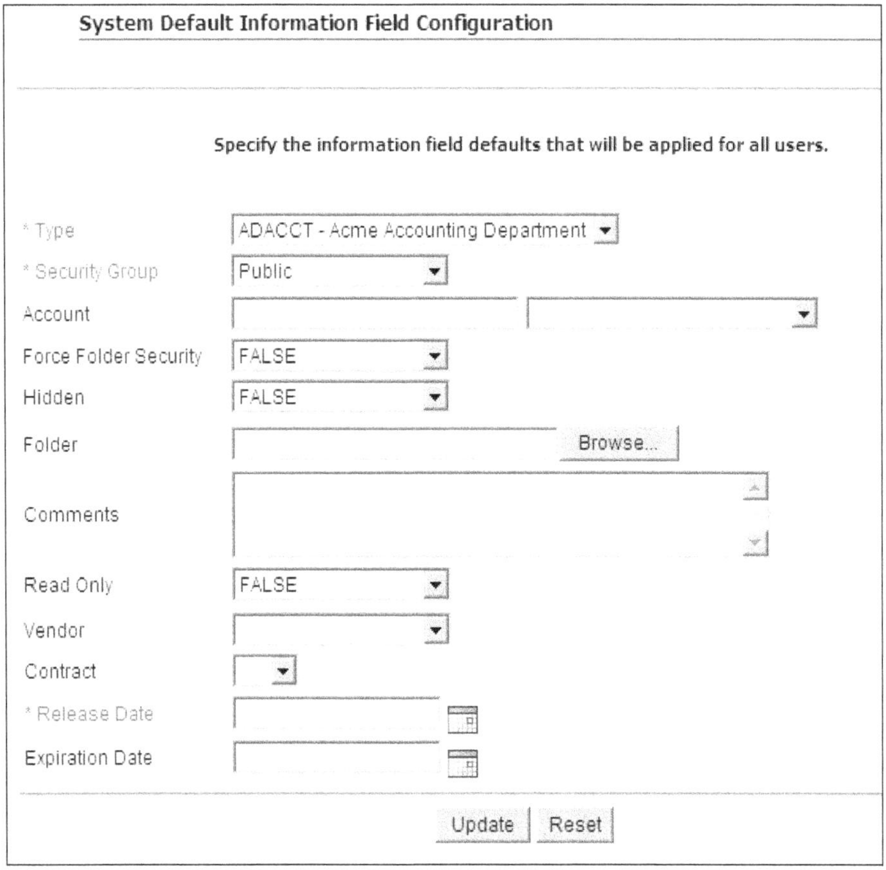

This is another screen that shows your metadata fields, looking like a Check In? Why is this screen important?

You see, in the next section we'll be using Windows Explorer to drag and drop new documents into the Content Server. Yes, you can simply drag and drop a document from your computer and it will get checked in! But there's a little caveat.

Your Standard Check In form may have a few fields marked as *required*. When you drag and drop a document there's no way to collect the values for some or all of these fields. So you need to specify the defaults. If a folder where you are dropping content has those values then it's perfect. But if it doesn't, the check-in will fail. So you need to set default values for those required fields.

But don't set anything for Release Date; it will be set to the actual date and time of your check in.

How to use WebDAV and Desktop Integration

In case you haven't heard of WebDAV, it's an industry standard protocol for editing and managing files remotely. Content Server supports WebDAV and so do Microsoft Office, Windows Explorer, and countless other products. You can integrate Content Server into your users' desktop and make document management easy and seamless.

The only problem is that when contributing content from third-party applications via WebDAV, the check-in screen will not come up, and the check-in process may fail because the required field values are missing. It may also become a bigger issue, when the content is checked in without other important metadata values and that makes it hard to locate and classify.

But the good news is that you can actually do something about it.

Just set up your default metadata values like I've shown you in the previous section. And there's also a way to set up your own default metadata values.

So let's pause here for just a moment to see the controls you have for customizing folder behavior.

Customizing folder behavior

There are two things you can do to customize your folder behavior:

- Define the values that metadata fields should take when you contribute content via WebDAV, where no check-in form is displayed (those will override the system default values)
- Customize user interface features when working with Folders in your browser

Let me show you both.

Defining the user default metadata values

Once again, note that these default values are only used when you contribute content via the WebDAV link and no check-in form is filled in.

There are two sets of them, one for creating new content items and one for creating new revisions of existing content items.

To set them up expand the **My Content Server** tray on your left and follow the links under **Folder Configuration** at the bottom of the tray (as shown in the following screenshot):

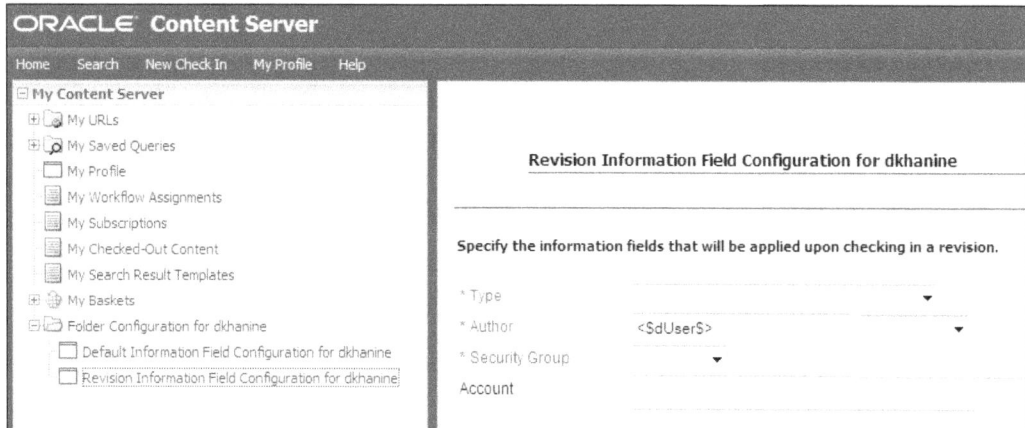

And here's how to access the screen for customizing folder user interface features.

Customizing Folder user interface features

Once again, this screen, as opposed to the ones we've just looked at only deals with the Content Server interface, the one that you see in a browser.

To change these settings, expand the **My Content Server** tray on the left and click on the **Folder Configuration** link towards the bottom of the tray. The **Folder Configuration** screen comes up (as shown in the following screenshot):

Folder Configuration for dkhanine

Behavioral options affecting how content is displayed and managed.

Content Style
- ⦿ Native
- ○ Web Viewable (Browse only)

Hierarchical Virtual Folder Options
- ☐ Show hidden when browsing
- ☐ Remove items immediately when deleted
- ☐ Show only items that user has deleted in trash virtual folder

Update   Reset

Quick Help

Default Information Field Configuration for   Revision Information Field Configuration for
dkhanine   dkhanine

You can now change things such as what file will come up when you click on the link, whether or not do you want to see hidden folders and if you need to use the Recycle Bin functionality.

Using Oracle Desktop Integration

Oracle Desktop Integration is a lightweight integration product that makes it easy to consume and contribute content directly from your Windows desktop, Microsoft Office, and Lotus Notes applications.

> At the time of this writing, Oracle Desktop Integration only runs on Windows. If your client base is running Linux or MacOS you might want to skip past the following section.

Desktop Integration is also easy to set up. Let me walk you through...

First, you need to download the product. Here's how you go about it. There are two ways of downloading Oracle Desktop Integration.

Downloading Oracle Desktop Integration

First of all, you can download it from the **Oracle UCM Downloads** page. Just Google for **Oracle UCM Downloads** and search the page for **Desktop Integration Suite**. If for some reason you're unable to find it, here's a little bit longer way of getting it:

1. Go to E-Delivery website. (You might want to check *Chapter 1*, *Getting Up and Running*, for a refresher on how to get there).

2. Download **Content Server Document Management** bundle (the one shown in the following screenshot):

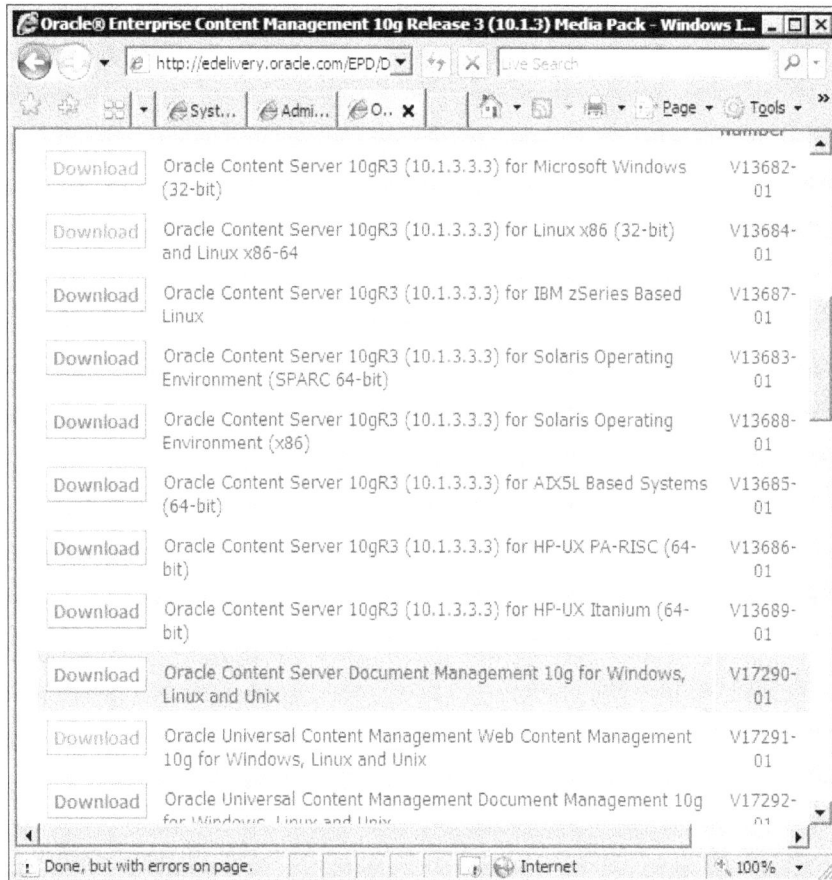

3. Once completed, look inside the `.zip` file. You need a file named something like `Desktop_10gR3_20090702.zip`.

4. Extract and unzip it.

Now we ready to proceed to the next step.

Installing the Content Server component

It's actually easier than it sounds. Here are the steps you follow:

1. Unzip the Desktop Integration archive. Go to the `Component` folder. It should contain a file named something like `DesktopIntegrationSuite.zip`.

2. Bring up the **Admin Server** screen (See *Chapter 2, Major Controls,* for instructions).

3. Click on the **Component Manager** link on the left. Component Manager comes up (as shown in the following screenshot):

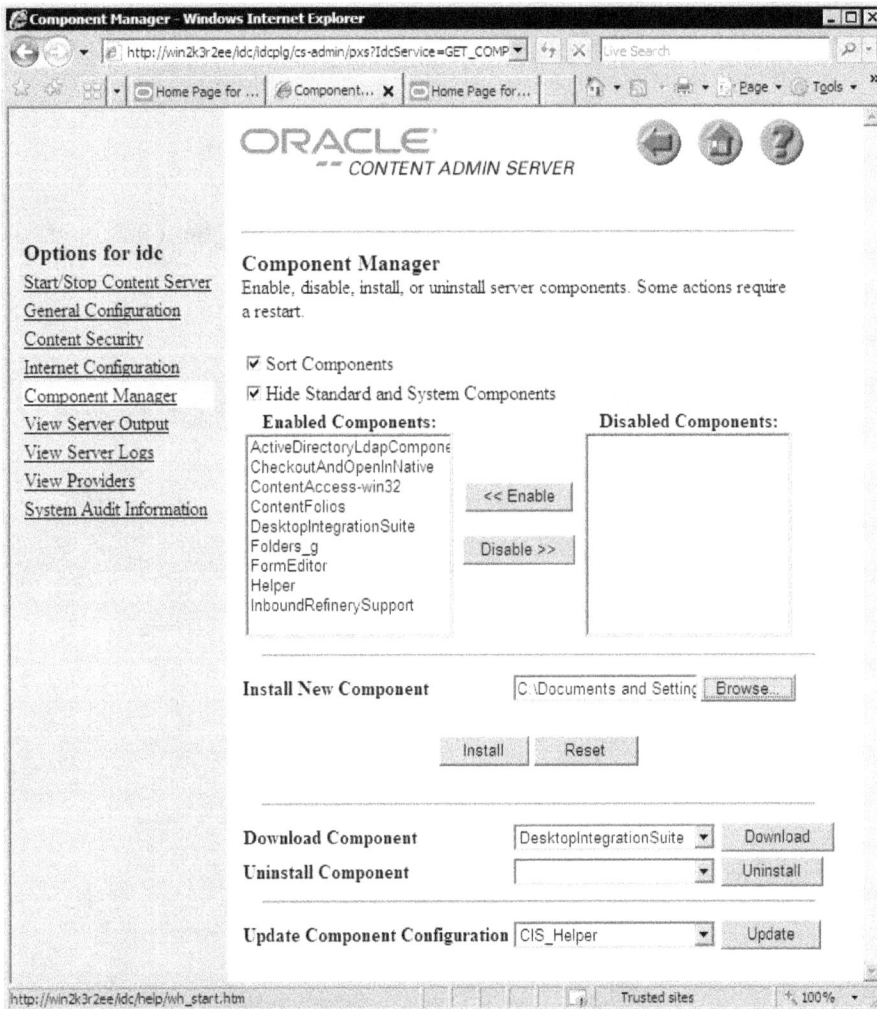

4. Click on the **Browse** button and locate the ZIP file you located in the previous step.

5. Click on **Install**.

6. Enable the Component and restart Content Server.

All done! Now it's time to install a client component on your desktop PC.

> If you're running in a virtual environment, you can install your client component there. Nothing prevents you from running your Desktop Client on the same machine as your Content Server.

Let's proceed to installing the client component.

Installing the client component

This one is even easier:

1. Copy `OracleDesktopIntegrationSuite.msi` to the client machine where you'll be installing Desktop Integration and run it.

2. You can select programs that your end users will use to contribute content (as shown in the following screenshot):

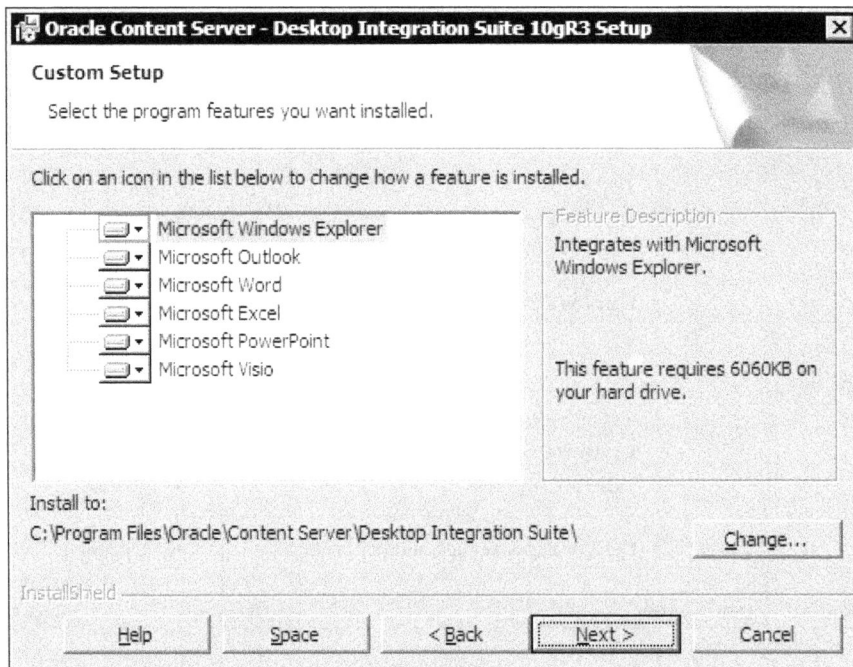

3. Once installation is complete, you'll notice an **Oracle Content Servers** icon placed on your desktop (like the one shown in the following screenshot):

4. Right-click on it and select **Add Server...**.
5. The **Add Server** Dialog comes up (as shown in the following screenshot):

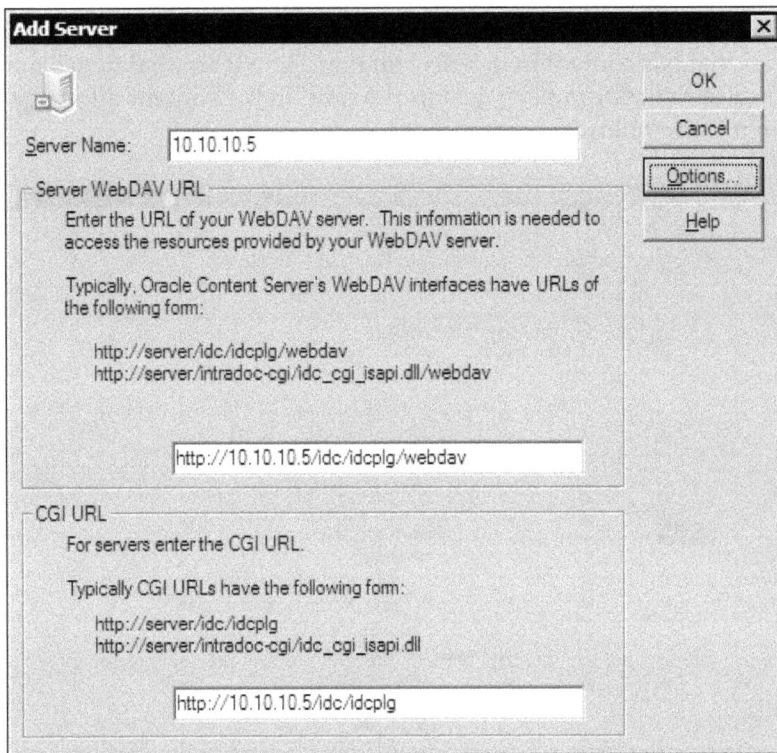

6. Simply type in your server name or IP address in the **Server Name** box at the top. The other two text boxes will get populated automatically.
7. **OK** the dialog.

Your installation is now complete! Let's see what Desktop Integration can do for you. Let's proceed to Lab 5.

Lab 5: Contributing content using WebDAV and Windows Explorer

Let's start with Windows Explorer. You might not be paying much attention to it, but I bet this is the top application you use.

Windows Explorer supercharged

Carry out the following steps:

1. Double-click on the **Oracle Content Servers** icon on your desktop. Windows Explorer opens. Go to **View | Explorer Bar | Folders**. You don't have to show folders, but it makes it convenient to explore virtual folders.

2. Expand your Content Server. Expand **Contribution Folders** and select a folder that has content in it. Select an item. You'll see that item's metadata appear in the bottom pane, just as it would in the content info page (as shown in the following screenshot):

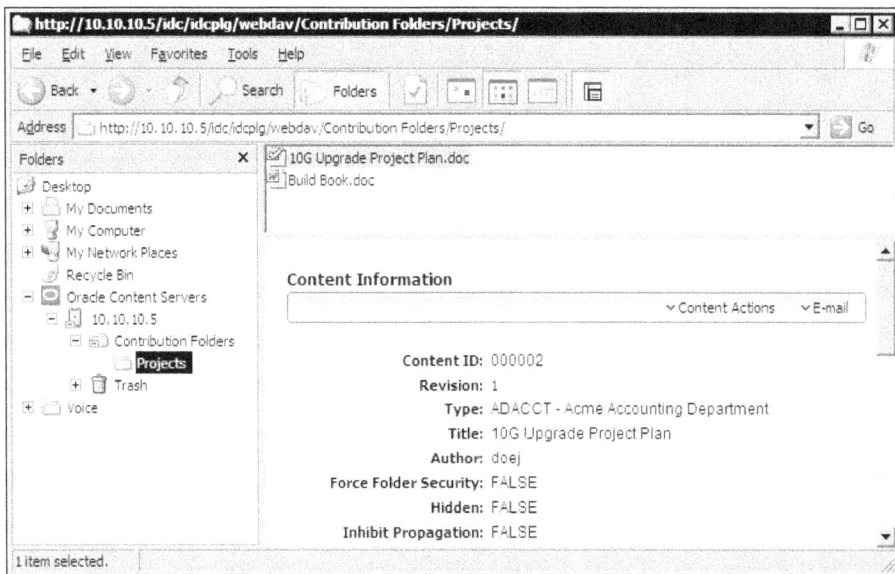

3. If you don't have any content items in this folder, it might be a good time to put one there. Simply drag or copy-and-paste a small document from My Documents (or some other place on your machine). The item will be checked in and will show up in the folder.

> If the item doesn't show up check your Content Server log for error messages. Did you forget to specify System Defaults?

4. Right-click on a content item and pick **Check Out** (as shown in the following screenshot):

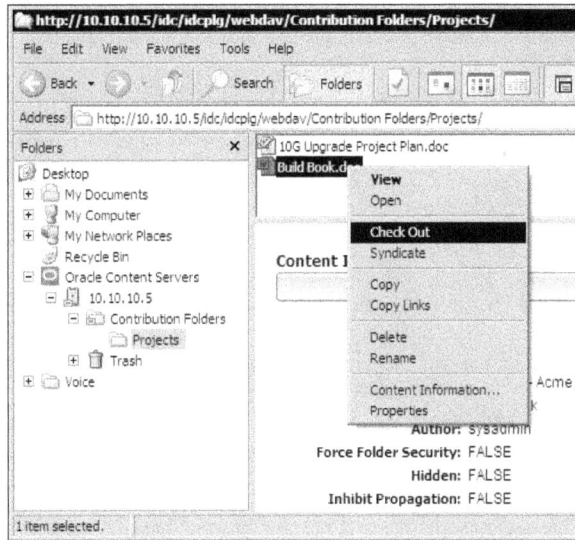

5. The icon changes to confirm that the item is indeed checked out. Now you can double-click on it to modify and save changes (as shown in the following screenshot):

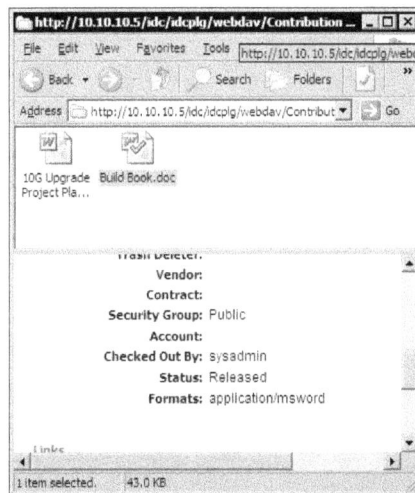

6. Select **View | Details** from your menu. Now right-click on a column heading (such as **Name**), and pick **Column Settings**. You'll see Content Server metadata fields that you can conveniently show in columns (as shown in the following screenshot):

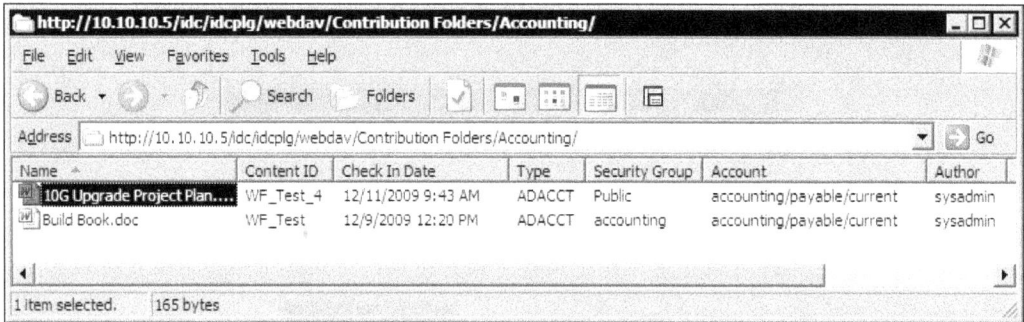

Pretty neat, isn't it? And that's not all! If you have MS Office Installed, here's what you can do with Outlook. Let's take a look at Outlook e-mails.

Checking in Outlook e-mails with just one click

Let me show you how it works:

1. Launch your Outlook. Notice the **Check In Mail Item** button added to your toolbar (as shown in the following screenshot):

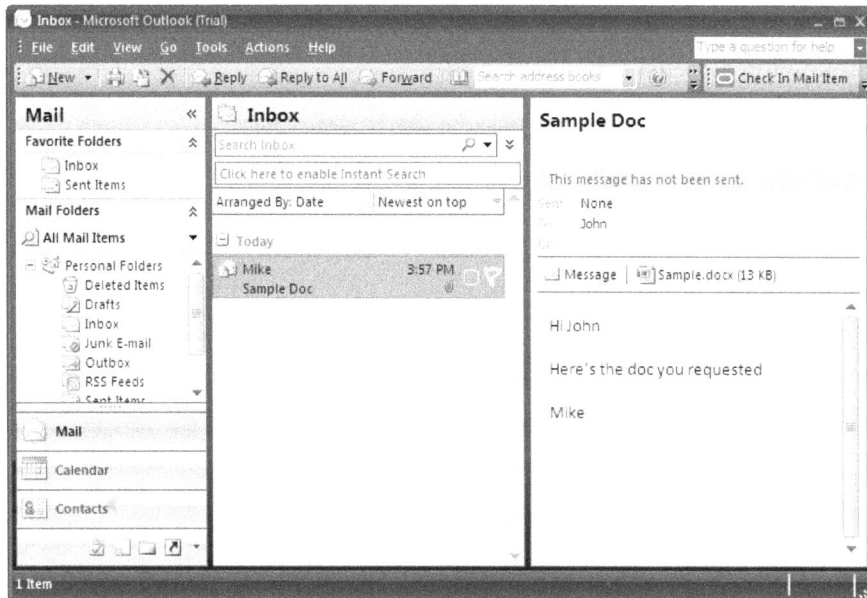

2. Select an e-mail and click on **Check In Mail Item**. This brings up a familiar Check In form in your Outlook! And your **Title** is already prefilled with the subject of the e-mail (as shown in the following screenshot). You will also see your default values prepopulated and your required fields displayed in dark red — just like the regular Check In form that you're used to seeing in the main Content Server interface:

3. Fill in the info you need to and click on **Check In**. A confirmation dialog displays (as shown in the following screenshot):

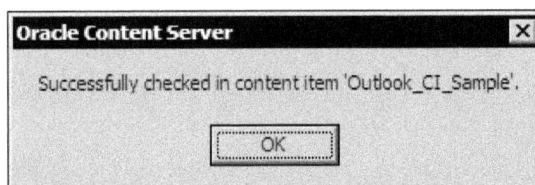

4. Congratulations! The check-in is now complete.

There's one more point I want to make about Outlook integration: Yes, you can separate attachments and check them in as content items in their own right. Go to **Tools | Email Client Integration Settings** in your Outlook to configure this behavior.

If you're using Lotus Notes—you too will be able to reap the benefits of one-click e-mail check-in and seamless Content Server integration.

Perfect! Now let's see how other Office Applications are integrated with Content Server.

Contributing documents from Word

Since Word is by far the most used application in from Microsoft Office, let's look at Word. The integration is really very simple. When you save a new document, a dialog box comes up, offering you to save the document in Content Server (see screenshot below):

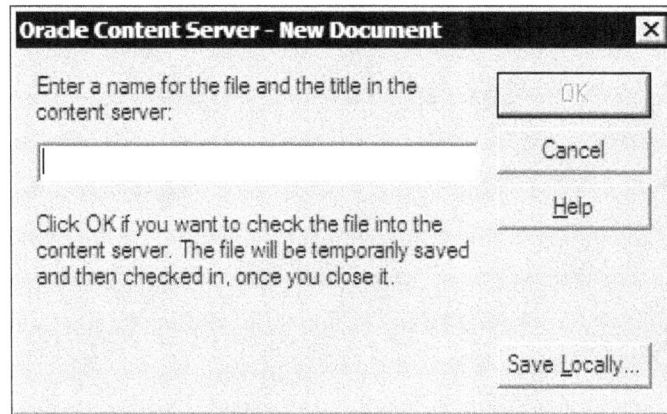

You can agree or decline. If agreed, a check-in form comes up (as shown in the following screenshot). Doesn't it look like the one you have just seen come up in Outlook? It sure does—it's the same form!

That's it!

I told you it would be a quick chapter. And all that's left to look at is just a quick Summary.

Summary

You've just learned why Virtual Folders are "virtual", how content items are linked to them, and what they can do for you. You've also seen how to install Windows Desktop Component and how to use it for seamless integration with Explorer and MS Office applications.

In the next chapter we will have some fun and take a deep dive into the inner workings of Content Server to see how things really work, and get some helpful insights too. See you soon.

7
Under the Hood

Welcome back! This chapter has a ton of time-saving tips and new approaches that you can start using right away. I'll take you "behind the curtain" on two major aspects of Content Server—its physical installation and its user interface. Here're some of the things you'll learn:

- How to automate tedious and mind-numbing manual updates and "roll them out" to thousands of items almost instantly

- A quick and easy way to debug configuration changes and custom components that make hidden errors "pop right out"

- A little handy utility that makes changing global settings a breeze; no more risky edits of the cryptic global configuration file

- A sneak peak at how documents are physically stored and what makes Content Server so efficient

Let's get started with the nine important directories.

Nine important directories: Which ones will make your life easier?

In *Chapter 3, Metadata*, we looked at the database structure. We've seen how metadata values are stored in the database. What about the items themselves? Let's explore Content Sever installation folder. I'll show you where the actual content is stored, and we will discover a ton of goodies along the way.

If you're using a virtual machine we built in *Chapter 1, Getting Up and Running*, then browse to `C:\oracle\ucm\server` folder. If you've changed the folder during installation, or if you're running on UNIX, your installation path will be slightly different. You'll see a bunch of subdirectories. Let's explore the critical ones. Let's start with `admin`.

admin

This is where Admin Server is installed. If you need a refresher flip back to *Chapter 2, Major Controls*.

Here's what the directory looks like:

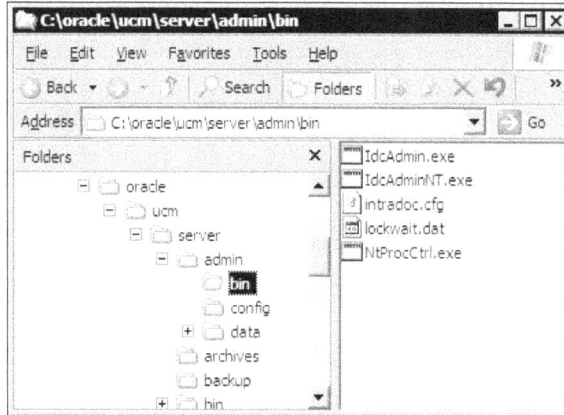

Admin Server can handle multiple Content Server instances, and allows you to start and stop them and to change their configuration. But there is no easy way to start and stop Admin Server itself. So here's how you do it.

On Windows `IdcAdminNT.exe` is running as a service. You can start and stop it from **Administrative Tools | Services**. (On UNIX it's just `IdcAdmin`.)

The following screenshot shows how you can remove it and add back in:

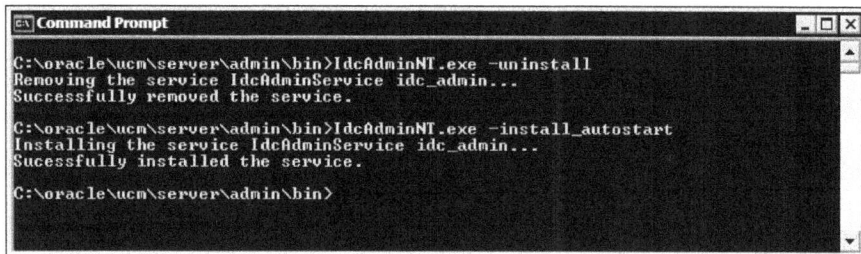

- `-uninstall` option removes the service registration.
- `-install_autostart` option installs the service with an option to start automatically.

Great! Now let's look at the next directory: `bin`.

bin

This is where the executable for Content Server itself resides. The directory also contains a few valuable admin apps and utilities (as shown in the following screenshot):

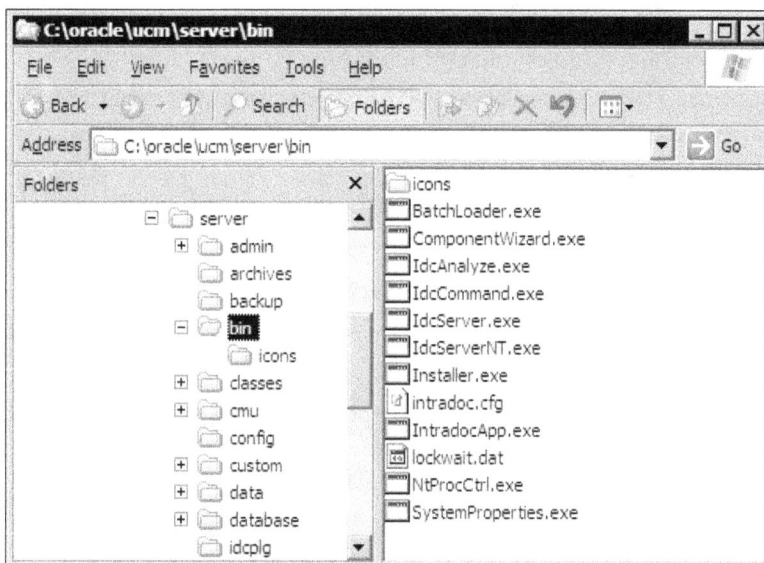

Let's look at the most important ones:

- BatchLoader — a handy tool that lets you do mass-check-ins, updates, and deletes. I will show you how to use it in the next chapter.

- ComponentWizard — a wizard you can use when developing your own custom components.

- IdcAnalyze — a consistency and error-checking tool for your file store and database.

- IdcCommand — a tool for executing Content Server services. We will look at it later in this chapter.

- IdcServer and IdcServerNT.exe — the actual Content Server executables.

- SystemProperties — easy enough, it's a tool that lets you edit system properties so you don't have to do dangerous direct edits directly on a configuration file.

Let's pause here for just a moment and see how a couple of these tools can make your life a lot easier. The first one we shall look at is SystemProperties.

SystemProperties: An easy way to manage configuration

As I mentioned in *Chapter 2*, you should be extremely careful when changing the main Content Server configuration file. On top of that, some of the property names are not self-explanatory and some such as DB password, you just can't change directly in the file. The SystemProperties utility offers an easy solution.

Let's use it to update **IP address filter** — a setting that controls what IP addresses can initiate a trusted connection into your instance. If you didn't change that during installation, your filter setting will be set to 127.0.0.1. Let's append a pipe character and the IP of the server itself; you'll also need this in place for work will do in the next sections.

Start SystemProperties. The utility main screen will come up (as shown in the following screenshot); switch to the **Server** tab and make the edits.

As you can see, the tabs across the top represent different sections of Content Server configuration. The **Server** tab, that we have open, shows you the **Server Configuration** page, where you can change the system locale, time zone, menu label, enable support for JSP, and, most importantly for us, edit the server IP Address filter.

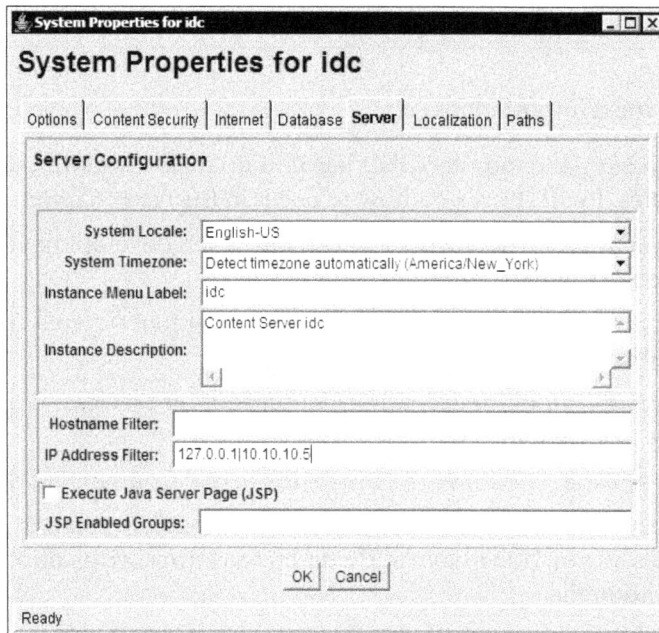

When you are done, restart Content Server for the changes to take effect. And here's another handy trick you might like.

Starting Content Server as a standalone process

Sometimes you face a serious error that prevents your Content Server from starting. It might happen after a component installation or after a configuration change.

If that happens, it's critical for you to see the output of the Content Server process itself, and you can't see it because the actual user interface depends on it being up and running. So how would you do it?

The answer is quite simple. Just start IdcServer from a command window.

> Make sure your Content Server is not running before trying this. Otherwise you'll be trying to start a second instance and it won't start because the first instance is using the port where it needs to listen.

You'll see it starting right before your eyes and any errors will pop up (as shown in the following screenshot):

And now let's continue exploring our Content Server installation. The next directory we shall look at is Config.

config

This is the directory where main Content Server configuration file resides. If you didn't guess, it's called config.cfg.

This is a typical UNIX configuration file and it also looks very similar to Windows INI files. You can comment out unwanted values by placing a hash character in front of them. Here's a little fragment showing the IP Filter changes we just made with the System Properties utility:

```
#Content Server System Properties
IDC_Name=idcm1
IdcProductName=idccs
SystemLocale=English-US
InstanceMenuLabel=idcm1
InstanceDescription=idcm1
# SocketHostAddressSecurityFilter=127.0.0.1
SocketHostAddressSecurityFilter=127.0.0.1|10.10.10.3
```

Make sure you back up this file before editing it or running the `SystemProperties` utility. You may also choose to comment out the old values and insert new rows for the new settings, just like I did with the `SocketHostAddressSecurityFilter` in the example above.

After you run `SystemProperties` or manually edit the file—restart Content Serer for the changes to come in effect.

The next directory we shall look at is `custom`.

custom

`custom` is a home for Content Server components. Every one of them has its own directory underneath it. We will be looking at custom components in *Chapter 10, Customizing Oracle UCM*, so let's proceed to the next directory, `database`.

database

This is where all database creation scripts reside. If you chose to skip creating a database during setup, these are the scripts you'll need to use to create your database schema and initialize your tables.

They may also be handy when migrating to another database vendor, in which case you can use the scripts to create the structure in your new database, and then copy your data over (you may also choose to use the content migration tools, described in *Chapter 9, Migrating Configuration*).

The following screenshot shows the content of the `database` directory:

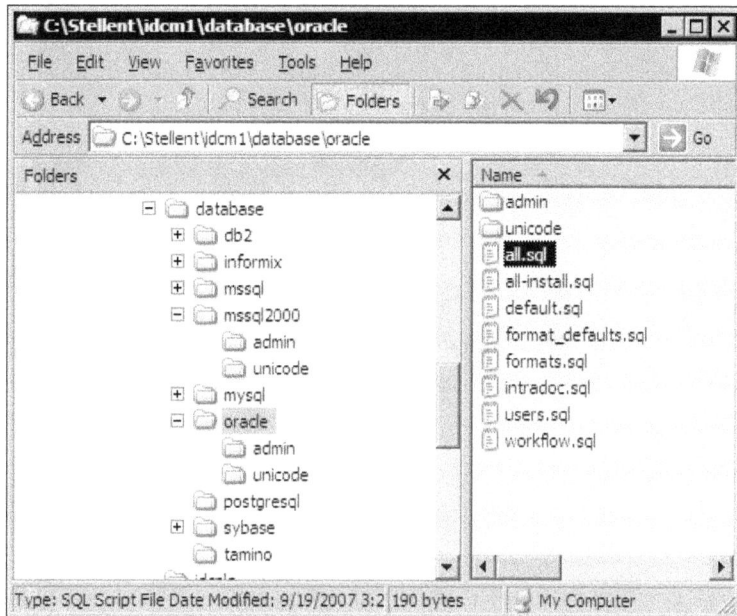

Use your database SQL execution utility to run these scripts, such as `sqlplus` with Oracle and `isql` with MS SQL Server. When running the scripts, always make sure that you run them in the following order:

```
intradoc.sql
default.sql
formats.sql
format_defaults.sql
users.sql
workflow.sql
```

For some databases there may also be an `all.sql` script (shown on the previous screenshot), which runs all the above scripts in a single operation and in the correct order.

The **Database** section of the Content Server Installation Guide has more information for each respective database.

And now let's look at the next directory, which is `idcplg`.

idcplg

You must've noticed `idcplg` in almost every single URL of the Content Server user interface (as shown in the following screenshot):

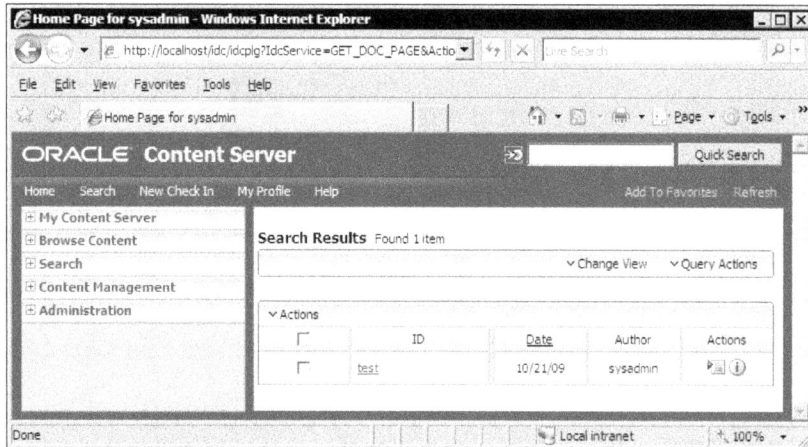

This is because it relies on a web server filter to intercept and handle all the requests. There're many benefits to this approach. One is that you don't need to incur a slow and resource-intensive database query just to check permissions and fulfill a document request.

To cut a long story short—the actual filter resides in this directory. Good to know when your web server configuration "gets out of whack".

The next directory we shall look at is called `install`.

install

We've seen this directory in *Chapter 1*, when we were installing Content Server. The critical file here that comes very handy is `log.txt`. Make sure you check it for lines beginning with ERROR when installing new Content Server instances. If errors are found in this log file then your installation will most likely fail.

So be sure that before you select **proceed with install** in the Content Server installer, you browse to the `install` directory and check `log.txt`. Every error has a detailed description that makes it easy for you to rectify the situation just like this one below:

```
ERROR:  Unable to create database connection... Unknown server
host name ...
```

(You've seen this error in *Chapter 1*.)

And now let's look at `weblayout`.

weblayout

And here's where the actual content is stored. In fact, content is stored in two places. The web-viewable version or **rendition** is stored here and the **native file** along with its version history is stored in the Vault. Why?

Support of multiple renditions is actually one of the strongest features of Oracle UCM Document Management. Here're a few examples that should bring it home for you:

- When you have a large scanned document stored in UCM, its web-viewable rendition may be a thumbnail version of the document. This will let the user see the image almost instantly without having to wait a long time for entire image to download over a slow connection.

- When you store an engineering document that requires a custom viewer to open and the user machine may not have that viewer installed—a PDF or GIF version may be displayed as a web-viewable rendition.

- When a company publishes a press release in a form of the MS Word document, but would like it to become an HTML page on their website— UCM's Dynamic Converter does just that instantly and automatically.

In fact, I'm sure you've been asking yourself a question; what **Primary** and **Alternate File** boxes are for on a check-in screen. Now you know the answer. The Primary File becomes a *web-viewable rendition* and the Alternate is its *native file*.

So here's how web-viewable renditions are stored (as shown in the following screenshot):

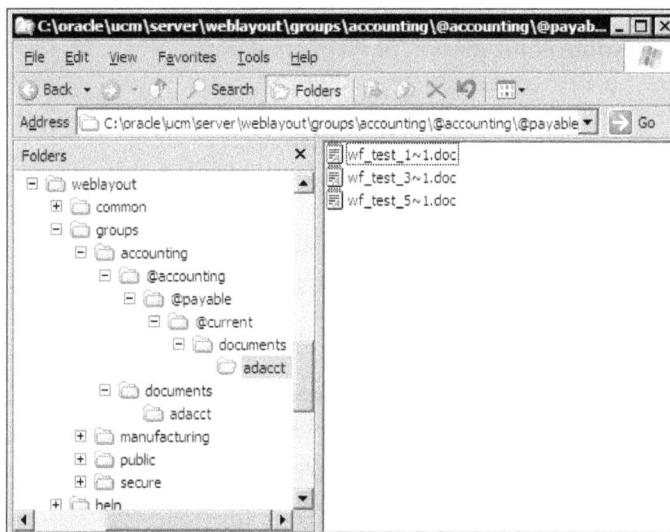

Wow! This structure has a lot of levels in it! But wait, it's not as complex as it seems. It's simply one directory per security group, then one directory per content account, and one per content type. Inside there is an actual file of a web-viewable rendition. The name of the file is its Content ID. That's all.

Why such a structure? The answer is really simple. It's optimized for very fast retrieval. So there's no need to query the database to determine whether a user can access a document.

And now let me bring up a question that many of our clients ask me: Do you have to store your content in the file system? You will find the answer in the next section.

Exploring your options for physical content storage

So do you have to store your content in the file system? The answer is "Nope, you don't have to". Depending on your specific situation, you may reap sizable rewards by choosing not to go with the default option and not to store your content in a file system. At least not all of it in the same one. The reasons include:

- You can store your content in the database to make for much easier to backup and recover.
- You can store some content on the file system and some in another device like an NAS or SAN or database, or other device.
- You may chose to store your content in a distributed, round-robin manner across a bunch of network storage devices.
- You may store just the native files and not web viewables.

Or you may go for some combination of all of the above.

And another old-time myth shattered:

Contrary to the common belief, storing content in a database may work faster than the file system-based storage.

When using Oracle 11g Database Secure Files (the ability to store unstructured content in the DB) the file system I/O speeds have been benchmarked faster than Linux file system I/O for read/write objects!

Imagine being able to store only your frequently used items on the file system, because they are optimized for quick retrieval by the web server. Other items can be stored in the database or on lower-cost storage tiers, so that you get all the power of UCM without the need for storing old content on high-cost storage devices.

This is especially good for enterprise systems and systems where you have a combination of archival and high use content.

You can even make the Content Server move your content from one device to another with a simple metadata field update! Such an update can be done automatically, manually, or through a workflow.

So how would you go about setting up one of these configurations in your own system? Pick up a copy of the **File Store Provider Installation and Administration Guide** from the Oracle online documentation page. That's right—**File Store Provider (FPS)** is the tool you need.

And now let's look at the next directory, the one that often goes hand-in-hand with `weblayout`. It's called `vault` and we shall look at it in the next section.

vault

And here's where the *native* files are stored. There're a lot more files stored here, than there are in the `weblayout`. `vault` contains all the historic revisions. Here's what the file structure looks like:

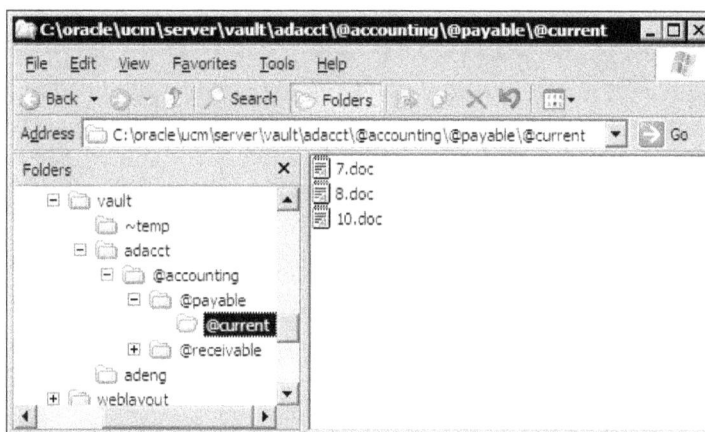

One directory per content type and one per content account, then there are the native files. File names this time are the `dID` values; globally unique Document Identifiers, *one per revision*.

Just move your mouse over a **Native File** link or **Revision** labels on the **Content Info** page, and watch the status bar for link URLs. Notice the `dID` values change to reflect unique document identifiers for every revision as shown in the following screenshot:

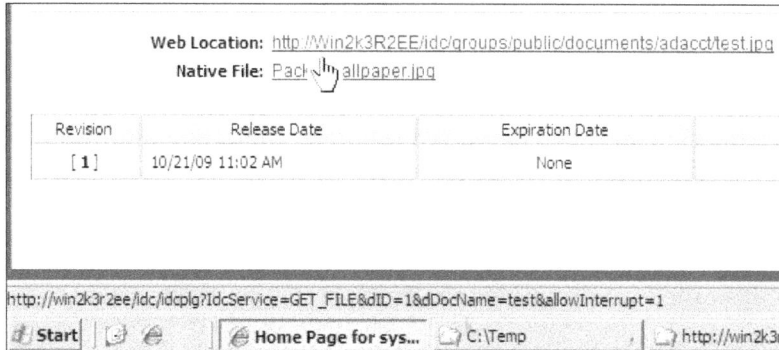

Didn't you notice what a mega-time-saver there is in the status bar at the bottom of the screenshot? The next section shows you a mega-time-saver you can spot by simply looking at the status bar.

Introducing Content Server services

A Mega-Time-Saver? I'm not kidding! Have another look at the URL on the status bar in the previous screenshot. Did you notice `IdcService=GET_FILE` right after the question mark? Yes, it's true. Every page display, every file retrieval, every update operation, and everything a Content Server does is a service call. Why is that such a big deal?

It's because we're no longer confined by the User Interface. We don't have to make 600 mouse clicks and wait for 200 server calls if we need to add 100 new users to the system. We can simply run a script that calls `ADD_USER` service and work on something else while it runs!

Let me tell you more in the next section.

Services architecture

Service Oriented Architecture is a buzzword these days. You have probably heard it or its acronym **SOA**. The reality is that long before it became a buzzword, the Content Server had been built that way (going way back to 1996). This means it is perhaps one of the most mature SOA systems out there today.

So here's how Content Server documentation defines **Service**:

A service is a function or procedure that is performed by the content server. Calling a content server service (making a service request) is the only way a client can communicate with the content server or access the database.

There are literally hundreds of them. There's one group of services for every aspect of Oracle UCM. For example, there're a dozen or so services that deal with virtual folders. So how do you find their names and instructions on how to call them?

Here's how. Begin by downloading a copy of the *Services Reference* from the UCM online documentation page.

Type "oracle universal content management documentation library" into Google. Search for **Services Reference Guide** under **Content Server.**

> At the time of this writing, this guide has over five hundred pages. It doesn't make it hard to use, because the services are very well organized by feature, such as workflow, folders, core content server services, and so on.
>
> The size of this guide simply gives you an idea of how granular and flexible the Services Architecture really is. It's hard to imagine a Content Server task that you cannot accomplish with a sequence of service calls.

Here's what the page should look like:

In the following sections I'll show you a way to use the Content Server services, and to make your life as UCM administrator much easier.

And now let me save you a couple of hours and help you to get started. Let's begin by understanding the structure of the HDA files.

Understanding HDA files

Before you can call services, you need to understand how to pass parameters to a service call. Most often, the parameters are simply passed on the URL, but sometimes, it's done via an **HDA file**. You will need to understand this simple file format, so here's a five-minute primer. It will be even more helpful for you to grasp, considering that most of the Content Server configuration files are also in HDA format.

HDA stands for Hyper Data. It's a compact way for storing name-value pairs and tabular data. It's a specially formatted text file. An HDA file can have three types of sections:

- `LocalData` sections that contain key-value pairs
- `ResultSet` sections for tabular data
- `OptionList` sections that simply list the options in a list

Here's a sample HDA file, used to add users to Content Server:

```
<?hda version="5.1.1 (build011203)" jcharset=Cp1252
encoding=iso-8859-1?>
# Add users

@Properties LocalData
IdcService=ADD_USER
dName=jdoe
dUserAuthType=Local
dFullName=John Doe
dPassword=password
dEmail=jdoe@testco.com
@end

@ResultSet UserAttribInfo
2
dUserName
AttributeInfo
jsmith
role,contributor,15
@end

<<EOD>>
```

Notice that the file starts with an XML-like header. Every line beginning with a number sign is considered a comment and ignored.

A `LocalData` section is declared with the line `@Properties LocalData` and terminated with `@end`. Inside are simple name-value pairs of metadata field names and their values.

A `ResultSet` section is declared by `@ResultSet <Result Set Name>` and terminated with `@end`.

Groups of sections in the file are terminated by `<<EOD>>`. If I wanted to add two users, my file would look like this:

```
<?hda version="5.1.1 (build011203)" jcharset=Cp1252
encoding=iso-8859-1?>
#User 1
@Properties LocalData
. . .
@end
@ResultSet UserAttribInfo
. . .
@end
<<EOD>>
#User 2
@Properties LocalData
. . .
@end
@ResultSet UserAttribInfo
. . .
@end
<<EOD>>
```

The `ResultSet` section does look confuting but it's really quite simple, once you understand how it works:

The first line after `@ResultSet <Result Set Name>` contains the number of fields in the result set (or columns in your table). Let's say, we have three fields. The next three lines then will have the names of the fields, and the rest of the section is the table data.

If line zero was the number of columns, then lines one to three are the column names, the lines four to six will have the values in the first row of the table, the lines seven to nine will have the second row and so on:

```
@ResultSet SampleTable
3 #number of columns
# Column names:
Column1
Column2
Column3
# Row 1
```

```
Row1_Col1
Row1_Col2
Row1_Col3

# Row 2
Row2_Col1
Row2_Col2
Row2_Col3

@end
```

The following table illustrates how this result set would look in a database:

Column1	Column2	Column3
Row1_Col1	Row1_Col2	Row1_Col3
Row2_Col1	Row2_Col2	Row2_Col3

Now it looks simple, isn't it? Just one comment though—in real life you don't want to put blank lines and comments inside your record sets!

> If you need more information on HDA file format refer to *The Definitive Guide to Stellent Content Server Development* © 2006 by Brian Huff.

That's it. We're now ready to make our first service call. So here's an easy way to do it.

An easy way to call Content Server services

There are many ways to call the services. To me, the easiest one is by using the `IdcCommand` utility. That's right, the one we've seen in the `bin` folder in Content Server installation.

Before using `IdcCommand` make sure that the IP Address Filter setting includes the IP address of the server itself. See the section on *System Properties* earlier in this chapter for instructions on how to change it.

> You may want to check out the *Idc command reference guide* available in the UCM Document Library if you need more info on the IDC Command

Let me give you a couple of examples to get you started:

Example 1: Creating folders

Let's see how we can create a bunch of folders using script:

Begin by creating an HDA file:

```
<?hda version="5.1.1 (build011203)" jcharset=Cp1252
encoding=iso-8859-1?>

@Properties LocalData
IdcService=COLLECTION_ADD
hasParentCollectionID=true
dCollectionName=DK Test Folder 1
dParentCollectionID=2
dCollectionOwner=doej
@end
<<EOD>>

@Properties LocalData
IdcService=COLLECTION_ADD
hasParentCollectionID=true
dCollectionName=DK Test Folder 2
dParentCollectionID=2
dCollectionOwner=doej
@end
<<EOD>>
```

Nothing fancy here. Two groups of sections, one for each folder we create, both containing only the name-value pairs. Each contains the following fields:

- `IdcService=COLLECTION_ADD`, the name of the service we're calling
- `hasParentCollectionID=true`, to specify that we're adding a sub-folder
- `dCollectionName=DK Test Folder 2`, the name of the folder we're creating
- `dParentCollectionID=2`, Collection ID of the parent folder that we can see in the browser's status bar when moving the mouse cursor over that folder
- `dCollectionOwner=doej`, the owner of that virtual folder

Let's say we name it `create_folder.hda` and put in `c:\temp`.

Here's how to put it into action:

```
C:\oracle\ucm\server\bin>IdcCommand.exe -f c:\Temp\create_folder.hda -u
sysadmin  -l c:\Temp\log.txt -c auto
```

Here's a list of parameters we've used:

- `-f` — the path to the HDA command file
- `-u` — the name of the user performing the change
- `-l` — the path to the log file
- `-c` — Content Server connection mode, which you can always keep at `auto`

And here's how a successful call should look:

A quick mental note, if you delete the folders and call the service again be prepared to see something like this:

```
1/4/10: Error executing service COLLECTION_ADD. Unable to create virtual
folder. Item with name 'DK_Test_Folder' already exists in folder '/
Contribution Folders /Accounting/Payable/'.
```

Why? The folders were not really deleted. They were moved to the **Trash** folder. Delete them from there and re-run `IdcCommand` to see it succeed.

And here's another example of using services.

Example 2: Mass-updating content info

This one is really simple. Just put the content IDs, Revision IDs (`dID`), and the metadata you want to change in an HDA file, and you're ready to roll.

This one will change the security group, content account, and document title:

```
<?hda version="5.1.1 (build011203)" jcharset=Cp1252
encoding=iso-8859-1?>
@Properties LocalData
IdcService=UPDATE_DOCINFO
dDocName=test
dID=1
dDocTitle=Packt Wallpaper
dSecurityGroup=accounting
dDocAccount=accounting/receivable/current
@end
<<EOD>>
```

And here's the result of the service call:

And here're the familiar "before" and "after" screenshots of the Content Info page.

Before:

4

And after the update:

```
Content Information
                                                    ⌄ Content Actions    ⌄ E-mail

                  Content ID: test
                    Revision: 1
                        Type: ADACCT - Acme Accounting Department
                       Title: Packt Wallpaper
                      Author: sysadmin
        Force Folder Security: FALSE
                      Hidden: FALSE
          Inhibit Propagation: FALSE
                      Folder:
                    Comments:
                   Read Only: FALSE
            Trash Delete Date:
        Trash Delete Location:
       Trash Delete Old Name:
               Trash Deleter:
                      Vendor:
                    Contract:
              Security Group: accounting
                     Account: accounting/receivable/current
               Checked Out By:
                      Status: Released
                     Formats: image/jpeg

Links

       Web Location: http://Win2k3R2EE/idc/groups/accounting/@accounting/@receivable/@current/documents/adacct/test.jpg
        Native File: Packt_Wallpaper.jpg
```

Revision	Release Date	Expiration Date	Status	Actions
[1]	10/21/09 11:02 AM	None	Released	Delete

And here's another scenario where calling services can save you time; I've mentioned it earlier in this chapter.

Example 3: Batch—creating users

The following command file executes the ADD_USER service to create two new users complete with their data, role membership, and security accounts:

```
<?hda version="5.1.1 (build011203)" jcharset=Cp1252
encoding=iso-8859-1?>
# Add users
@Properties LocalData
IdcService=ADD_USER
dName=jdoe
dUserAuthType=Local
dFullName=John Doe
dPassword=pwd
```

```
dEmail=john@testco.com
@end

# ResutlSet that specifies user attributes:
@ResultSet UserAttribInfo
2
dUserName
AttributeInfo
jdoe
role,contributor,15,account, #all, 7
@end
<<EOD>>

@Properties LocalData
IdcService=ADD_USER
dName=dbrown
dUserAuthType=Local
dFullName=Derek Brown
dPassword=password
dEmail=derek@testco.com
@end

@ResultSet UserAttribInfo
2
dUserName
AttributeInfo
dbrown
role,contributor,15,account,manufacturing,7
@end
<<EOD>>
```

Note that for every user record you will need to create a LocalData section to store user information such as their name and e-mail address, and one ResultSet to specify their roles and accounts.

Use the following values for the Access Numbers that define user permissions:

- 1: Read only
- 3: Read and write
- 7: Read, write, and delete
- 15: Administrative permissions

You can also use #all, the special value that gives the user access to all accounts.

And here's the result of the service call—the users have been created (see the following screenshot):

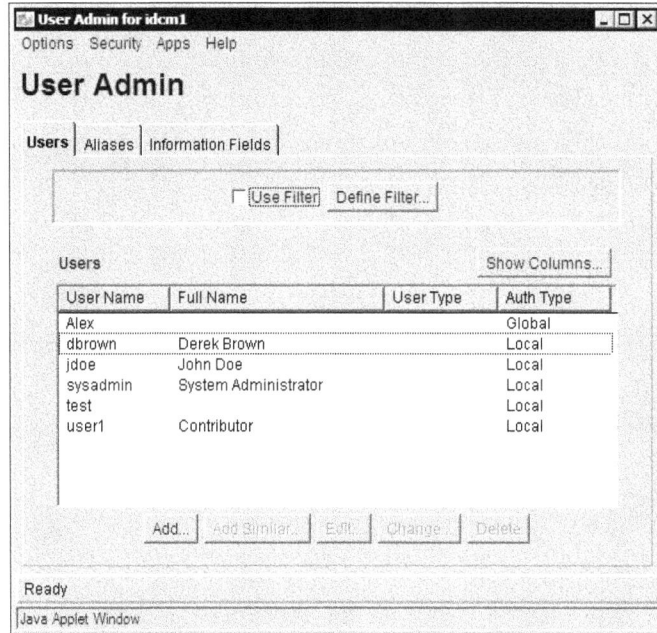

And here is the **Accounts** tab for John Doe, showing his Read/Write/Delete permissions for All Accounts:

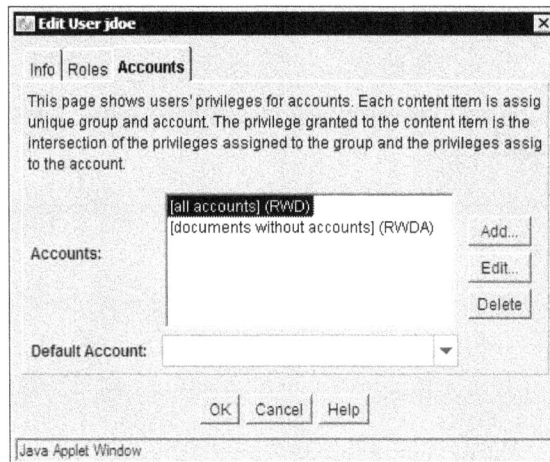

And now let's take a quick look at something even more exciting, creating your own services!

Creating your own services

That's right. You can extend Content Server functionality to perform custom tasks and integrate in your overall enterprise infrastructure. In *Chapter 10*, I'll give you a head start, but you don't have to do those customizations on your own.

I can give you dozens of specific examples when we were able to point our clients in the right direction, and help them avoid costly customizations with original and creative use of existing out-of-the-box functionality. We may also be able to help you minimize your investment when custom development is the only option to achieve the result you want. Use your Free Critique Certificate and I'll be happy to personally assess your approach at no cost to you.

And here's another option you should always keep in mind. If you *cannot* possibly avoid expensive customizations with out-of-the-box UCM functionality, you may still be able to avoid them with reusable components and pre-built custom solutions that are readily available from Oracle Partners. If this is the route you are considering, check *Appendix B, Detailed Oracle UCM Resource Directory*, for Value-Added Products and Services.

That's it! And all that's left of this chapter is just a quick summary.

Summary

There you have it. I hope it was a fun chapter. You've also learned how to automate tedious tasks, what services are all about, how content is physically stored, how to debug Content Server start-up problems like a pro, and where the global configuration settings are actually stored.

In the next chapter I'll show you more ways for automating mind-numbing tasks, and how to back up and restore your content.

8
Backup, Restore, and Content Migration

In the previous chapter we took a good look at the Content Server file system. We now know where and how the content is actually stored. If you were following the sequence of chapters, by now you're likely to have some configuration changes, metadata and content that you need to back up. And almost certainly, you have a bunch of existing content that you'd like to bring over to your new Oracle UCM. If any of this is true, this chapter will be very timely, because it will show you:

- The best strategy for protecting your system from user errors, software malfunctions, and hardware crushes (skip this step and you'll inevitably lose some critical data forever).

- A simple coding shortcut that gives you an almost unfair advantage when migrating content. I've used it to migrate content over 16 times faster than my client's previous (large and reputable) consultant planned to.

- How to avoid placing your sensitive business content on public facing servers so even if they do get compromised the attacker will leave empty handed.

- Quick and easy way to archive older content, save disk space, and keep your system at its peak performance. If you don't adopt this practice, your content store will grow almost exponentially and you'll constantly face hardware upgrade issues and new license fees.

- A handy tool that lets you mass-check-in thousands of content items at once, this is included free with your Content Server.

And yes, you will learn all of these in the next half an hour or so. But we must get into it.

First of all, let's make sure that your content and your configuration are safe. Let me show you how to backup and restore.

How to backup and restore

I hope you realize that your data can only be really safe when you back it up regularly. If you lose a document to user error, your system gets corrupted by an OS patch, your hard disk crashes or your building burns down, you should have a recent copy of your system stowed somewhere off-site and ready for a quick restore.

That actually brings up a vital lesson I've learned some years that might save you a few sleepless nights.

These companies were "completely protected" but lost their data anyway

Don't be lulled into a false sense of security when your network group reports that your servers are backed up, they may not be. The wrong directories might be selected, leaving your critical content unprotected, or the old tape may be sitting in a tape drive, or no tape at all! I've seen people get very creative when it comes to doing things *wrong*! So never assume. Make sure! How?

With these two simple words: demand a periodic **Restore Test.**

Ask for your last week's content. Get it restored on a virtual machine and test it. Do you see the revisions you need to see or you've got an older copy? Is everything working as expected? Only then you can be sure.

Let me show what you need to back up. The next section walks you through this.

Backing up filesystem and the database

Content Server System Migration Guide says: Caution: Do not use Archiver as your primary method of disaster recovery; use standard backup systems for the database and file system.

It means you don't use Content Server tools. Backup your entire Content Server installation directory and your database. (Combine full and incremental backups to conserve space. Full backups make a copy of your entire directory, while incremental ones only store changes made since the last full backup).

And pick your least active time like 4 a.m. when no updates are made. If you backup a new content item in your filesystem but your database backup was taken earlier and doesn't contain it then you won't be able to retrieve it or you'll get errors. The same thing will happen if you get an item in a database, but not in a file system. You must have both. Hence there should be no updates while the backups are running.

If there's no way to make sure, write a script to stop the service `IDC Content Service` on Windows, or call `idcserver_stop` on UNIX prior to beginning the backups. When complete start the service on Windows or call `idcserver_start` if you're running in a UNIX environment.

> If you've customized your File Store Provider and storing your content in a database, you don't need to stop the Content Server and worry about synchronization. A single backup of the database covers everything.

Perfect. Now that we got full backups and disaster recovery out of the way, let's see what partial backups can do for you, partial backups and their three important applications.

Content Server provides a complete toolset for backup and restore of your content and configuration. In this chapter will have a look at the main tool, **Archiver**. In the next chapter will cover the rest of the toolset.

Archiver is your first choice when it comes to making partial backups. Here're the three most important things it can do for you.

Moving content to another server

You can copy or automatically replicate some of your content from one server to the other. For instance, you may not want *all* of your content copied over to your public site or extranet.

Another very common use of this feature is moving content from Development to Staging and then to Production and vice versa.

Removing inactive content

You can archive your older or inactive content for permanent or temporary storage, or delete altogether. This will save your disk space and your CPU cycles. Your `weblayout` and your `vault` file systems will not grow as fast. Your indexer will not take as long and your database will stay smaller.

In some cases old *revisions* of content items have to be removed on a scheduled basis. Your company may only want to keep certain content for X number of years and then permanently delete it, or in case of a lawsuit it can potentially be used against it.

In fact, legal, industry and compliance regulations may dictate storage and disposition rules and timeframes, how long should the content be stored, and what action needs to be taken when that period is over.

And here's one more important thing that Archiver can do for you. It can help you with mass-updating metadata.

Mass-updating metadata

Yes, you can use Archiver to mass-update your metadata. It is actually pretty simple. Just export the content you'll be updating, set up the metadata changes you need to make in a form of an import map, and then import it right back. I'll show you how to do just that later in this chapter.

Let's see how all of this fits together.

Lab 9: Using Archiver

Before we get started with the lab, you need to see a couple of term definitions. They sound familiar, but when it comes to Archiver, they mean totally different things:

- **Batch File**: A result of a single export operation. Every time you export to an archive, a new export folder and a new batch file is created.

- **Collection (Archiver)**: Collection of archives (not virtual folders!). It is a file folder with a set of archives in it. Each one containing its own export folders.

One more glance at the Content Server file system will help you internalize these definitions. Take a look at the screenshot below:

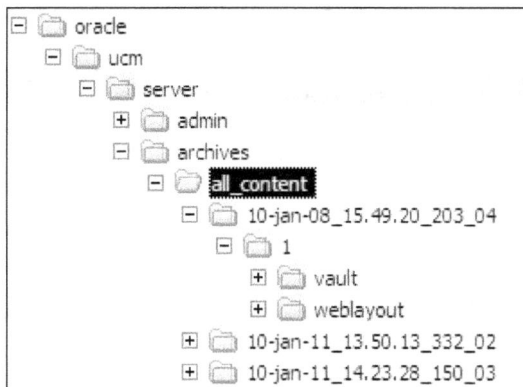

By default, the folder `archives` under root Content Server installation serves as default archive collection.

I've created an archive called `all_content`. I've then ran an export three times, so you can see three export folders. If you expand them you'll see that they contain their own partial snapshots of `vault` and `weblayout` directories.

Great! We're now ready to start the Archiver.

Exporting content

Let me walk you through:

1. Go to **Admin Applets** and click on **Archiver** as shown in the following screenshot:

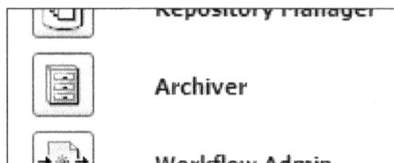

2. **Archiver** applet starts as shown in the following screenshot:

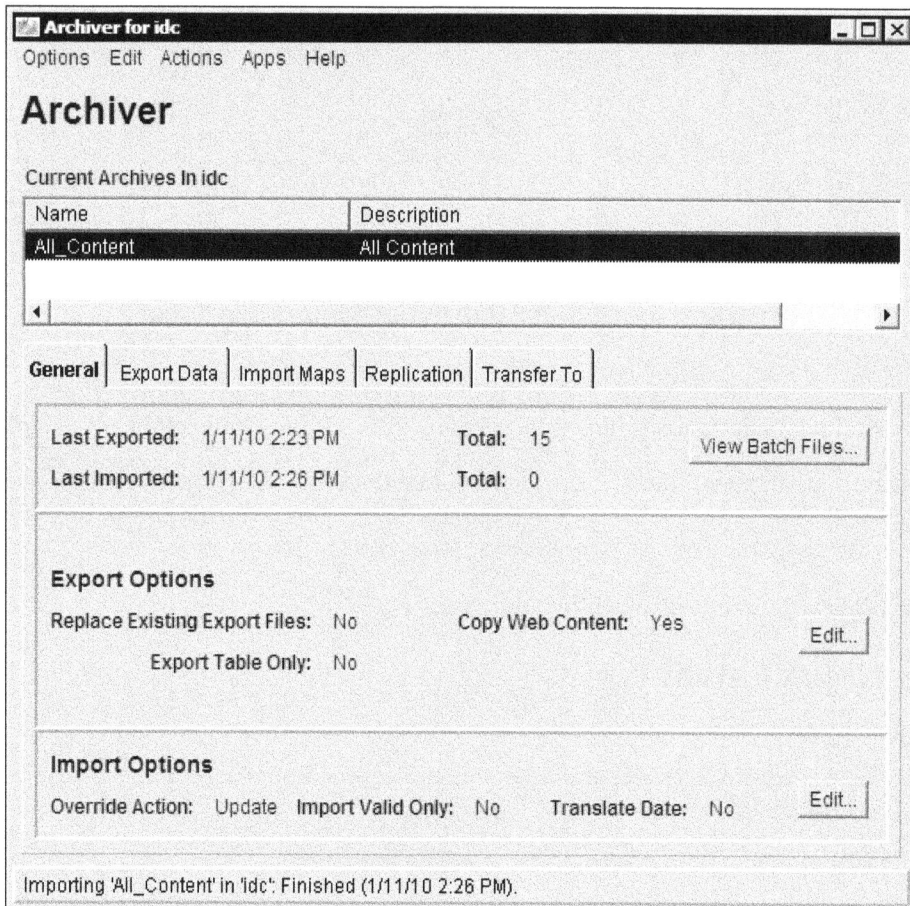

> If you're trying to create or remove collections or copy archives - you'll need to start Archiver in a stand-alone mode. See *Content Server System Migration Guide* for more information

3. Go to **Edit | Add. Add Archive** dialog displays as shown in the following screenshot. Enter the name for your archive (no spaces allowed) and its description:

```
┌─────────────────────────────────────────────┐
│ ▓ Add Archive                            [×] │
├─────────────────────────────────────────────┤
│  Archive Name: [                          ]  │
│  Description:  [                          ]  │
│                                               │
│              [ OK ]  [ Cancel ]  [ Help ]     │
└─────────────────────────────────────────────┘
```

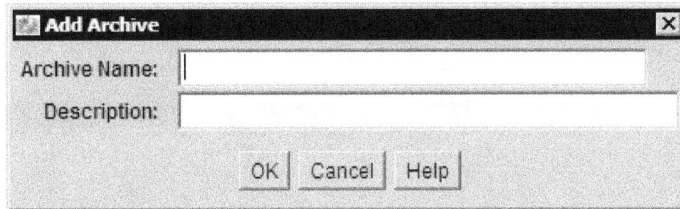

4. Go to **Actions | Export. Export Archive** screen comes up as shown in the following screenshot:

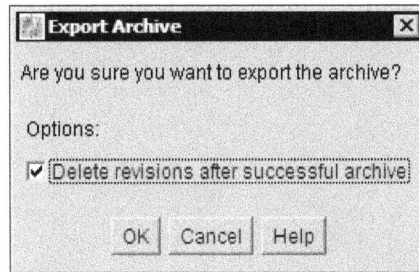

```
┌──────────────────────────────────────┐
│ ▓ Export Archive                 [×] │
├──────────────────────────────────────┤
│ Are you sure you want to export the   │
│ archive?                              │
│                                        │
│ Options:                               │
│                                        │
│ ☑ Delete revisions after successful    │
│    archive                             │
│                                        │
│        [ OK ]  [ Cancel ]  [ Help ]    │
└──────────────────────────────────────┘
```

> Archive operations may take a long time when you have a significant number of content items to process. To save time you might be better off running these examples on a test system with under 500 content items.

5. You can choose to move your content to archive (**Delete After Successful Archiving** option) or copy it there when the box is not checked. Let's check **Delete After Successful Archiving.** When you click on **OK** export operation begins.

6. And here comes the heart attack! Your content store is now EMPTY! (as shown in the following screenshot):

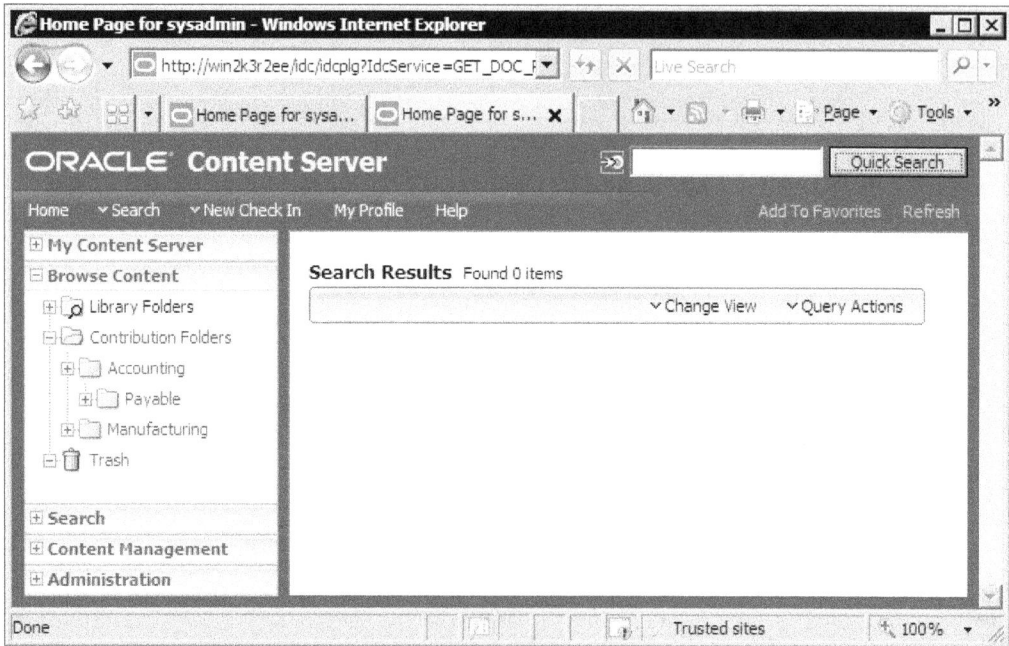

> If you don't see results of your export or import operation you may need to force-rebuild an index to see the changes right away. Here's how you do this:

7. Go To **Admin Applets** and start **Repository Manager**.

8. Go to **Indexer** tab.

9. Click on **Start** button under **Collection Rebuild Cycle** as shown in the following screenshot:

Repository Manager

Content | Subscriptions | **Indexer**

Automatic Update Cycle

Finished indexing.

State:	Initialization	**Indexer Counters**
Status:	Active	**Total:** 0
Start Date:	1/8/10 3:53 PM	**Full Text:** 0
Finish Date:	1/8/10 3:48 PM	**Meta Only:** 0
Active Date:	1/8/10 3:53 PM	**Delete:** 0

Start | Suspend | Cancel | Configure...

Collection Rebuild Cycle

Finished indexing.

State:	Finished	**Indexer Counters**
Status:	Idle	**Total:** 0
Start Date:	1/8/10 3:50 PM	**Full Text:** 0
Finish Date:	1/8/10 3:50 PM	**Meta Only:** 0
Active Date:	not active	**Delete:** 11

Start | Suspend | Cancel | Configure...

No content items matched the criteria. | Finished indexing.

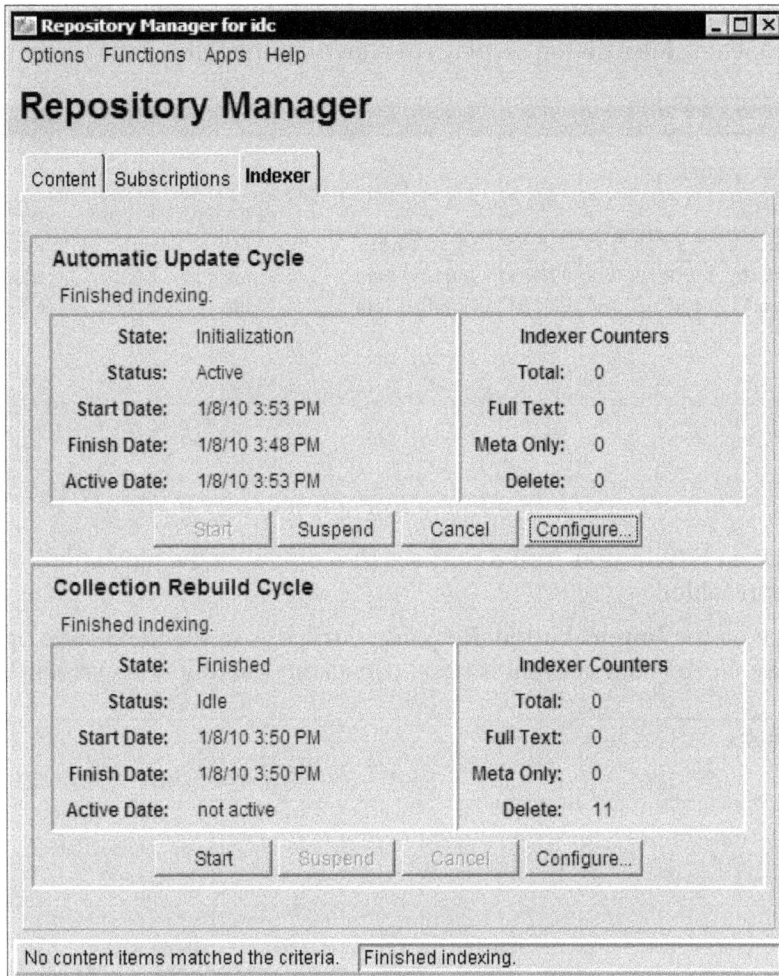

Warning! If you have a lot of items in the system then this will take a while.

10. On the **General** tab of your **Archiver** applet click on **View Batch Files** button. View Batch Files dialog displays as shown in the following screenshot:

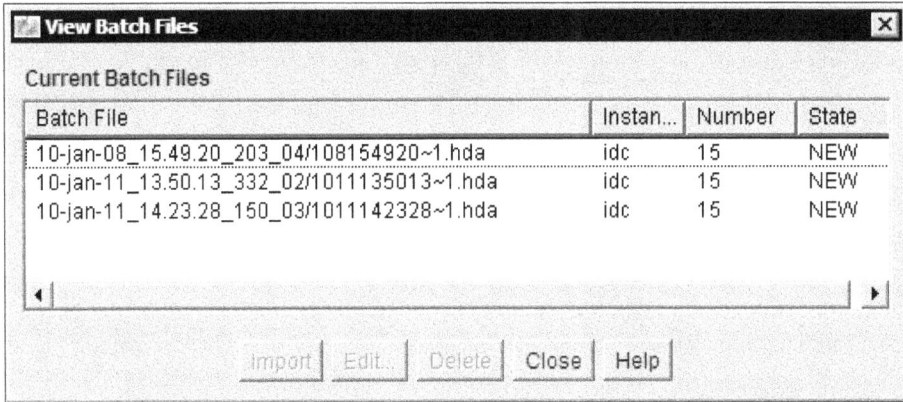

11. Click on **Edit** button. You'll now see the content of the batch file's export folder.

12. Click on the **Import** button. Rebuild your index to see the results right away. Voila! Your content is back! (Checkout the following screenshot):

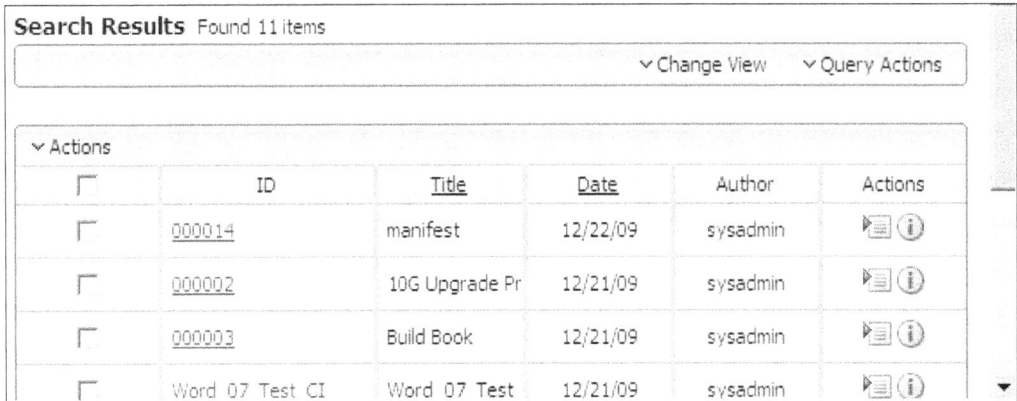

13. Expand **Administration** tray. Select **Log Files | Archiver Logs**. You can now see exactly what Archiver is doing. This is especially useful for troubleshooting, as shown in the following screenshot:

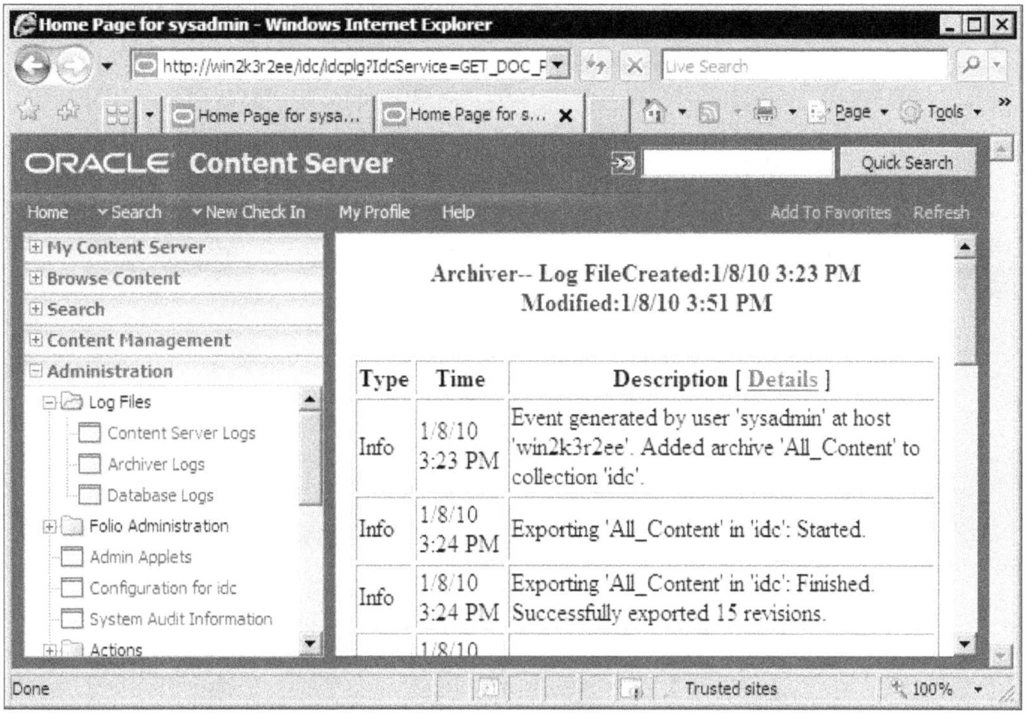

That's it for exporting content. In the next section we will look at Importing content.

Importing content

Are you up for a little magic? Here it comes. Let's say, you'd like to change the author on all the documents you're about to import from `sysadmin` to `doej`. Here's how you'll do it:

1. In Archiver's **Import Maps** tab click on **Edit** button next to **Value Maps** box as shown in the following screenshot. Specify the value you need replaced under **Input Value**, specify your field and the new value under **Output Value**. And yes you can replace multiple values in multiple fields all at the same time!

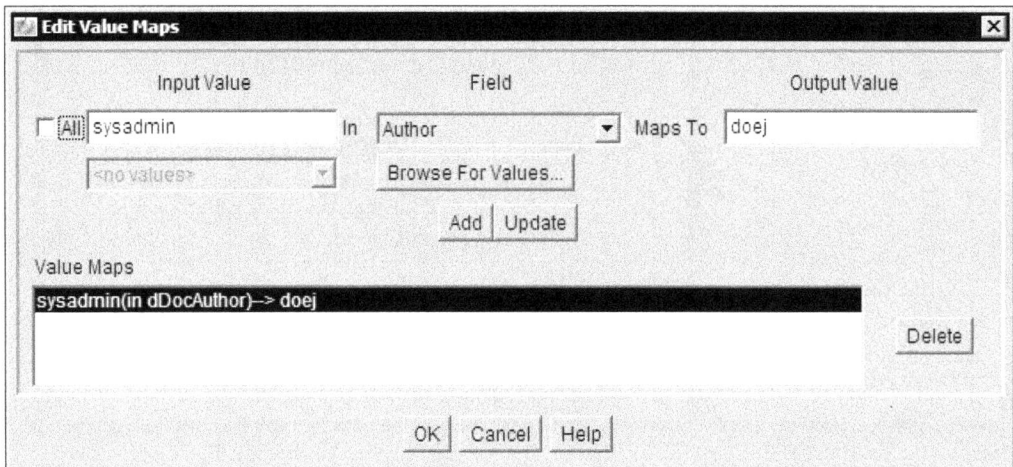

Sometimes, you'd want to copy or move ALL values from one field over to another. Let's say, you need to copy the value of the document's title (`dDoc-Title`) to a custom Vendor Name field we've defined (`xVendor`).

2. Click on **Edit** button next to **Field Maps** box. **Export field** is the original field in your archive (remember to click on **Add** to add your expression to the list of field maps!) as shown in the following screenshot:

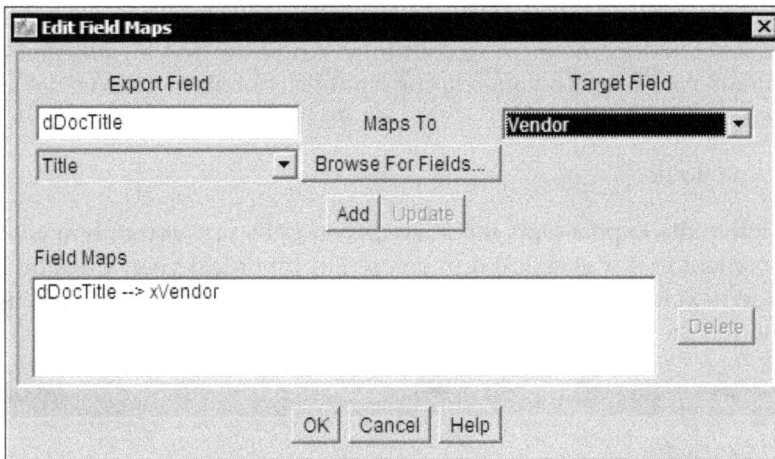

3. Rerun your import and re-index repository. You'll see the new values in Author and Vendor fields as shown in the following screenshot:

Search Results Found 11 items

∨ Change View   ∨ Query Actions

∨ Actions

☐	ID	Title	Date	Author	Actions
☐	000014	manifest	12/22/09	doej	▸▤ ⓘ
☐	000002	10G Upgrade	12/21/09	doej	▸▤ ⓘ
☐	000003	Build Book	12/21/09	doej	▸▤ ⓘ
☐	Word_07_Test_CI	Word_07_Tes	12/21/09	doej	▸▤ ⓘ
☐	Outlook_CI_Sample	Sample Doc	12/21/09	doej	▸▤ ⓘ
☐	000013	launcher-local	12/14/09	doej	▸▤ ⓘ
☐	Basic_Test_1	Test	12/11/09	doej	▸▤ ⓘ
☐	WF_Test_4	Bypass test	12/11/09	doej	▸▤ ⓘ
☐	WF_Test	Test documen	12/9/09	doej	▸▤ ⓘ

But wait! Do you always have to archive your *entire* repository? How do you update metadata on *just* the documents in Accounting? And how do you *only* archive expired content? And how do you *only* copy public content to an extranet and keep all sensitive documents private?

Here's how you do it:

1. Switch to the **Export Data** tab in Archiver. Let's say, you only want to archive the content that was checked in before Jan 1st or last year. Click on **Edit** button next to **Export Query** box. **Query Definition** screen comes up as shown in the following screenshot:

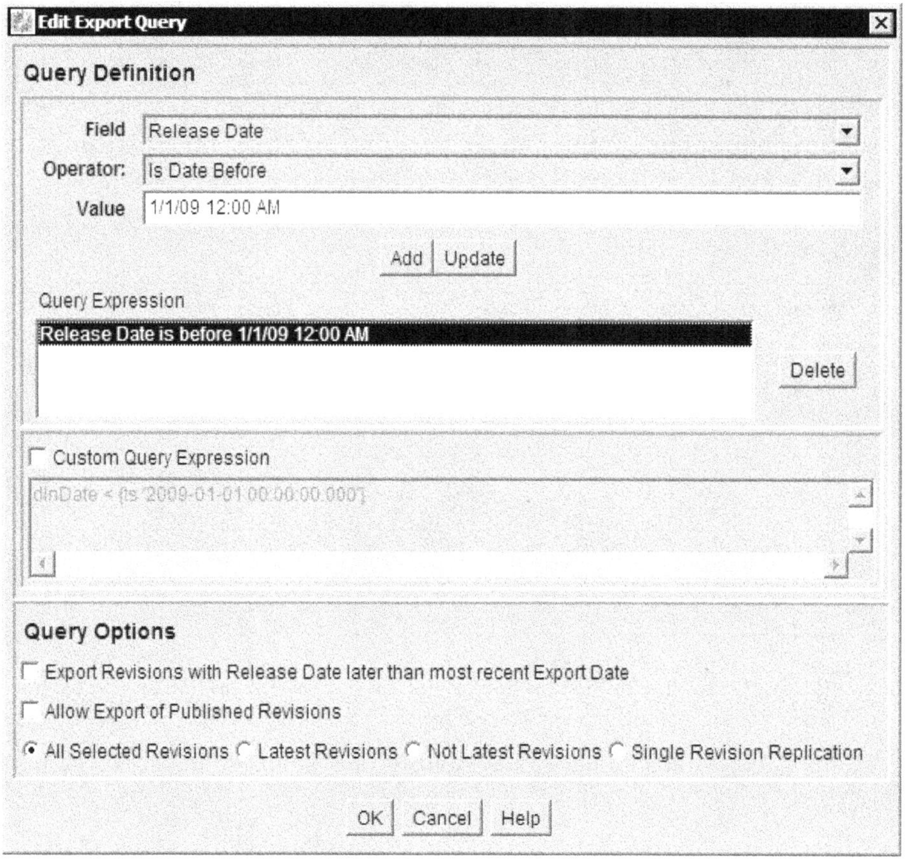

2. Specify **Release Date** as your input **Field**, **Is Date Before** as **Operator**, and **1/1/09** as your **Value**. Click on **Add** and **OK** to close the dialog.

3. Click on **Preview** button to test how your query works. If you don't see any results go back and check the criteria. What you see in the preview is what will be exported into the archive (see the following screenshot):

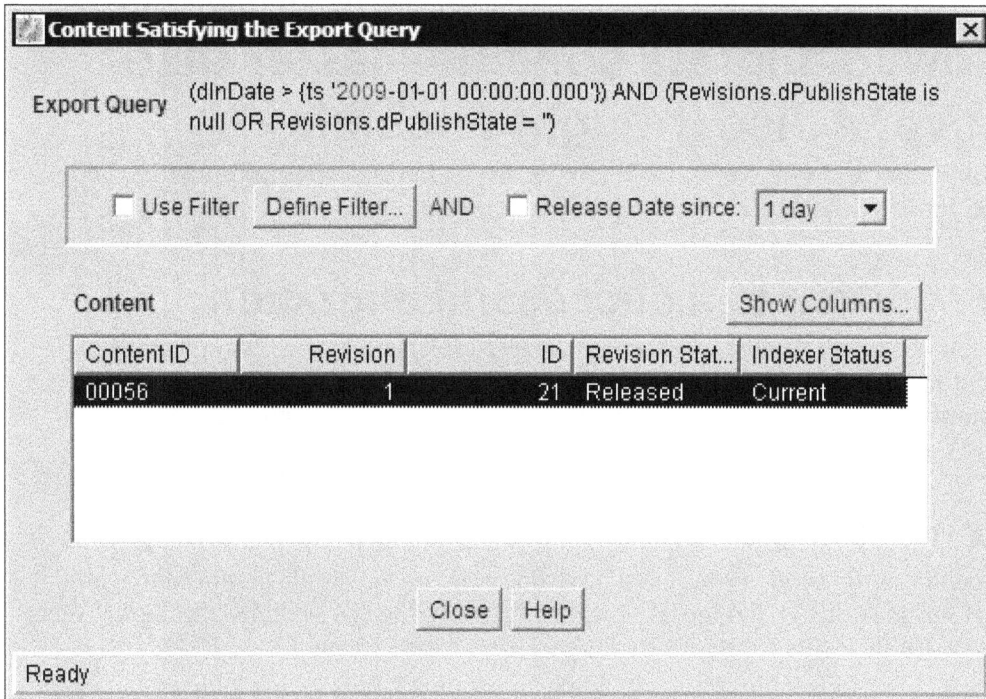

> You can use the **Define Filter...** button to filter results and search for specific records.

That's it! You've now seen all major things that an Archiver can do for you. Well, almost all.

Setting up real-time content replication

If servers one and two are set up for replication, the moment a content item gets checked-in or updated on server one it gets archived, transferred over to server two and imported there. And, yes, if you need, you can only replicate a sub-set of your content, such as public documents.

See *Content Server System Migration Guide* for more information and instructions on how to set up replication between two Content Servers.

Now let me tell you more. The minute you're ready to roll out your Oracle UCM you'll be asking yourself this big question: How do i bring my existing content in? The next section tells you about this.

How to migrate content—faster than anyone else thought possible

Hold on to your hat! Not only I'll tell you how to bring existing content in, I'll tell you how to do it *fast*.

A shortcut to a successful migration

Before we take a plunge into Content Server tools, here's a really important topic to consider: Are you talking about just *bringing existing content in* or do you need a *content migration*? What's the difference? There's plenty. First, check out Content migrations.

Content migrations

A content migration is when you have one or more existing Content Management systems to consider. On the day of the migration, the old systems become obsolete and all of the content "magically" appears in the new system.

There may be some down time in between. There may also be a **content freeze** in the middle, when your old systems become read-only and you have the time to bring content over.

More often than not, content migrations need to be *repeatable*. This means that you write down your *migration process*. You develop a sequence of scripted and manual steps, required to bring the content over. And you follow them by **content verification** steps. You make sure that it has indeed migrated correctly.

You go through the migration process more than once. You test it in a development environment. And when you like the results, you schedule the day of the migration and repeat your process in production.

A well-planned process is your best shortcut to a successful migration. Script it as much as possible. Run it in a test environment until you get it right. It's much easier to tweak the process than clean the content after!

Simply uploading existing documents

If all you need is to upload a bunch of documents then your task is really simple. There is no content freeze and you don't have to migrate all the content *at once*. It's a major benefit. You can bring the content in small batches.

But never the less, spend the time and test each little step in development environment first. It's still easier then fix the content by hand later!

There you have it. Now let's explore the migration tools. First let's take a look at Batch Loader.

Using Batch Loader

Batch Loader is your first choice of a content migration tool. It allows you to mass-check-in content. You can also use it to update metadata and delete large number of content items in one shot.

Watch. I'll show you how to use it:

1. Go to the /bin folder in your Content Server installation directory. Start BatchLoader. It will ask you for user name and password. Use sysadmin and idc for the password (unless you've changed it).

2. **Batch Loader** comes up as shown in the following screenshot:

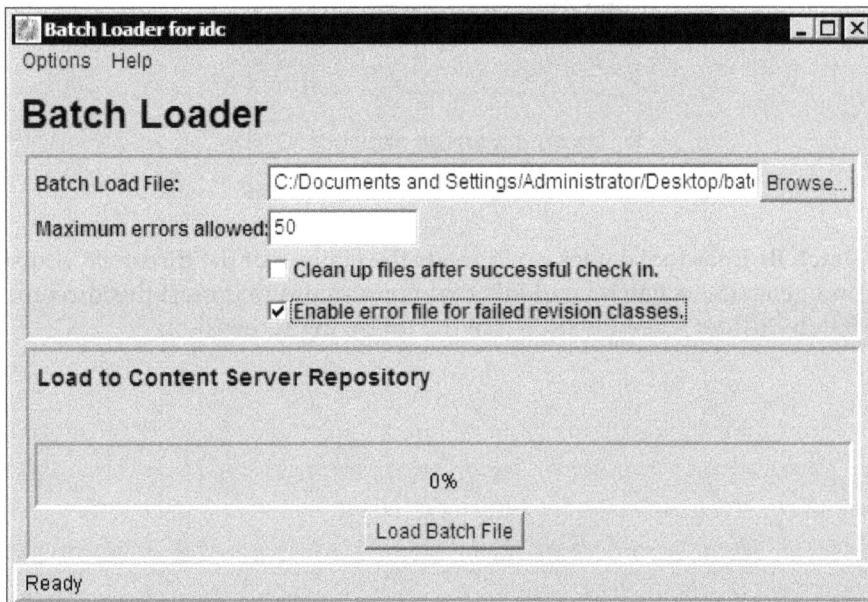

Looks pretty simple, doesn't it? It takes a **Batch Load File** and processes it. Actually, there are just three controls I want you to note:

- **Clean up files after successful check in** box: Treat it like nitro-glycerine. When checked, if the file was successfully checked in - it will be wiped out. So keep the box un-checked if you're not sure.

- **Enable error file for failed revision classes** box: This one is actually very useful. I always make sure that it's checked. It makes your Batch Loader to move failed records into a new Batch Load File where you can fix the errors and re-run it.

- **Maximum errors allowed** text box: This is the number of errors you allow before the batch load operation gets terminated. If your content is inconsistent, you can bump it up. But in most cases, default value is fine. I've loaded thousands of items with just a couple of errors. If it works it works.

I bet you're curious about how Batch Load File works and how to make one. First, I'll show you the tool that does all the grunt work:

1. In Batch Loader select **Options | Build Batch File** as shown below:

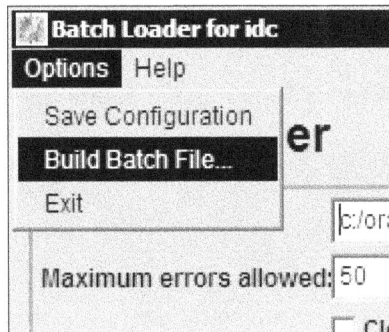

2. **Batch Builder** tool comes up. It reads the content of the directory you specify and generates a Batch Load File that you can use to import this directory. **Batch Builder** screen is shown in the following screenshot:

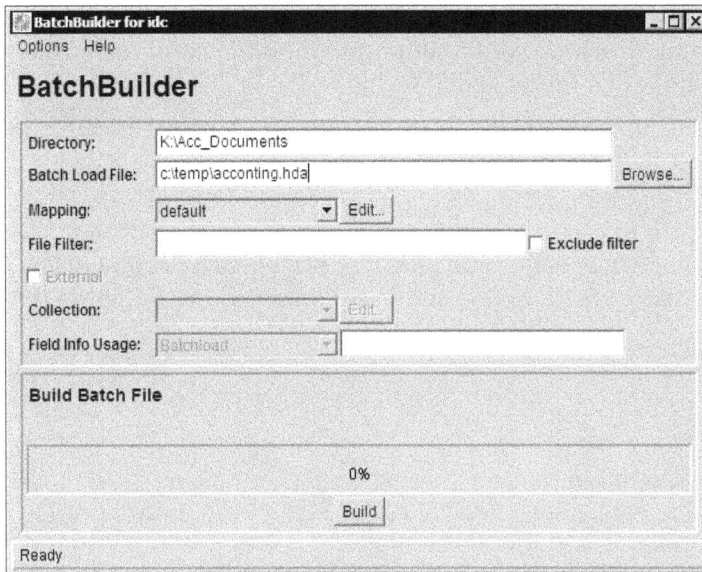

3. Type up a directory where you will be importing the documents from. Then browse for location of your future Batch Load File.

4. If you like, you can edit the Field Mapping, hit the **Edit** button next to **Mapping** drop down. Select **Default Mapping** and hit **Edit** again. **Edit Mapping** dialog displays as shown in the following screenshot:

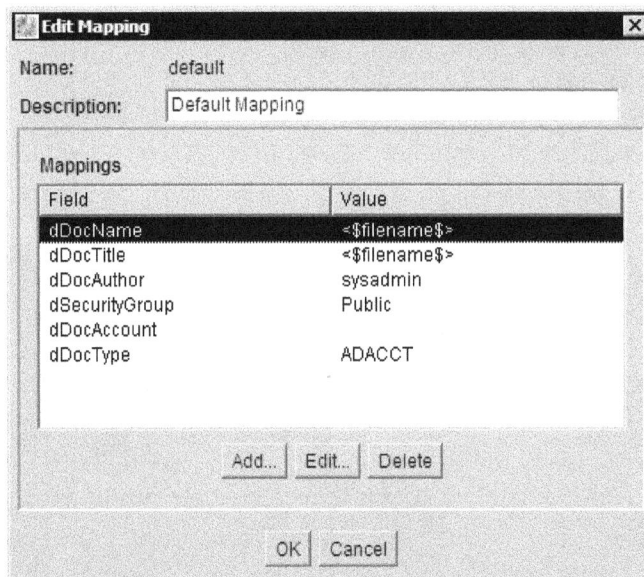

As you see, Field Mapping dialog allows you to map *metadata fields* in the documents you are about to import to their file name, extension, directory name, and other file system information.

5. That's all. Now you're ready to get your Batch Load File built. Hit the **Build** button at the bottom.

6. Let's see what's inside the Batch Load File:

I've kept the matters simple and only placed two documents in `K:\Acc_Doc-uments`: `Invoice_234.doc` and `Name Change.doc`. So here's the Batch Loader file:

```
Action = insert

dDocName=Invoice_234
dDocTitle= Invoice_234
dDocAuthor=sysadmin
dSecurityGroup=Public
dDocAccount=
dDocType=ADACCT
dInDate=1/13/10 4:41 PM
primaryFile=k:/Acc_Documents/Invoice_234.doc
<<EOD>>

dDocName=Name Change
dDocTitle=Name Change
dDocAuthor=sysadmin
dSecurityGroup=Public
dDocAccount=
dDocType=ADACCT
dInDate=1/13/10 4:41 PM
primaryFile= k:/Acc_Documents/Name Change.doc
<<EOD>>
```

It looks like a name-value section of an HDA file (See *Chapter 7, Under the Hood*, for HDA Syntax). It's just a list of metadata field names and values, terminated by `<<EOD>>`. And there's `Action = insert` in the first line to tell the Batch Loader that we actually want to insert the documents.

7. At last, we're ready to import the content. Go back to Batch Loader and run your file. Here's what I've got on the screen after running my script above:

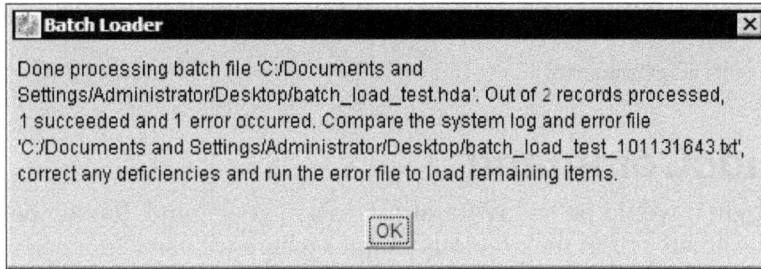

Ouch! One document didn't import. What happened?

Here's where the error file really comes handy. Look in the directory where your Batch Load Script is. The file name is something like `<Batch Load File Name>_101131650.txt`.

Here's how the error file looks like:

```
#Internal error version
#!csUnableToCheckIn,name change!
#csCheckinIDHasSpaces!csCheckinIDNotValid,name change
#
#External error version
#Content item 'name change' was not successfully checked in.
#It contains spaces. The content ID 'Name Change' is invalid.

dDocAuthor=sysadmin
dDocName=Name Change
dInDate=1/13/10 4:49 PM
dDocType=ADACCT
dDocAccount=
dSecurityGroup=Public
dDocTitle=Name Change
primaryFile= k:/Acc_Documents/Name Change.doc
<<EOD>>
```

It's simply a portion of our original Batch Load Script that didn't work! Yes, we can fix it and use the error file itself as a new Batch Load Script! And it tells you what went wrong. In our case, we simply need to remove the space in `dDocName` value.

It's time to check the results. It might take a while for the new content to get indexed, so if you in a rush, start indexer's Auto Update Cycle (no need to rebuild the entire index in this case).

Voila! Your batch loaded documents appear in the search results! Is that a neat tool or what?

But wait! What about folders? Are you forced to create all the folders by hand?

The answer is in `idcCommand`.

Using idcCommand

Nope! I thought it would be handy to refresh this in your mind. Remember the example I've shown you in the previous chapter where we used `idcCommand` to create virtual folders? So here's your answer.

And I kept the best for the last. Here's the final bit that will really bring these tools to life for you.

A secret "catalyst" that triples the speed of your migration

OK. It's not a secret any more. The Catalyst is Code Generation. No longer you have to type up your HDA files for use with `idcCommand` and only rely on the Batch File Builder to create a perfect Batch Loader Script.

You can use your text editor's search and replace function, a Perl script or a programming language of your choice to *generate* those. How?

In my recent article for Independent Oracle UCM Knowledge Center at `http://stellentexperts.com/ioukc`, I'm revealing exactly how we managed to migrate content 16.9 times faster than a large and reputable vendor was planning to accomplish with a "standard" solution. Dozens of readers reported some massive time savings with this technique, so I'm reprinting it here.

How we got a project over a finish line 16.9 times faster

Last year we ended up migrating 38 websites and major site sections (10,710 pages in total) in just over a week each, while a nation-wide reputable vendor estimated each of them to take three to six months. How did we do it?

The short answer is this: we used Batch Loader, easy enough. Am I simply comparing a manual import to the use of a tool? Nope. I'm writing this article to waste your time. After all, that vendor was also using the batch loader. But what we were really using was the batch loader turbo charged.

Batch loader turbo charged

When it comes to a mass-check in the batch loader is a nice and useful tool, but when you're loading tenths of thousands of files from dozens of locations, and when each file has unique derived values in its metadata Batch Loader won't be of much help.

I guess that almost any enterprise-scale content migration will have you fall flat on your face if you're simply relying on Batch Loader to "magically" load your content into the UCM.

The quickest way to automate a migration

It's simple. The answer becomes obvious when you look at how the batch loader works. It processes a typical HDA file, one record at a time. It picks up a file from the location you specify in `primaryFile` field, sets metadata values to the ones you tell it to use, and calls a Check In service. Again, it reads batch loader script one record at a time and checks in files one by one.

What if we could create some cool batch loader script that will import all the files we want imported? All at once! Sure, that would be nice, but how do we go about creating one?

The Batch Builder utility that comes with Batch Loader is very limited. It builds simple files based on a content of a single directory and lets you use file system data as metadata. It won't let you pick up files from multiple locations or create complex metadata values.

So, here's the biggie, to turbo-charge your content migration effort, you need to consider generating your own batch loader scripts.

And here's how to use code generation effectively.

How to use code generation effectively

First of all—how do you go about generating it?

For simple migration you can get away with using your editor's search and replace function on a comma-separated list of files. Let's say, your excel file has the following columns:

```
Content Id, Title, Author, Security Group, Account, Doc Type, Date,
File Path.
```

After you save it in a comma-separated (CSV) format, you'll end up with something like this:

```
A2561405,Migration Project Plan,Bill,Public,abstract,8/12/09 4:20 PM,
C:/Migration/Project Plan v.3.4.doc.
```

Now, you could use a `RegEx` like this to produce a batch loader script out of your CSV file. Replace this:

```
^([^,]*),([^,]*),([^,]*),([^,]*),([^,]*),([^,]*),([^,]*),([^,]*)$
```

> If you're new to regular expressions, this RegEx says:
> Begin at the start of a line, select every character until you see a comma repeated eight times and you must end up at the end of the line.

With this replacement string:

```
dDocName=$1\n dDocTitle=$2\n dDocAuthor=$3\n dSecurityGroup=$4\n
dDocAccount=$5\n dDocType=$6\n dInDate=$7\n primaryFile=$8\n <<EOD>>
\n
```

You may need to test the RegEx in your own editor as everyone has a slightly different syntax. After you run it your comma-separated line will transform into an HDA entry that will look like this:

```
dDocName=A2561405
dDocTitle=Migration Project Plan
dDocAuthor=Bill
dSecurityGroup=Public
dDocAccount=
dDocType=abstract
dInDate=8/12/09 4:20 PM
primaryFile=C:/Migration/Project Plan v.3.4.doc
<<EOD>>
```

I hope you get the idea.

How to scale it up

You can easily adapt this technique to any complexity. Just use Perl, Ruby, or another scripting language of your choice to generate metadata values, file names, and locations.

Be sure to use subroutines, structure your code well, and store it in source-control system. Code generation script can get quite complex really quickly.

And now consider these important last minute tips.

Important last minute tips

Today, there will be three:

- You'll very likely need to debug your code generation script and run your batch load file more than once so be sure to:
    ◦ Add a custom meta field or a special value like `batch_loader` for the `dDocAuthor`, so you can find your new loaded test files quickly, and delete them when it's time to start fresh.
    ◦ Test on a small sub-set (under 200 items) so you don't have to wait for eight hours for these 500 Gb to import.
- Be sure to CLEAR the **Clean up files after successful check in** box. If you leave it checked your source files will be deleted and you won't find them in **Recycle Bin**!
- Be sure to mark **Enable error file** box. This will create a detailed log file and a smaller batch loader script file for the files that didn't load. This option is absolutely essential!

I hope you enjoyed this neat technique that can hopefully save you buckets of time off your busy content migration schedule. Take a quick break now and check the Independent Oracle UCM Knowledge Center (`http://stellentexperts.com/ioukc`) for latest insider tips and career-boosting secrets of effective use of Oracle UCM. Check it out now as the information is still fresh in your mind.

Welcome back! Let's spend a few more moments in this chapter. Let's go through this quick summary.

Summary

Now you know how to backup and protect your content and system configuration, how to create partial backups, promote content between environments, and mass-update metadata. You've also seen the secret behind efficient and fast content migrations so it will be easy for you to bring your existing content in.

In the next chapter you'll learn how to backup your configuration, your complete, and partial folder structures, and how to transfer them to other servers.

Migrating Configuration

In the previous chapter you've seen how to do full and partial backups and how to migrate data to another Content Server instance. What we didn't cover is how to back up your system configuration, your workflows, and virtual folders. It's time to explore the rest of the toolset. In this chapter you will:

- Learn how you can back up, restore, and migrate system configuration — your custom metadata fields, profile information, workflows, and other customizations — over to another system, so you can create a complete replica or just deploy a few selected customizations.

- Discover two different options to back up, restore, and migrate your virtual folders with and without content.

Let's get into it.

First, let's see what *other* tools are available to help us with backup, restore, and migration:

Completing your backup, restore, and migration toolkit

So far, we've seen Archiver, which allows us to export, import, and migrate our content items and to update metadata. We've also seen how we can use Batch Loader, Content Server Services, and idcCommand to migrate content to another server instance.

Now let's look at the tools that complete your toolkit:

- **Configuration Migration Utility (CMU)**: This is the tool that exports and imports your Content Server configuration and customizations.

- **Folder Archiving**: This is a feature that allows you to export your entire virtual folder structure into a single HDA file. The content is not included and you're forced to export and import complete folder structure, not a subset.

- **Folder Structure Archive Component**: This is a free add-on component that enables you to cherry-pick and export only selected folders you need—complete with their content.

Perfect. Now that you know what the tools are, let's see how we can use them.

How to migrate your configuration

I bet you know the answer. We will need to use **Configuration Migration Utility**, the **CMU**.

One of the things that's great about the CMU is that you can export all of your settings out of system A and bring them over to system B. And you don't have to just apply all of your settings there. You can choose exactly what sections and values to import into system B. It is very handy to have such granular control over the configuration.

It's a common practice to share a content archive and a CMU bundle (explained in the next section) with each other to see a particular demo or feature set. It's very quick and convenient.

I'll walk you through it. But first, you need to see a couple of new terms, which CMU uses extensively:

Using the CMU

There are only two definitions to understand:

- **Configuration Bundle** is a set of configuration information that you're exporting or importing. A bundle is stored in a single ZIP file. You can copy it over and *import* on another Content Server instance.

- **Configuration Template** (or **Export Rule**) is a stored set of options that you'd otherwise have to manually select every time you export a bundle. It's a time saver, so you can repeat your export with the same settings more than once.

That's it. And now just couple of important tips before we start using the CMU:

> The CMU does NOT erase configuration in the target system. It simply adds the settings you're migrating.
>
> Also, it won't overwrite your target configuration settings with matching values from the bundle — unless you set the **Force Overwrite** to true when you import a bundle. Only then will the matching values actually be overwritten.

All set. Let's start the CMU now. I'll walk you through it in the next section.

Exporting your settings

Expand the **Administration** tray. Now click on the **Config Migration Admin** folder at the bottom of the tree as shown in the following screenshot:

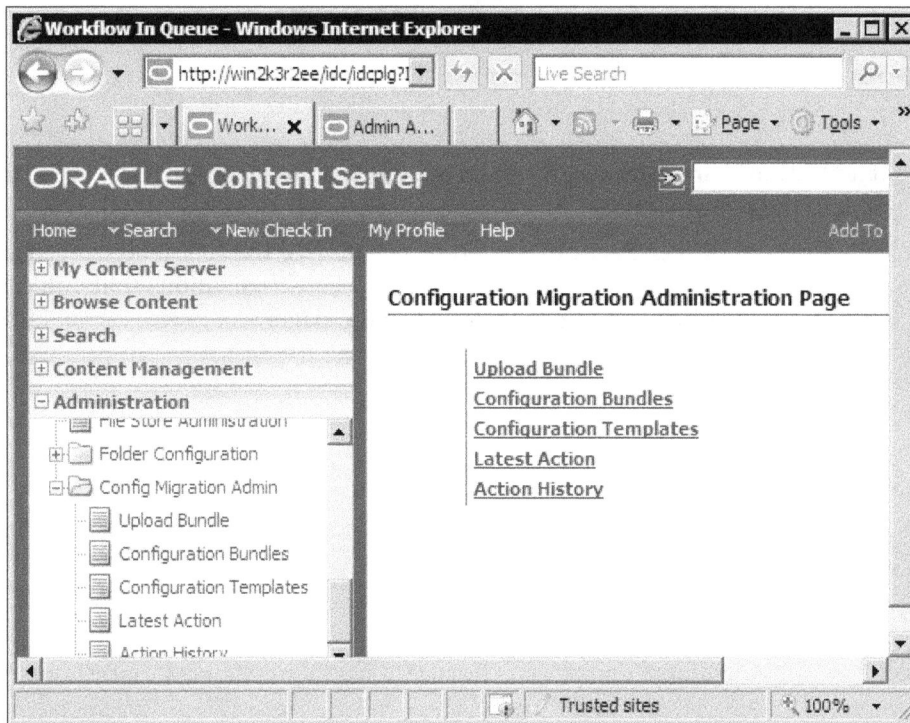

Here's how you export configuration into a configuration bundle:

- First, you need to create a *Configuration Template*. Click on the **Configuration Templates** link on the left. Then pick **Create New Template** from the **Actions** dropdown on the top right (see the following screenshot).

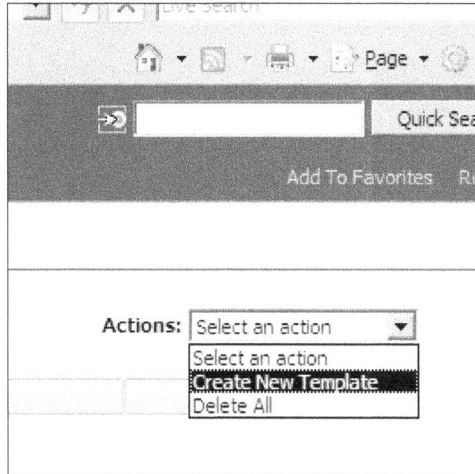

- The **Define Template** screen comes up. Click on the **Content Server Sections** link in the bottom left.
- The **Content Server Sections** screen comes up (see the following screenshot). It has a list of all configuration, metadata, and customizations that you can export—the **Child Sections** table lower in the page:

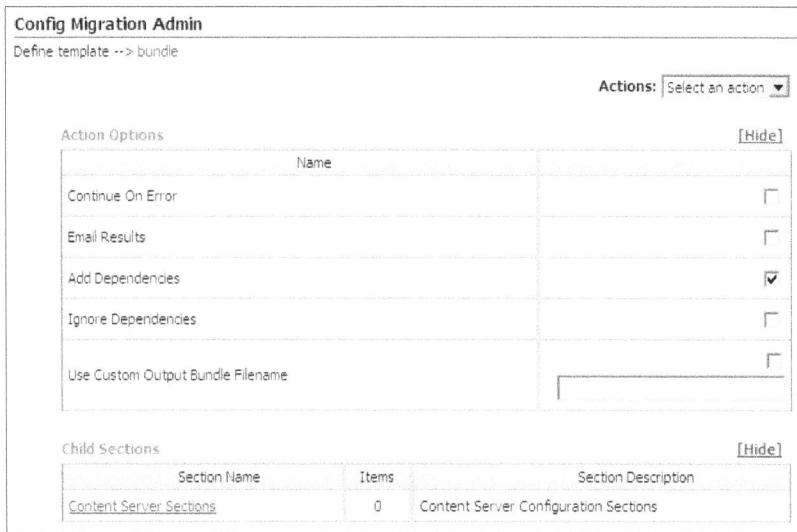

You can also change values in the **Action Options** section:

- **Continue On Error**: This forces the export or import to continue—even if an error is encountered.

- **Email Results**: This mails results to the user who initiated the export or import.

- **Add Dependencies or Ignore Dependencies**: This controls whether the dependencies are added to the export or import bundle.

- **Use Custom Output Bundle Filename**: Allows you to change the file name that will be used to store your configuration bundle.

Now take a look at the following **Child Sections** table. Notice the zeros in the **Items** column. It indicates that your template still has no configuration settings selected. You can now add all configuration settings to your template or cherry-pick just the ones you want to export.

1. Select **Actions | Select All**. Notice the numbers in the **Items** column now reflect your selection. Pick **Actions | Save** to save your selection. You will be prompted to give your template a name and description (see the following screenshot):

Add Export Rule

Name	All_Config
Description	All CS Configuration Settings

Save

2. Your template now has all of configuration settings in your Content Server.

3. Let me show you how you pick just the ones you want. Select **Actions** | **Unselect All**. Select **Metadata** and place a checkmark next to the **xVendor** field that we created in *Chapter 3, Metadata* (see the following screenshot):

Config Migration Admin

Define template --> All_Config --> Content Server Sections --> Content Metadata

Actions: [Select an action ▼]

> Page has been modified. Any changes made on this page or any children pages will be recorded, but not permanently saved. Unless the task is saved or updated, all changes will be lost when navigating from the definition page.

Action Options   [Hide]

Name	
Continue On Error	☐
Add Dependencies	☑
Ignore Dependencies	☐

Items for section 'Content Metadata'   [Hide]

dName	dType	dCaption	
xCpdIsLocked	Int	apCpdIsLocked	☐
xCpdIsTemplateEnabled	Int	apCpdIsTemplateEnabled	☐
xForceFolderSecurity	Text	apxForceFolderSecurity	☐
xHidden	Text	apxHidden	☐
xInhibitUpdate	Text	apxInibitMetadataUpdate	☐
xWebFlag	Text	apFsWebFlag	☐
xStorageRule	Text	apFsStorageRule	☐
xVendor	Text	Vendor	☑
xContract	Text	Contract	☐

---

4. Pick **Actions** | **Save**. You're now ready to export your settings into a configuration bundle.

5. Pick **Actions** | **Preview** to see exactly what settings will be exported (see the following screenshot).

Export Preview

Actions: Select an action ▼

Action Options   [Hide]

Name	
Continue On Error	No
Email Results	No
Add Dependencies	Yes
Ignore Dependencies	No
Use Custom Output Bundle Filename	

Preview

Content Metadata   [Hide]

dName	dType	dCaption
xVendor	Text	Vendor

6. Select **Actions** | **Export**. The export operation begins. It may take a while. The screen will refresh at the interval you specify in the dropdown at the top right (see the following screenshot). Or, if you're impatient, you can always click on the **Refresh** link on the top right, just beneath the **Quick Search** box.

erver   →□ [   ] Quick Search

My Profile   Help   Add To Favorites   Refresh

Latest Action

Page Refresh (In Seconds): 10 ▼

Time	Section	Message
1/22/10 3:14 PM		Starting export of 'All_Config'
1/22/10 3:14 PM	Schema Tables	Exporting 'Vendors'.
1/22/10 3:14 PM	Schema Views	Exporting 'VendorsView'.
1/22/10 3:14 PM	Content Metadata	Exporting 'xVendor'.
1/22/10 3:14 PM	wwCmuSectionLabe	Finished

7. The last thing left to do is to grab the actual bundle file, so we can copy and import it in our target Content Server instance. Go to the **Configuration Bundles** page (see the following screenshot). Click on the **actions** *icon,* next to the bundle you want. Pick **Download**.

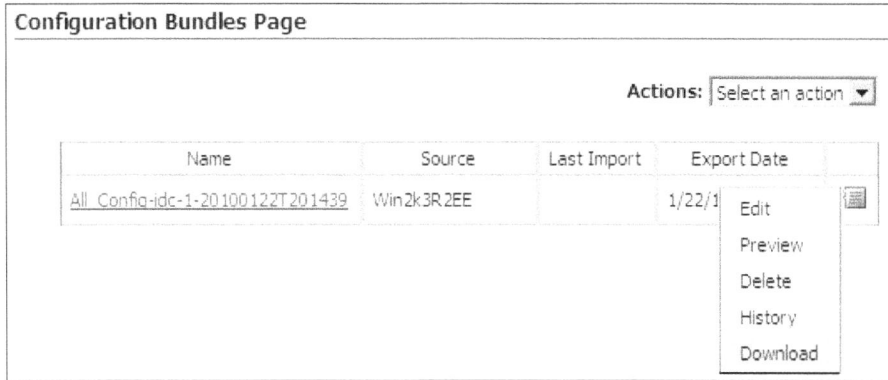

```
Configuration Bundles Page

                                          Actions: Select an action ▼

         Name              Source      Last Import    Export Date
  All_Config-idc-1-20100122T201439  Win2k3R2EE            1/22/1   Edit           🖼
                                                                   Preview
                                                                   Delete
                                                                   History
                                                                   Download
```

Perfect. Now let's see how we can upload the bundle on our target instance.

Importing a configuration bundle

Importing is the easy part. Follow these steps:

1. Pick **Upload Bundle** under **Config Migration Admin**. The **Upload Configuration Bundle** screen displays (see the following screenshot):

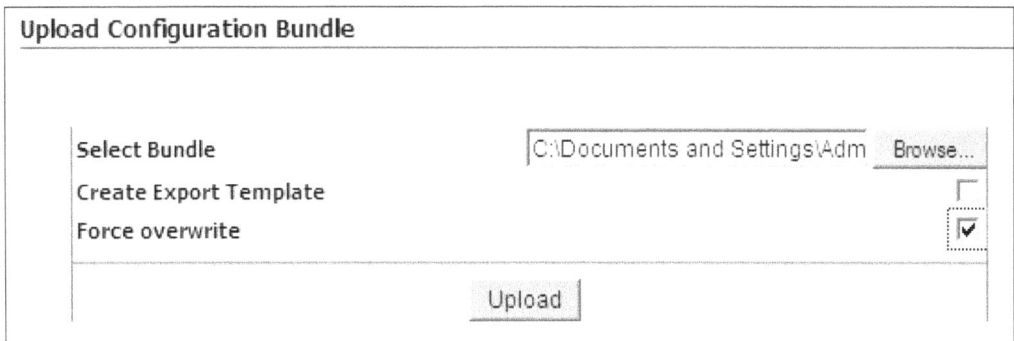

```
Upload Configuration Bundle


  Select Bundle             C:\Documents and Settings\Adm   Browse...
  Create Export Template                                    ☐
  Force overwrite                                           ☑

                       Upload
```

2. Pick the ZIP file of the bundle that you'll be uploading. Check the **Force overwrite** box if you want your bundle to replace an existing bundle with the same name.

3. Click on the **Upload** button. The bundle appears in the list on the **Configuration Bundles** page.

You can now preview and import the bundle. If you like, you can change some settings such as setting **Overwrite Duplicates** to **True**. Select **Actions | Edit** and change the options before you select **Action | Import**.

That's all. Pretty easy, isn't it? But what if something goes wrong when you export or import? How do you find out why it failed? I'll give you a hand in the next section.

Troubleshooting configuration migration

You can see exactly what went wrong. Here's how:

1. Expand the **Administration** tray on the left and click on **System Audit Information**.

2. In the **Active Sections** dropdown under **Tracing Sections Information**, pick **cmu**. Note that section names are not sorted by alphabet! (See the following screenshot.)

3. Click on **Update** and then repeat the import or export operation that produced an error.

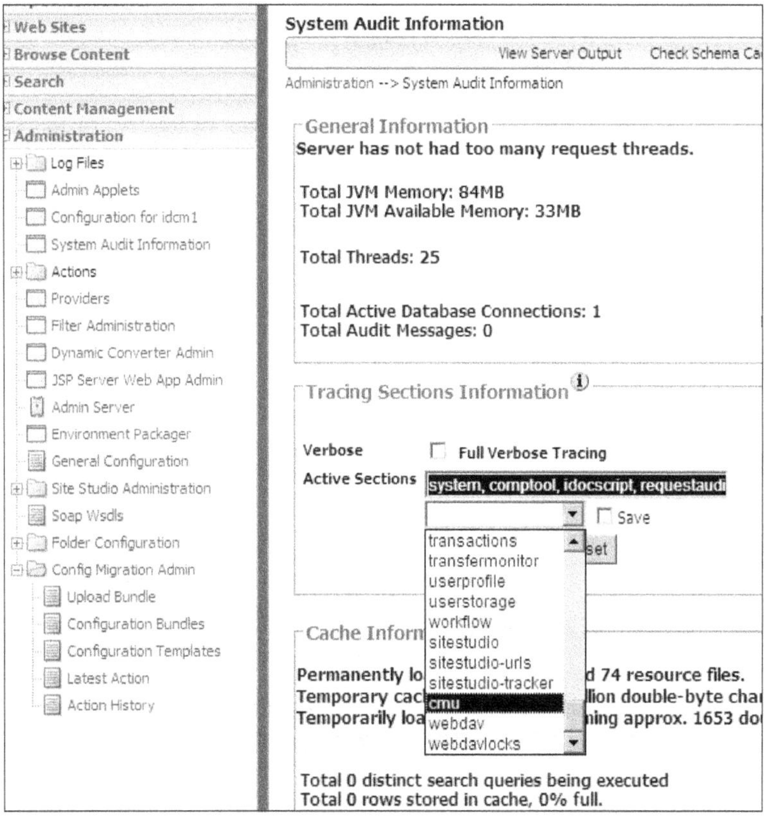

4. Bring up Admin Server (see *Chapter 2, Major Controls*, if you need a refresher) and go to **View Server Output**. Notice that everything CMU was doing is now logged for you—step by step (see the following screenshot).

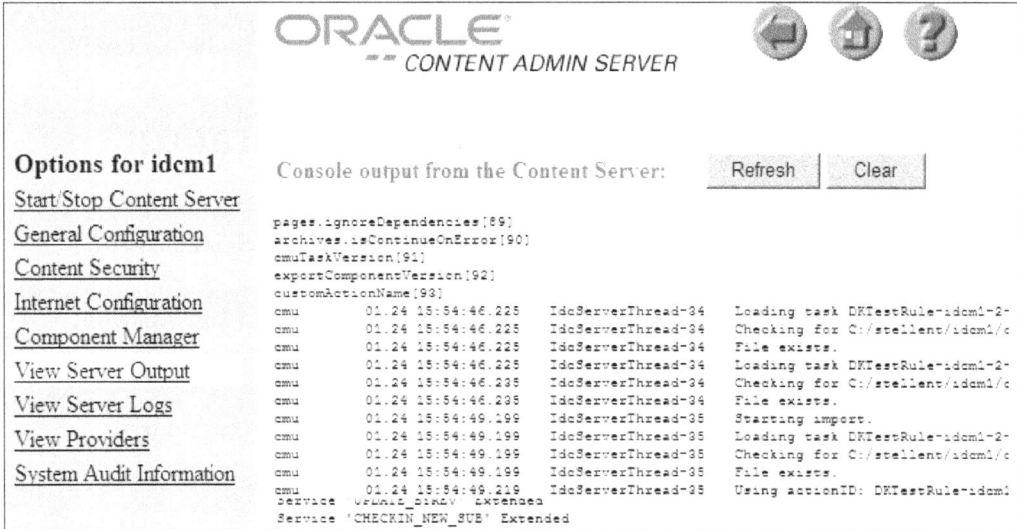

If you see any error messages in the server output, you will find them pretty self-explanatory and easy to fix. Many times, the error will be due to a missing metadata field or a duplicate value. In the case of a duplicate, you may choose to ignore the error by setting the "Continue on Error" flag. In the case of missing metadata field—you can create it and re-run the import—or, better yet, update your export bundle to include the missing field.

That's great. Now, that you know how to migrate your configuration settings and your customizations, let's look at archiving your folders.

How to migrate folder structures

When it comes to migrating folders, you have two options: Migrating all folders in one shot or selectively migrating a subset of folders. Let's check out both options:

Migrating all folders in one shot

The big advantage of this approach is simplicity. You just export your entire folder structure with literally one click of a button into a simple HDA file. And then you can import it on the target system with just one more click. But it has its own limitations:

- It doesn't migrate your content, just the folders themselves.
- It erases all folders in your system and then creates the ones from the import file.

It's great if you need to migrate a copy of your entire folder structure over to a new instance. Here's how to do it:

1. Expand the **Administration** tray. Click on **Folder Configuration**.

2. Click on the **Export Archive** button. This will export your complete folder structure as a single HDA file and place it in the location of your choice (see the following screenshot):

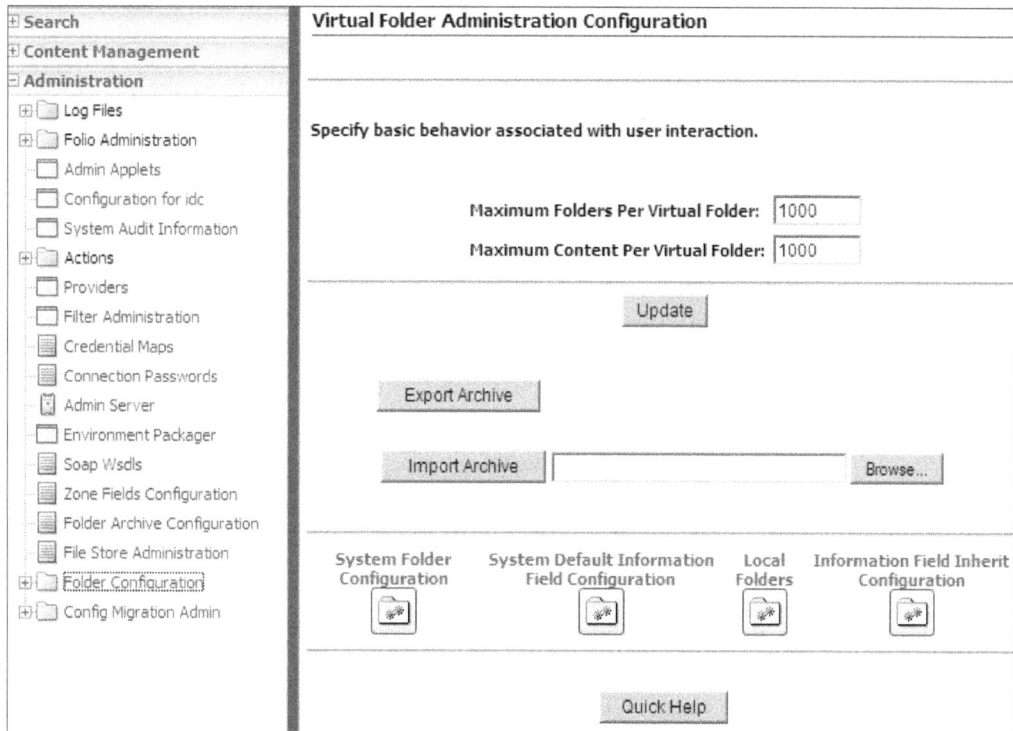

3. To import it go to the **Folder Configuration** page on the target system, click on **Browse** to locate your folders HDA file. Then click on the **Import Archive** button.

I told you, it would be simple.

How to migrate only the folders and content you select

Yes, you can archive and migrate just a select set of folders—including their content. Here's how.

You'll need to install an optional (but free and included with your Content Server) Folder Structure Archive Component.

Let's go ahead with this simple installation:

1. Go to the `extras` directory in the main Content Server ZIP file (a file like `ContentServer_Windows_10gR3_20080807.zip`) and grab `FolderStructureArchive.zip`.

2. Launch Component Manager and install `FolderStructureArchive.zip`. If you need a refresher on how to install a Content Server component, go back to *Chapter 6, Understanding Virtual Folders and WebDAV*.

3. Restart Content Server. Close and reopen your browser. Log in to Content Server.

That's all. You should now have a **Folder Archive Configuration** link under the **Administration** tray (see the following screenshot).

Here's how to archive and migrate selected folders:

1. Click on the **Folder Archive Configuration** link. You'll see the Folder Archive page loading in the right pane. (See the following screenshot.)

2. Pick the Archiver **Collection Name**. If you didn't create additional collections, you'll only have one collection in the dropdown. The Folder Archive component uses Archiver and this is the collection where your archive will reside.

3. Select an **Archive Name** or type in a name for the new archive you want created. Do this first! (Don't try selecting folders before you pick or type in your archive name. Your selection will be lost when you change anything in this field.)

4. Now you can go ahead and pick the folders you'd like to archive.

5. Click on the **Add** button when you're done.

And you can always update an existing folder archive. See the following screenshot:

Your archive is now created and ready to export. Launch an Archiver and export it (see *Chapter 8, Backup, Restore, and Content Migration*, if you need a refresher on how to use an Archiver).

That's great. And before we close, let's test how the Folder Archive component works:

It's best if you do this on your "sandbox" system where you can afford to lose data and you have a small number of content items.

1. Create a new folder archive and only export a section of your folder structure.

2. Export the archive. Make sure the export operation is finished by looking at the status bar in Archiver.

3. Delete a folder or a subfolder within your selection and some other folder outside your selection that you can afford to lose. (See the next screenshot.) I'm going to delete `Accounting` and `Manufacturing`.

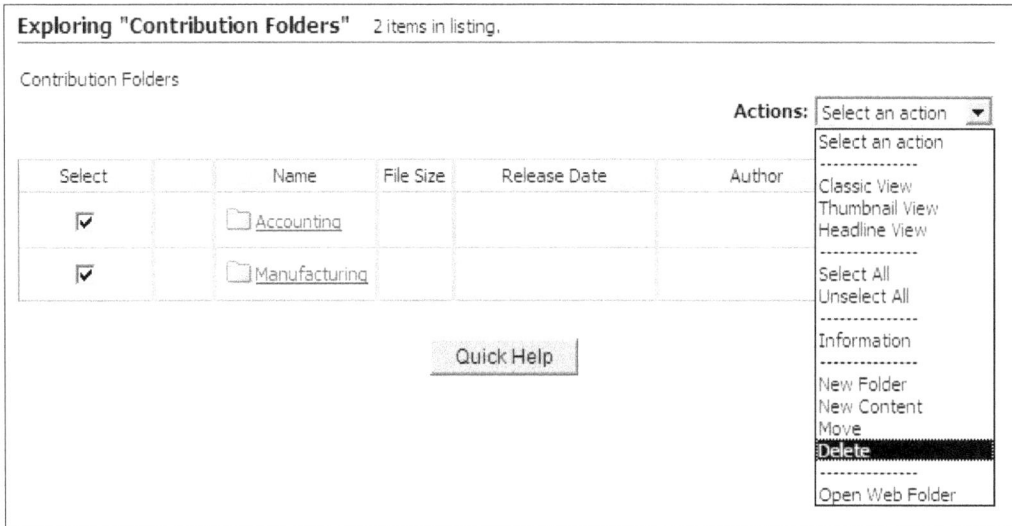

Make sure none of the content is in the workflow or you won't be able to delete the folders.

When you delete them also delete them from Trash! The regular delete operation just moves them there and is not really deleting anything!

4. Launch Archiver and **Import** the archive you've just created (see the following screenshot):

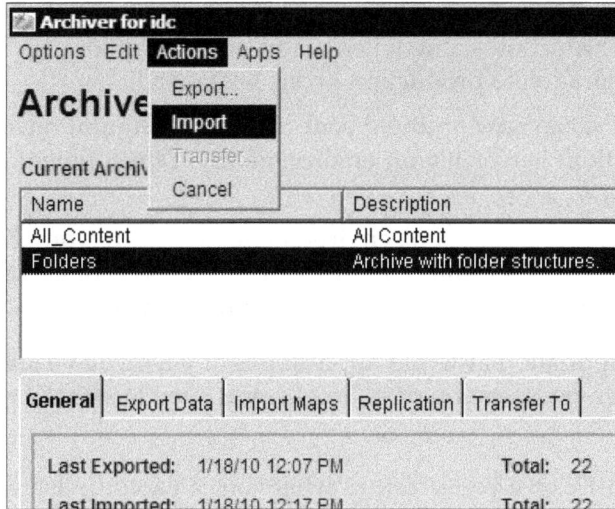

5. Refresh the left pane (or close and reopen your browser). Notice that the folders that you've archived are now restored in their original location. And folders that you haven't selected for archiving are now gone! My `Accenting` folder is back, but my `Manufacturing` one is gone for good.

That's all for the Folder Structure Archive component. Now you have the power to pick and choose what folders you want to migrate.

Summary

Congratulations! You now have a complete picture of all the options for backup, restore, and content migration. You've just seen the last two bits you were missing — how to migrate your configuration and your Content Server customizations to another instance, and how to migrate folder structures.

You've also seen the two options you have for migrating them — simple full-structure migration and more comprehensive, selective migration with the optional Folder Archive component.

This chapter completed our study of backup, restore, and content migration. Think of the power I've just given you:

- You now can easily build a system prototype, migrate content in there, and then clone it — completely or in part.

- You can easily create additional servers when needed — for increased capacity and failover.

- You can migrate and refine content, and test your migration—without affecting production—and, when ready, promote all of your new content and configuration to production in one fell swoop.

- In short, you can now promote your content, configuration, and customizations between your environments—Development, Staging, and Production.

- You can also create sandbox environments whenever you need to test your customizations, dry-run upgrading to a new version of UCM, or simply play with the content of configuration—without worrying about affecting others.

All of these are important real-world applications of what you've just learned, and this knowledge can save you days, weeks, and even months of rework and frustration.

In the next chapter I'll give you a taste of what you can accomplish with Content Server customization. And here's a quick tip—you can customize *everything*!

10
Customizing Oracle UCM

In the previous chapter you learned how to migrate content and configuration. Now, that you're ready to open the floodgate of your UCM let's see how you can customize it and integrate into your overall Enterprise Architecture. *You'll need some development background in Web Development, Java or .NET, and/or scripting languages to customize Oracle UCM.*

Unlike all the previous chapters though, this one has a different purpose. I'm not trying to teach you how to customize and integrate Oracle UCM in an hour or two. It just won't be possible but what I *can* do well here is give you a few pointers and insider tips that will save you hours and days down the road. Here's what you'll learn:

- How to smoothly integrate Oracle UCM into your enterprise — to wipe out dreaded manual double data entry and multiple "source of truth" repositories.

- How to customize the Content Server interface by tapping into its powerful scripting and Dynamic Server Page resources.

- How to maximize the value you get from a UCM consulting vendor, reduce your risk and avoid severe penalties to your budget, timeline, and your system functionality.

- How to boost your efforts with the steady flow of inside information directly from Oracle. Most people miss out on this absolutely free, project-accelerating consulting time, available to all UCM clients.

- The tools you have available to alter Content Server behavior and time-saving pointers on how to use them.

I'll be referring you to a lot of documentation. And I've seen how a great majority of people get discouraged and intimidated when put in front of a pile of 300-page manuals, if you too feel that you can use some help — check out the following section.

Documentation and support—the unexpected treasures

Oracle has provided us with very detailed and complete documentation. A lot of documentation! Maybe that's why most people are failing to use it to its full potential. The next section will help you get the most out of Oracle documentation, and save you hours of frustration when looking for stuff.

How to find what you need in ninety 300-page manuals—in three minutes or less

If you know the answer, feel free to skip to the next section, but if you're not sure—this will save you many hours of frustration.

At the time of this writing, there are over 90 manuals posted on the central Oracle UCM Documentation Library.

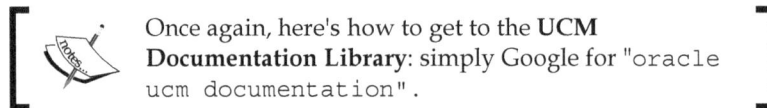

> Once again, here's how to get to the **UCM Documentation Library**: simply Google for "oracle ucm documentation".

Most of the time, you have to find what you need really fast. But if you'd try to *read* any of the manuals—it will take you days to get a simple question answered. You have to *speed-read*.

Nope. I'm not insisting that you take Evelyn Wood's course right now, even though, it might actually help. I'm just asking you to become very *selective* and *skeptical* when you read documentation. Here're a few practical tips that will let you find information in Oracle UCM documentation library faster than ever before:

- First of all, I personally prefer to read my manuals in PDF rather than linked HTML pages (both options are available for most of the guides). This helps me see (and search) the *entire document* and I can be sure that I haven't missed anything on the subject at hand.

- If you find yourself reading some PDF documents over and over again, you may choose to save them locally and not wait for them to load off the net when you need them.

- Every one of these online guides comes with a section called **About This Guide** and/or **Overview**. They're just a few paragraphs long at the most. I know, it sounds obvious, but *read them first*. A lot of times, you'll either realize that you're reading the wrong document or you'll see the purpose and the main features of the tool.

- Read the entire Table of Content (TOC). You may notice several sections conveying similar information like a chapter on **Installation** and a paragraph with **Simple Installation Procedures**. In many cases, that paragraph is all you need!

- Mark the sections you'd like to read while scanning the TOC. Resist the temptation to jump into them until you've seen all of the TOC. There might be a faster way to learn the same thing later in the document.

- Flip through the pages you're about to read first. This will give you a better sense of what you're going to read. You'll look at the screenshots and illustrations more often than not—it will let you skip a lot of pages when you actually do read the section.

Plan your reading diligently and be smart about it. Unless you truly enjoy reading documentation, there's a massive amount of time to be saved here.

Now what if documentation doesn't answer your question? Do you have to shell out a few thousand bucks and bring in a consultant?

Not necessarily! Even though, you might be the only person on the project, if you have at least one Oracle UCM Support license, you are not on your own.

How to get free consulting from Oracle

Yep. You read it right. Oracle is happy to help out. They'd spend hours on the phone and e-Conference helping you troubleshoot issues and addressing your product concerns. This book's Technical Reviewer, Billy Cripe, and I can personally attest to how good and diligent the UCM support team is at Oracle. They have many years of experience, are very willing to help out, and are good at what they do.

If you ever suspect that any of the UCM products are not doing exactly what you think they should—don't "be a hero" trying to fix it on your own. Log a support ticket and let a pro from Oracle help you out for free.

How? It's actually quite simple. Just browse to: `https://support.oracle.com`, register and log a ticket.

The application is easy to use and it comes with step-by-step guidance (see the following screenshot):

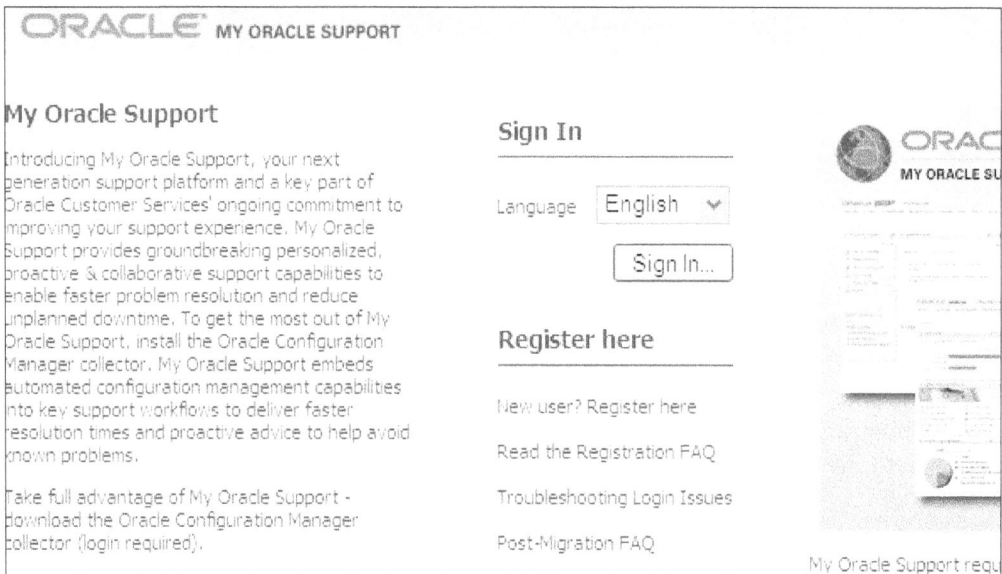

Perfect. It's off my shoulders now. It's really important that you follow these guidelines. You see, if you're stuck on a technical issue, it's easy to ask for assistance. You know exactly what to ask or search for.

But if you end up not using the right tool or product feature because you *missed it in a document*—that may really turn into something scary for your project and your organization. Now you have the tools to never let that happen.

With that in mind, let's jump back into customization and integration.

Integrating UCM into larger architectures

Imagine that you need to store a vendor invoice in Content Server. The transaction itself is entered in your *Vendor Management* ERP system and you're trying to avoid making your procurement staff enter data in two places. And, of course, you'll need to be able to get that invoice document out of Content Server from within the ERP, should they decide to view or print it. What are your choices?

The first one I'd consider is SOAP Web Service, which we will discuss in the next section.

SOAP web services

As we've seen in *Chapter 8, Backup, Restore, and Content Migration*, the Content Server itself is a completely Service-Oriented Architecture (SOA) system, where each action the server takes is a discreet service call. And each of these calls can be done remotely, assuming you have the correct permissions and authorization, or chained together. This makes it extremely powerful and easy to integrate.

Let's review a couple of definitions before we proceed:

Simple Object Access Protocol (SOAP) is one of the most popular standards for calling remote services over the Web. It uses XML to encode data. Almost every major programming language and development environment such as MS .NET and Java supports it. Many offer wizards that generate all supporting code and let you call remote services as easy as if they were local and running on the same machine.

Web Services Definition Language or **WSDL** is another XML-based protocol that lets you define the services, methods you call, their return values and parameters. Web Services wizards use WSDL file to generate a wrapper class—a block of code that actually lets you call remote services as if they were local.

Content Server comes with a **WSDL Generator** component—a tool that lets you generate a WSDL file for any of the Content Server services. This makes all of the functions of the UCM available to be called remotely via the SOAP protocol.

You don't have to use it, but it's a really helpful tool.

How do you get started with using SOAP? The fastest way I know is to start with a working sample. WSDL Generator comes with a ton of step by step, well documented samples.

On your Content Server file system go to `\oracle\ucm\server\custom\`
`WsdlGenerator\samples` (see the following screenshot):

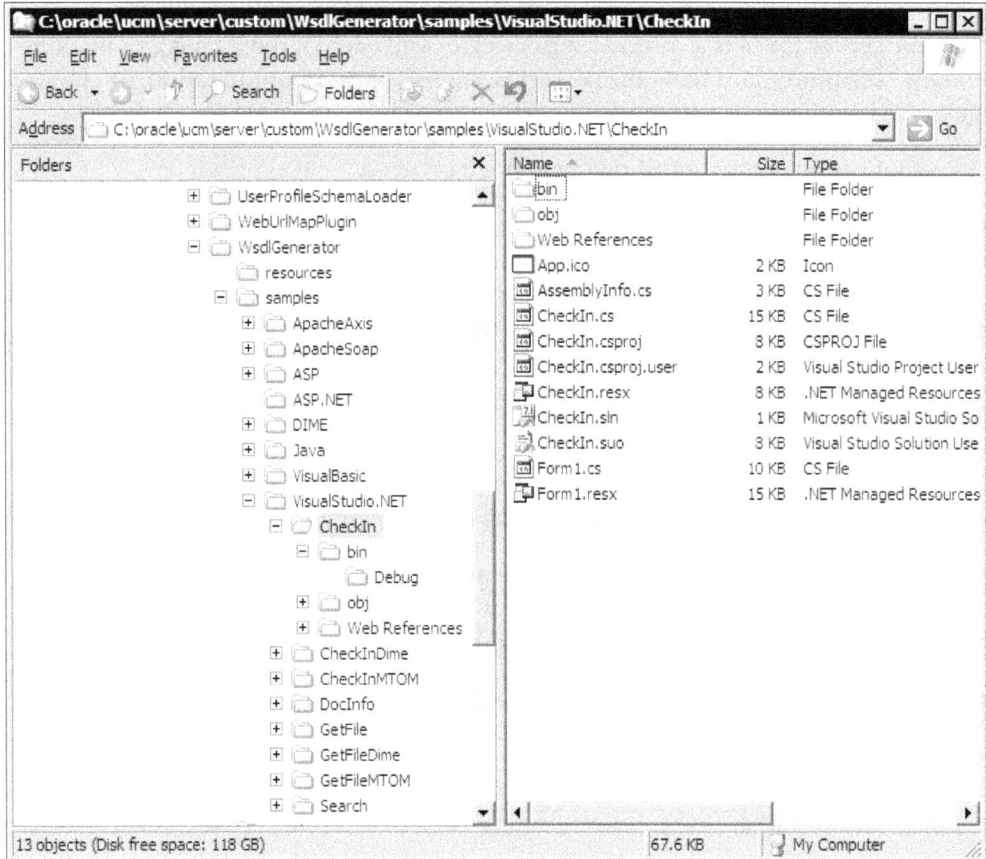

If you don't see `WsdlGenerator directory` under `custom` you may want to grab WSDL
Generator component (`WSDLGenerator.zip`, located in `packages/allplatform` inside
the main Content Server distribution `.zip` file) and install it using the Component Manager.

You'll see a variety of samples in several programming languages — for most of the
core Content Server services, like check-in and check-out, downloading files, getting
content info, and others.

Now what if you need another way of calling the services that runs faster than SOAP
and hides the details of Content Server service calls? I'll give you an answer in the
next section.

Content integration suite and remote intraDoc client

It's a Java toolset that can be deployed on a number of J2EE application servers. You can also use **Content Integration Suite** (the **CIS**) from a standalone Java application.

The biggest benefit of the CIS is that it has its own high-level API, **Universal Content and Process Management API** (**UCPM API**) which, in turn, uses the Content Server API. This allows developers to focus on the task at hand, instead of getting concerned with the mechanics of calling individual low level Content Server services. Believe me, it can get pretty involved.

If the application that you're using to communicate with the UCM is written in Java, I suggest that you start by evaluating the CIS. It's free and well documented. To get started, scan the **CIS Administration Guide** in **Oracle Universal Content Management Documentation library**.

And if you're considering the CIS, you should actually start by looking at newer (just over a year old at the time of this writing) **Remote IntraDoc Client API** (**RIDC API**). Just like the CIS, it designed to allow remove Java application to interact with the UCM, but it's a lot smaller and more intuitive to use.

It also doesn't wrap the UCM services as Java classes so you can easily call any service you like — including new and custom services. For example, the following code snippet shows the CIS code to get document info by the dID:

```
ISCSDocumentInformationAPI documentInfoAPI =
m_cisApplication.getUCPMAPI ().getActiveAPI
().getDocumentInformationAPI ();

// create the document ID
ISCSDocumentID documentID =
(ISCSDocumentID) m_cisApplication.getUCPMAPI ().
createObject (ISCSDocumentID.class);

documentID.setDocumentID("12345");

ISCSDocumentInformationResponse docResponse =
documentInfoAPI.getDocumentInformationByID(m_context, documentID);
```

And here's the corresponding RIDC API call:

```
// create and initialize data binder object
DataBinder binder = client.createBinder();

binder.putLocal("IdcService","DOC_INFO");
binder.putLocal("dID","12345");
// Make the service call
```

```
ServiceResponse response = client.sendRequest(new
IdcContext("sysadmin"), binder);
```

It's easier to understand, more flexible, and a lot more intuitive. Notice that the names of the classes are a quite a bit shorter too.

And let me also show you a really simple and elegant way of including editable Site Studio content into any of your web applications (if you're new to Site Studio and Web Content Management, you may want to skip this section and come back to it after reading the next chapter).

Consuming site studio content in third-party web applications

Imagine that you have an enterprise portal built with some third-party software such as WebSphere Portal or Liferay, and you want to include your Site Studio-managed content. There is a really easy way to do this—just use the following code to include a contributor data file, rendered in a specified region template:

```
<iframe src=" http://stellentdev/idc/idcplg?IdcService=WCM_
PLACEHOLDER&dataFileDocName= TEST_DATAFILE&templateDocName=TPL_TEST_
SITE_EXT"></iframe>
```

The content ID of the contributor data file is `TEST_DATAFILE` and template is `TPL_TEST_SITE_EXT`.

> The only caveat to using this feature is that it's new in Site Studio 10g R4, so you will need to upgrade your server-side component in order to use it. It will not work in 10g R3 and earlier versions of Site Studio.
>
> You will also need to brush up on Placeholders and Region Templates (These and other new features of Site Studio 10gR4 and upcoming 11g will also be covered in your newsletter. See Appendix A for subscription information).

I've created a sample HTML file to illustrate this. The screenshot below shows a rendered Site Studio data file inserted into an existing sample html page:

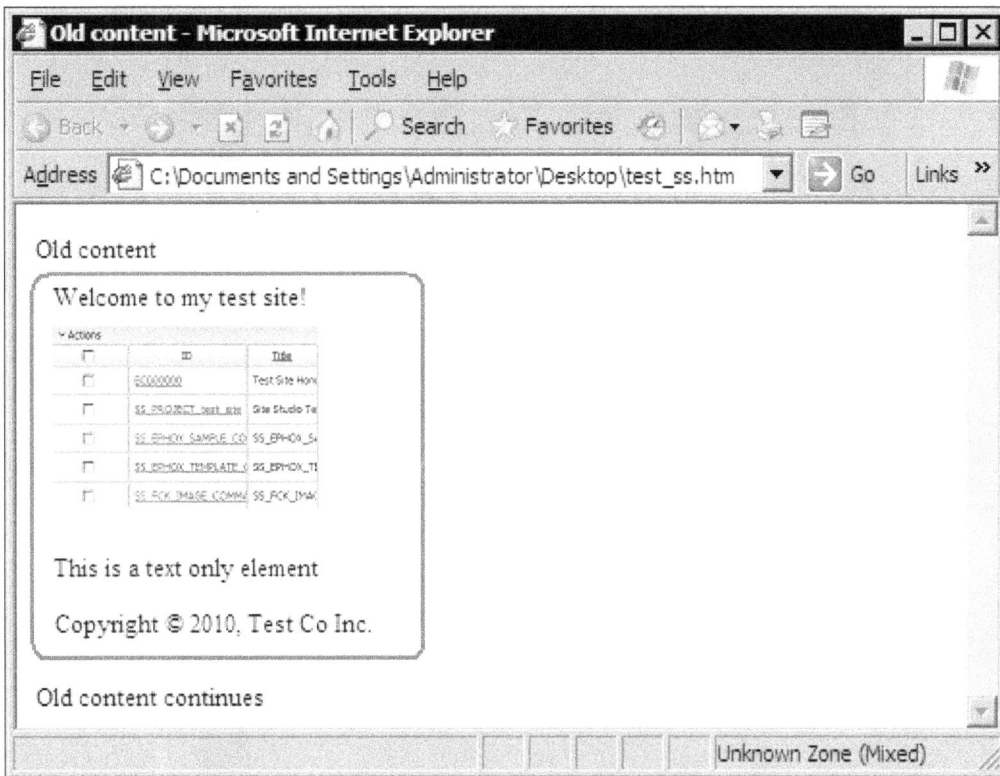

And here's how to include the "edit" link:

```
<a href="http://stellentdev/idc/idcplg?IdcService=WCM_BEGIN_EDIT_
SESSION&dDocName=TEST_DATAFILE">Edit content</a>
```

This link brings up your familiar Site Studio Contributor application as shown in the following screenshot:

That's it. Simple and intuitive!

For more information, Google for "WCM_PLACEHOLDER" and "WCM_BEGIN_ EDIT_SESSION" services or else get this Oracle whitepaper called *External Application Options* (available at http://www.oracle.com/technology/ products/content-management/ucm/sitestudio10gr4tutorials/ UsingSiteStudioInExternalApplications.pdf).

So those were your main choices for integrating with the UCM. Well, what about customizing the Content Server itself? How do you alter its interface or functionality? The next section tells you how.

Customizing the content server

When it comes to customizing the Content Server you really have the oceans of options in front of you. Almost any customization you can imagine you can implement with the tools and techniques I'm giving you in this section. Let us start with a few real-life examples.

Examples of common customizations

The most common customization I've seen is the need to apply some custom processing after check in. You may need to do things like applying new metadata values based on the item's location in your folder structure, or simply customizing its content ID based on the new value of content type.

Applying custom logic after check-in

Take a look at this snippet of java code. This is all the code it takes to write a custom component for temporary changing the value of AutoNumberPrefix Content Server configuration variable, based on the content type of the document you're just about to check in. This lets you generate more meaningful content IDs, like ACC_0247 for Accounting documents and MKT_0952 for marketing ones:

```
public class CheckinFilter implements FilterImplementor
{
    public int doFilter(Workspace ws, DataBinder binder,
                        ExecutionContext cxt)
        throws DataException, ServiceException
    {
        String type = binder.getLocal("dDocType");
        String prefix = binder.getEnvironmentValue(type + "_
                                                    prefix");

        if (prefix != null)
        {
            binder.putLocal("AutoNumberPrefix", prefix);
        }

        return CONTINUE;
    }
}
```

You can easily inject your custom java code exactly where you need it, get and update your metadata values, and run any custom pre- or post-processing. You will find out more about the custom java components later in this chapter.

And now let's go a full circle and look at some really simple customization.

Sending custom e-mails from Content Server

Let's say, you want your users to fill in a feedback from on your site and you want that to generate a nicely formatted e-mail to your customer service department.

You tried `<form action="mailto:support@yourcorp.com">` and it doesn't produce a nice looking e-mail, plus your e-mail address will be picked up by spammers.

Simply install the AcmeMail component, that comes with the HowTo Components (discussed later in this chapter) and use this line in your server page to send your email:

```
<!--$ sendAcmeMailDirect(From_address,Recipients,Subject,Message) -->
```

And you can use can use the following line to get the values that your correspondent has typed in:

```
<!--$fName = getValue("#active", "FirstName")-->
```

It retrieves the value they typed into your `<input name="FirstName">` and places it into your iDoc script variable named `fName`.

And again, I'll tell you more about using dynamic server pages later in this chapter.

But what if you need to create say, a completely custom user experience and change the way your users interact with the Content Server?

Creating completely custom user experiences

This sounds like a lot of work, doesn't it? But it may be much easier than it sounds. Simply create a Site Studio website and build your custom interface. Dynamic List fragments will let you display the results of the Content Server queries and you can continue to use iDoc to retrieve the values of metadata fields and user input (I'll introduce you to Site Studio and Web Content Management in the next chapter).

And who said you have to rebuild everything from scratch? You can use the chunks of existing Content Server user interface and simply plug it in where appropriate.

For instance, using these four dynamic `html` includes let you apply the standard Content Server look and feel to any of your custom pages.

Place `<$include std_html_head_declarations$>` in the HEAD of your page, `<$include body_def$>` in the BODY and simply wrap your content in `<$include std_page_begin$>` and `<$include std_page_end$>`.

And here're the "before" and "after" pictures:

This screenshot shows you a simple one-liner HCST page:

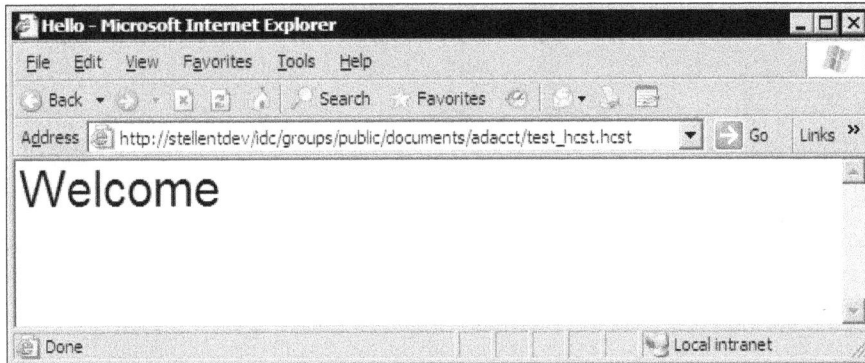

And here's how it looks after inserting the includes:

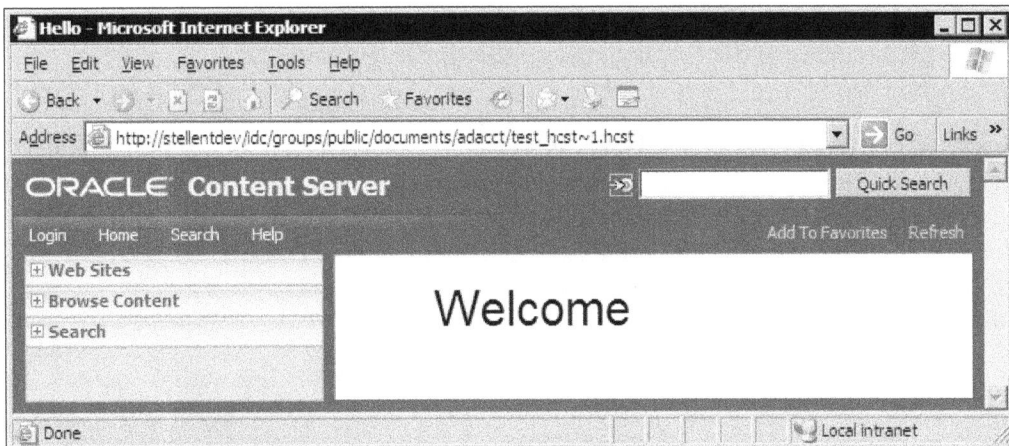

When it comes to customizing the Content Server, no resource comes close to *The Definitive Guide to Stellent Content Server Development* by Brian "Bex" Huff. Even though, it's slightly outdated (one version behind 10g R3), most of the content is still valid, so, if you need more guidance and information on any of the Content Server customizations we talk about here I recommend that you get that book (at least a free preview version from Google Books) and study it.

That said; let's look at your options for customizing the Content Server. Essentially, there are two things you can customize—functionality and look, and feel. Sometimes you'll need to do both. Let's start with customizing the functionality.

Customizing functionality

If you need to add a specific scenario when users get a temporary "boost" of their permissions or you need some scheduled checks performed on your content every night—you're looking at customizing functionality. But don't fire up your Java IDE just yet!

In many cases, you can save yourself a lot of work by simply using configuration instead of customization. If you need someone notified when a special type of document is checked in—consider creating a criteria workflow instead (See *Chapter 5, Understanding Workflows,* if you need a refresher). And if you need to show, hide, or alter meta values, consider using Profiles and Dependent Choice Lists (explained in *Chapter 3, Metadata*).

> There's also a bigger benefit in avoiding the actual customization. Your custom code may stop working when a new version of the UCM is released and you'll be forced to rewrite it.

Alright! You're sure that you can't accomplish it with profiles and the workflows. You're then looking at developing custom server components.

Content server components

In fact, you can think of the Content Server itself as a framework for running components. Most of the UCM modules such as Web Content Management, Records Management, the Dynamic Converter, and Virtual Folders, all are implemented as custom components. Components are also a great way to customize the core look and feel.

Here's a quick way to get started. Begin by scanning the **Working with Content Components** guide. It will help you understand the inner workings and how to use the Component Wizard to create and deploy skeletons for your new components.

Once again, you can enable and disable, install, uninstall, and download ZIP files from Component Manager page of Admin Server as shown in the following screenshot:

ORACLE·
CONTENT ADMIN SERVER

Options for idc

Start/Stop Content Server

General Configuration

Content Security

Internet Configuration

Component Manager

View Server Output

View Server Logs

View Providers

System Audit Information

Component Manager

Enable, disable, install, or uninstall server components. Some actions require a restart.

☑ Sort Components

☑ Hide Standard and System Components

Enabled Components:
```
ActiveDirectoryLdapCompone
CheckoutAndOpenInNative
ContentAccess-win32
ContentFolios
DesktopIntegrationSuite
Folders_g
FolderStructureArchive
FormEditor
Helper
InboundRefinerySupport
```

Disabled Components:
```
DynPrefix
```

[<< Enable]

[Disable >>]

Install New Component [_____] [Browse..]

[Install] [Reset]

Download Component [DesktopIntegrationSuite ▼] [Download]

Uninstall Component [DynPrefix ▼] [Uninstall]

Update Component Configuration [CIS_Helper ▼] [Update]

After you get an idea how to use Component Wizard, I suggest you understand the types of components you can create and look at some code samples. Let's see what's involved.

Creating content server components with Java

First, let's get the code samples and developer documentation. Try downloading them from: `http://www.oracle.com/technology/products/content-management/ucm/samples`. If the page has moved, just Google for "Sample Components for Universal Content Management".

Download *HowTo Components Sample* (also works with Content Server 7.5.2).

It's a tutorial that contains several advanced Java components for the Content Server, as well as documentation of common UCM Java classes. It shows you how to hook into the internal Content Server Java API and call custom Java code in response to the server events.

Below are the five primary methods for adding custom Java code (the first two are my favorites):

- **Service Handlers** allow you to create custom Content Server services and piggy-back on existing services.
- **Filters** are event handlers. You can intercept an event such as New Check In and Update Content Info and have your custom code executed then.
- **Service Classes** allow you to create your own Content Server services. They can then be called form the server pages or client applications just like the standard ones.
- **iDoc Script Extensions** let you add new iDoc Script functions. These functions will be available everywhere you can use iDoc — dynamic pages, profiles, and workflows.
- **Class Aliasing** is the most intrusive. It allows you to extend the functionality of the Content Server classes, for instance, when you need to call a filter and no event hook is defined for the event you need to handle.

Look at the samples that come in `ZIP` file. Be sure not to miss the main `readme.htm` file that has important information on Java components (see the following screenshot):

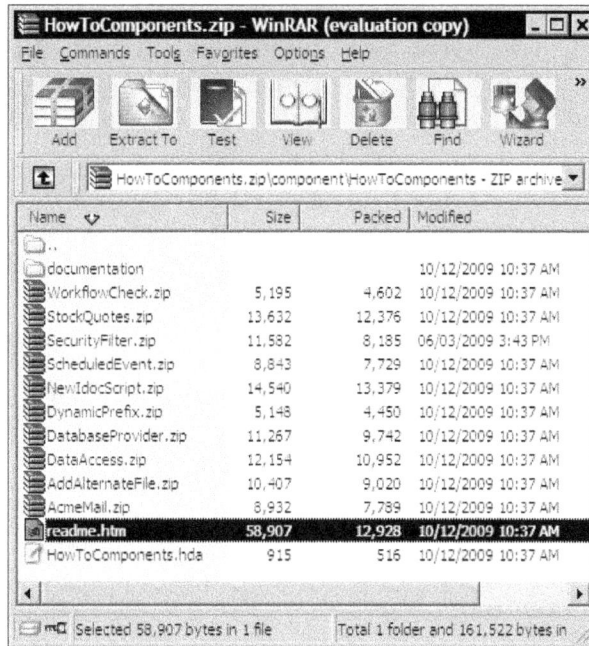

Anything similar to what you're trying to accomplish? Now you ready to fire up your IDE.

And here's the question most people are asking when getting into Content Server Java components.

How to setup Java IDE for debugging

I'll give you a few pointers. Content Server itself is a Java application so all you need is simply set it up as a main class that the debugger should start in your IDE. You then add your component's directory to the classpath, set your break points and off you go. See, It's not as complex as it seems!

Be sure to add Content Server classes to your project's classpath. They reside in `ucm/server/shared/classes/server.zip`. The main Content Server class that you want to run is `IdcServer`. (Make sure you stop the service or shutdown your regular Content Server process before starting it or you'll have two processes trying to listen on the same port)!

You may need to add more files from that directory if your project doesn't compile.

And I suggest that you always do your coding on a virtual machine where you can always undo your changes. For instance, Eclipse has a default `config` setting of "scrub output directory" that may delete Content Server class files and corrupt your installation. You yourself may accidentally delete or overwrite stuff. Better be safe than sorry.

> If you're using Eclipse, *The Definitive Guide to Stellent Content Server Development* book I recommended in the beginning of the section, has a step by step guide on setting up the debugging on page 203.

Now you should have a good feel of how to get started with developing custom Content Server functionality, but what about the presentation layer? Let's see what's involved.

Customizing interface

When it comes to customizing Content Server interface, you have four types of customizations to pick from:

- You can modify the skin and layout for search results, left navigation, the logo, color scheme, and so on. This is useful if all you're trying to do is apply branding on the Content Server interface or make style adjustments.

- You can develop custom dynamic pages that access Content Server functionality. This is exactly what you will be using if you're going to deploy Web Content Management (see next chapter for introduction to the WCM).

- You can create a Web Content Management site with Site Studio (covered in the next chapter).

- You can use a third-party application as your frontend and surface UCM capabilities in that application as appropriate (for example, Siebel, PeopleSoft, JD Edwards, Portal, or Web Applications).

> A lot of people confuse the Content Server user interface with UCM functionality. UCM is a powerhouse of services and reusable components, while the Content Server UI is just a skin placed on top of a few most common of those service calls, just the tip of the iceberg, take another look at *Services Reference Guide* on the Content Server documentation page.
>
> If you think about it that way, then your user experience can be easily changed per the needs of your users.

OK. Now that I've mentioned all the ways for customizing user interface, let's start with creating dynamic pages.

Dynamic pages

Here's another vast subject that would easily fill a few chapters on its own. So you can use a good "map" to help you avoid major mistakes and save a lot of hours. Let's explore the types of pages out there are and what they can do. You can find the rest of the details in **Dynamic Server Pages Guide** in Oracle UCM Documentation Library.

Before we dive into the different types of dynamic Content Server pages, let me show you the best part of all of them — they are managed content items. You can check them in and out and version them just like any other document. This means that they are highly portable, have full "source code version control" built in, can go through the workflow, have metadata, security and content policies applied to them and so on.

Let's start by looking at the most common dynamic page type: HCST.

HCST

Hypertext Content Server Template (HCST) pages are very much alike traditional ASP and JSP pages. They use the same structure as the GUI templates used by Content Server itself. HCSTs allow you to call iDoc Script functions, get values of the variables and execute Content Server services. You can create custom check-in screens and search pages and dynamically display content. HCSTs are widely used in Web Content Management where you use them to create page templates.

Here's an example of a simple page that displays name, user name, and security information of currently logged in user using iDoc Script variables:

```
<html>
<body>
Hello <strong><$UserFullName$></strong><br/>
Your login name is <$UserName$>,<br/>
your roles are <$UserRoles$><br/>
and your accounts are <$UserAccounts$>

</body>
</html>
```

And here's how to test it:

1. Save the code above into a file with .hcst extension. Check it into the Content Server.

2. Go to its **Content Information** page and click on the **Web Location** link.

3. Voila! The page displays, just as expected as shown in the following screenshot:

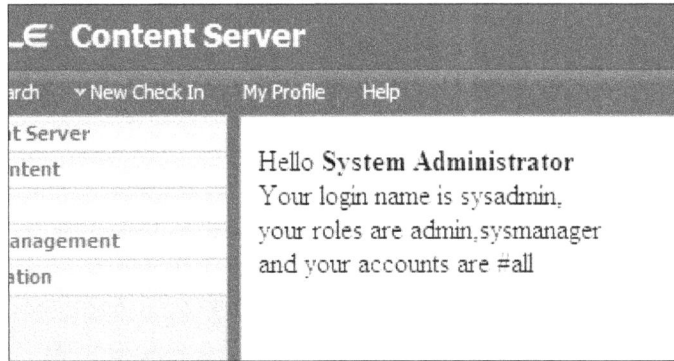

Remember me saying that HCSTs are a bit like JSPs? Actually, Content Server lets you use them too. Here's how to use JSP.

JSP

Java Server Pages or **JSP** is also supported. You can use them to access content and iDoc Script features. It may come really handy if you have existing JSP code and you just need to blend in some UCM features. You can continue using JSF, Struts, Spring, and similar frameworks as well as JSP Tag Libraries. Or you can simply use JSP if you feel more comfortable with them and would rather not code in iDoc.

UCM has an embedded Tomcat application server where you can deploy your WARs, and servlets.

The only caveat is that JSP support is not enabled by default so you need to turn it on. Here's how to do it:

1. Expand **Administration** tray and go to **Admin Server** page.

2. Click on **General Configuration** on the left. **General Configuration** screen comes up as shown in the following screenshot:

3. Place a checkmark next to **Enable Java Server Pages (JSP).**

4. In the **JSP Enabled Groups** type up the comma-separated list of Security Groups that you will use to check in JSP pages. You can use the groups you already defined or create new one, it's a common approach to create a separate group just for running JSPs.

Restart the Content Server. Now you are ready to check in JSP pages and they will render, just like you did with HCST. (*Be sure to check them into a JSP-enabled Security Group*)!

Let's continue with our example:

1. Save the following listing as a new `.jsp` file and check it in:

```
<%@ page import = "idcserver.*" %>
```

```
<jsp:useBean id="sb" class="idcserver.ServerBean" />
<%
  sb.init(request);
  String user = sb.evalIdcScp("UserFullName");
  String login = sb.evalIdcScp("UserName");
  String roles = sb.evalIdcScp("UserRoles");
  String accounts = sb.evalIdcScp("UserAccounts");
%>

<html>
<body>

Hello <strong><%=user%></strong><br/>
Your login name is <%=login%>,<br/>
your roles are <%=roles%><br/>
and your accounts are <%=accounts%>

</body>
</html>
```

2. Go to the **Content Info** screen and click on **Web Location** link to run it. I've opened the **Web Location** link in a new tab as shown in the following screenshot:

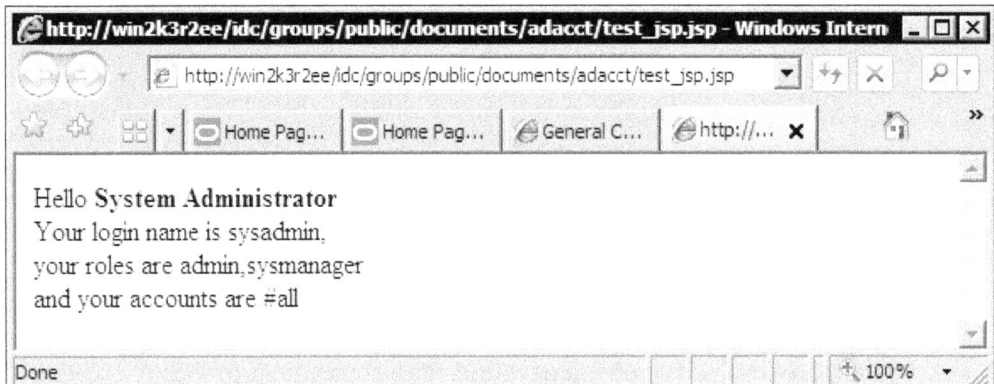

Note that you use the `idcserver.ServerBean` object to execute Content Server services. It has methods for performing requests, looping over the results and executing iDoc Script.

You can also bundle a bunch of JSPs and Servlets into a single WAR file, and deploy to the Content Server.

What about iDoc? Do you always have to embed it inside the HCST or JSP pages? Nope. You can separate it out into its own iDoc files.

iDoc files

While iDoc files cannot be rendered on they own, they are frequently used as include files for other types of dynamic server pages. This helps enforce the traditional best practice of separation of logic (iDoc Script) and presentation (HCST).

This is especially useful in HCSPs and HCSFs—the last two types of dynamic pages out there.

HCSP and HCSF

These pages are very similar to HCSTs that we looked at earlier in this chapter. Both **HCSP (Hypertext Content Server Page)** and **HCST (Hypertext Content Server Form)** are combination of HTML and iDoc Script and both can do the same things that HCST pages can. The difference is that they are fully XML—compliant and there for use XML iDoc Script, which is iDoc, embedded in HTML comments. The code to echo the username will now look like this:

```
<!--$UserFullName-->
```

Below is a fragment of Site Studio HCSP page template that inserts a copy of the TestCo_Copywrite fragment at the end of every page:

```
<br />
<!--SS_BEGIN_SNIPPET(fragment2,1)-->
<!--$ssFragmentInstanceId="fragment2", ssIncludeXml("lib_TestCo_
Fragments", "fragments/fragment[@id='TestCo_Copywrite']/snippets/
snippet[@id='1']/text()")-->
<!--SS_END_SNIPPET(fragment2,1)-->
</body>
```

HCSF pages are used to create web forms that users can fill in for surveys and other business applications. When user submits an HCSF form, Content Server creates a copy of the page in a new HCSP page with response values embedded in XML.

You don't have to create your HCSFs from scratch. The following section tells you about Using Web Form Editor.

Using web form editor

Web Form Editor is a free optional visual design environment for creating web forms. Once again, authoring web forms can fill a mini-chapter, so all I'm going to give you is a quick guide to help you hit the ground running.

Latest versions of Content Server come with the **Form Editor** component bundled in, but if you're using an older version, you'll have to download and install the Form Editor. It's easy to check if you have it.

Expand **Content Management** tray and see whether **Web Form Editor** link is present as shown in the following screenshot:

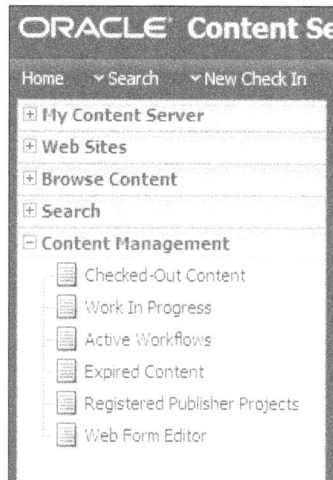

If you don't have it here's how to install the Web Forms Editor:

1. Download the latest Content Server `ZIP` file — see *Chapter 1, Getting Up and Running*, if you need a refresher.

2. Inside the archive, under `packages/allplatform` extract two files: `FormEditor.zip` and `FCKEditor.zip`. The latter is a lightweight web editor component used by the FormEditor as shown in the following screenshot:

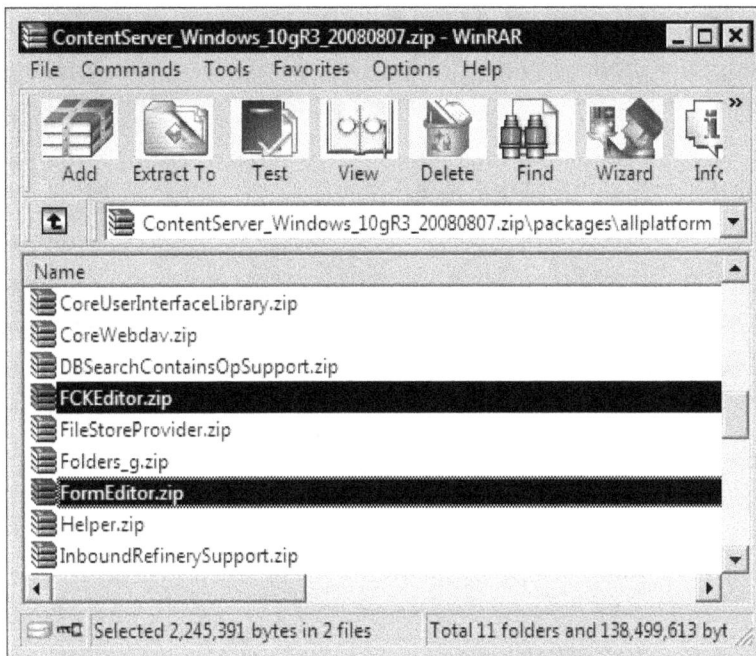

3.   Browse to Admin Server and load Component Manager. Install and enable FCKEditor first.

4.   Install and enable the FormEditor. Restart the Content Server.

You're now ready to launch the FormEditor.

Before you create your first form though, be sure to check out the *Web Form Editor Guide* a comprehensive manual that will get you started with HCSF forms much faster. Here's how to find it:

On the Content Server file system browse to `custom/FormEditor` — the directory where FormEditor component is installed. Locate file named something like `web_form_editor_10en.pdf` and also check out the `readme.doc` — a shorter version of the same document. Earlier in this chapter I've given you a refresher on speed reading. I bet it will come handy now.

And we're not done yet. The last type of customization we haven't looked at yet is the Content Server Custom Layout and Skins.

Custom layouts and skins

It's what you use for modifying the Content Server Interface. Let's start by getting a flavor of what they are:

1. Click on **My Profile** link on the top navigation bar. **User Profile** page loads as shown in the following screenshot:

2. Change **Layout** value to **Top Menus** and click on **Update**. You'll notice that the left navigation has disappeared, and the items that used to display in trays on the left are now forming the second row menu on the top (see the following screenshot):

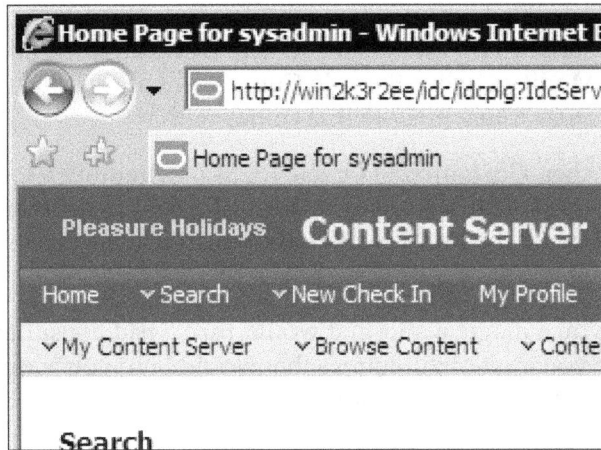

You can modify layouts by simply changing files under `weblayout\resources\layouts\Trays\Oracle` (be sure to make a backup first)!. For instance, if you replace the `HeaderLogo.gif` — you will change the Oracle logo in the top left corner with one of your own (see the following screenshot):

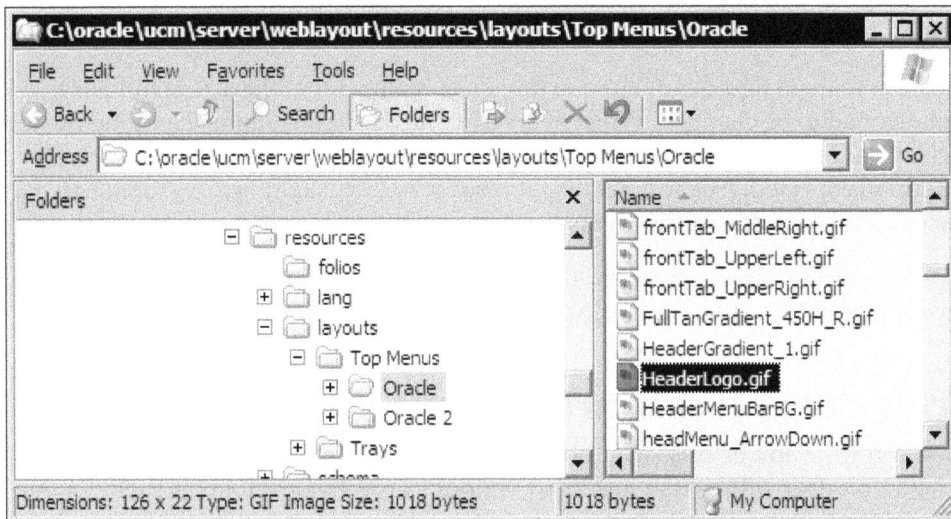

(Be sure you're modifying files in the directory of the layout that you have currently selected or you won't see your changes)!

But you don't even have to do that. Oracle, once again, offers you a helping hand. You can go to the UCM support website and download a free Create, and Modify Layout Sample Component. It shows you how to create new layouts to create your own custom interface.

Browse to: `http://www.oracle.com/technology/products/content-management/ucm/samples` (or Google for "oracle UCM samples"). Download and install **Create and Modify Layout Sample Component** and be sure to check out `modifying_interface_10en.pdf` file that comes with it.

And here's the clincher. Customizing Oracle UCM may require a lot of skills and resources, so many organizations engage consulting help to get them through, and many get scorched when the projects run longer than promised, cost significantly more and they're not getting the quality that they expected.

While I can't give you a magic wand that would turn a bad consultant into a good one, I still can give you a set of guidelines that would help you acquire some "x-ray vision" and get dramatically better results at the end.

Five ways to maximize results when working with a UCM vendor

As a UCM consultant myself, it used to drive me nuts to see some of my projects suddenly go under without any prior warning. Certainly, nothing related to quality of work.

It took me years to figure out, but one day I just realized that the actual industry standards had to be changed. When everyone is used to consultants charging by hour, the clients are virtually guaranteed to end up paying more and have their projects run longer than expected. (See my website at: `www.stellentExperts.com/consulting` for detailed discussion of exactly why is this happening).

Below are the few simple "secrets" that consistently help our clients get their projects delivered on time and on budget, and avoid the common IT project pitfalls.

Work out a fixed price project

I always get "It can't be this easy" objection when I recommend this but yes, it can, and you drop all the risk into your vendor's laps. Even if it takes them longer than anticipated you always end up paying exactly what you initially agreed on. I personally always take initiative and recommend our clients a fixed price option.

You also can't run out of budget when you know exactly how much it will cost you before the project is started, and it allows for better project scope control while taking full advantage of the modular SOA capabilities of the UCM. Your larger project then is delivered as a sequence of small incremental projects that can naturally fit into each other.

But what if you don't know exactly what you want? What if you want to try a few scenarios before you have your business people commit on a specific path of implementation? How can you make you price fixed then?

A short "discovery" mini-project may be a good idea

It will help you explore a few scenarios, do some prototyping and decide on a best solution. It will help your vendor better understand your unique requirements, and come up with a solid estimate. But the key is: *make this mini-project fixed-price too*!

This will prevent it from running two or three times longer than anticipated. I always recommend my clients to start with a short initial fixed-priced "discovery" phase.

A planning exercise like that will also help you eliminate the risk of "coding yourselves into a corner" — when, for example, consultants are doing three fixed projects with no visibility into the fourth one, that will depend on projects one and three.

Making the fourth project quick and easy becomes impossible as projects one, two, and three will have to be reworked to fit in the requirements for project number four.

But if the need for the project four was identified during the discovery phase, a shared program governance model can be developed to facilitate execution of our fixed price projects, and have them run in series toward a known and shared overarching goal.

And here's how to further protect yourself. Even if your vendor agreed to a fixed-price project — *you can still get burned*. How?

When your vendor's idea of what a "completed system" should look like is not the same as yours! So the way to protect you from this is to negotiate specific completion criteria.

Negotiate specific completion criteria

If project plan simply states that "UCM is up and running" is your success expectation — it's not specific enough and you're at risk. What modules should be present? What customizations complete? If data migration is in scope — what fields should be migrated over?

Completion criteria can get fairly complex so you may need some time to verify the results. And here's where another "industry norm" is set up to make clients vulnerable.

The norm I'm talking about is the conventional 90, 60, or even 15 day guarantees. This is how long the consultant gives you to verify that all the work was completed to your satisfaction.

Now what if you find a defect or major omission after this period is complete? You'll have to pay for fixing it! That's right. You'll have to pay for it again, even though you already paid for it to be delivered as part of the project.

You need to protect yourself. You need to negotiate longer guarantee.

Negotiate longer guarantee

The longer you have to weed out the errors and omissions the better is your chance that your vendor will fix most of their errors at no cost to you.

Of course, the ultimate protection would be the **Full Lifetime Guarantee** — when your vendor would fix their errors — no matter when you discover them. I personally feel that this is the only way the clients should be treated and this is what we at Stellent Experts offer to all our clients.

Your vendor may not (most vendors won't) agree to give you full lifetime guarantee so you just have to reduce your risk as much as possible, and negotiate a longer term with them.

And one last crucially important point is coming your way. It's training. We always include *free staff training* in our project plans. But even if your vendor is charging you for training, I recommend that you don't skimp on training.

Don't skimp on training but don't spend a fortune either!

If you don't train your developers, you'll have to shell out thousands of dollars and hire consultants. If you don't train your staff people, they won't put their important documents in UCM. They'll keep them in their e-mail and their shared drives or they'll put them there, but never update them.

On the other end, when important content is missing or outdated — people are not excited to search for it. The system then takes a down spiral, turning into scrap metal.

How can this be avoided: With training and education. So why almost everyone still avoid sending their business users for a meaningful UCM training program?

Because Oracle UCM training could be a massive expense. At $700.00 per person per day, sending 10 people for a five day course totals a handy sum of $35,000.00! And it never ends with just one course.

No wonder most managers are having bad feelings about it and skimp on training.

So the lesson here is this — your vendor can include the training into your fixed-price project. For them the added expense is five days of one senior consultant to conduct the training. For you, the savings are hundreds of dollars *per person* per day.

Another great way to reduce your training expenses is to encourage your folks to attend conferences, read blogs and articles (listed in the *Resource Directory* in *Appendix B*).

An even better option, that doesn't require constant effort on your part, is to subscribe to the UCM-related newsletters (See the end of *Appendix A* for instructions on how to get your free Oracle UCM continuing education).

Will this book itself help to reduce your training expenses? Absolutely! Will it shorten the duration of the training you require? Absolutely! But will it let you get by without training at all? No, it won't. No book will.

Summary

This sure was an unusual chapter. I've given you a complete roadmap of all major tools and options you have for customizing the Content Server and your UCM. You've learned how to alter the look and feel, and functionality of UCM, and how to seamlessly tap into its power from other enterprise applications. Last, but not least, I've explained how to maximize the value you get from a UCM consulting vendor, reduce your risk, and avoid severe penalties to your budget, timeline and your system functionality.

In the next chapter we will look at the second most popular UCM module next to Document Management, its Web Content Management capability, and I'll walk you through creation of a simple website, pages, and templates.

11

Web Content Management and Collaboration

In the previous chapter I've given you a complete roadmap of options and the tools you have for customizing Oracle UCM. I've explained how to reduce your risk, and avoid severe penalties to your budget, timeline, and your system functionality – when working with a UCM consulting vendor.

This concludes our review of Oracle Content Server and core Document Management. You now have a solid foundation and are ready to master any of the additional UCM modules that we didn't completely cover in this book. You've done all the hard work. Everything else in UCM such as Records Management (URM) and Web Content Management (WCM) come as add-on Content Server components. You understand Content Server and that instantly parachutes you many miles ahead of the clueless rookies fighting their way through the quicksand of confusion and documentation.

That said, nearly every single Oracle UCM deployment now includes Web Content Management and nearly every client I've spoke to in the last several years, were fascinated with the mojo of Web 2.0 and online collaboration. So I figured that you might like me to add a chapter about that, and help you to hit the ground running.

So here it comes. I'll guide you through using Web Content Management to create great websites from installing WCM itself – to planning – to the tools you use to design the actual site. Hold on to your hat! Will zoom you through over 500 pages of documentation in a short hour and save you a few more weeks of trial and error. In this chapter I'll show you:

- How to install and configure Web Content Management and get you ready to dive into development of your first UCM website.

- Seven website planning steps that will steer you clear from pain and agony of mid-project redesigns, and wasted weeks of un-necessary content migrations.

- How to use page templates, fragments, and region content. This will give you an instant knowledge of WCM site structure and how to get your site up at record speed.

- A step by step, easy way of actually creating your first Site Studio website.

- Insider look at online collaboration tools, features, and products, and how to best get them working for you.

Enough introductions! Let's start by getting ready for the WCM.

Getting ready for Web Content Management

In this section I'll show you how to install Web Content Management on your Content Server instance, and introduce you to its major components. In fact, there is only one—the product behind Web Content Management called Site Studio, and it has four parts to it. So let's begin by looking at these parts one by one.

Introducing Oracle Site Studio

Let's look at the parts that make up the Site Studio:

- **Site Studio Content Server Component**: This is what extends Content Server to enable WCM functionality. You need to install Site Studio Component before you can use WCM (see the next section for installation instructions).

- **Site Studio Designer**: This is an integrated development environment (IDE) for building websites. Designer is a Windows application and must run on the Developer's desktop. We will be using the Designer later in this chapter to create our first website.

- **Site Studio Contributor**: This is a thin-client editor application that runs in the client's browser. This is what actually allows contributors to manage content. I'll show you how it looks later on, when we'll be adding content to your site.

- **Site Studio Manager**: This is a limited, browser-based version of Site Studio Designer. It allows Site Administrators to create new pages and modify site navigation.

Great! We're now ready to get back to the keyboard. Let's proceed with the installation.

Installing Oracle Site Studio

Installing Oracle Site Studio involves three basic steps:

1. Downloading the WCM components.
2. Installing Site Studio Content Server.
3. Installing Designer Application.

Let's start with the first step.

Downloading WCM Components

Just as before, Google for "`Download Oracle Universal Content Management`". The page you want must look like this:

> **Oracle Universal Content Management Web Content Management 10g**
> *(requires Content Server installation)*
>
> ⬇ Complete UCM Web Content Management bundle for Windows, Linux, and Unix (V
> 419,978,708 bytes)
>
> **Alternatively, you can download the following Oracle Universal Content Man
> sub components separately:**
>
> ⬇ Connection Server 10gR3 (Version: 10.1.3.3.0 | Date: 20070406 | Size: 30,903,202 by
>
> ⬇ Content Portlet Suite 10gR3 (Version: 10.1.3.3.5 | Date: 20090715 | Size: 107,128,84
>
> ⬇ Content Publisher 10gR3 (Version: 10.1.3 | Date: 20071031 | Size: 153,062,568 bytes
>
> ⬇ Site Studio 10gR3 (Version: 10.1.3.5.0 | Date: 20090715 | Size: 53,449,136 bytes)
>
> ⬇ Site Studio 10gR4 (Version: 10.1.4.5.0 | Date: 20090702 | Size: 43,638,910 bytes)
>
> ⬇ Site Studio Publishing Utility 10gR3 (Version: 10.1.3.3.0 | Date: 20070406 | Size: 31.
>
> ⬇ VCR/SPI for Site Studio 10gR4 (Version: 2009-05-01 (10g) (Rev: 2864) | Date: 200905

Just scroll down to Web Content Management section and download a file named something like `Site Studio 10gR4`. (10g R4 is the latest version of Site Studio – at the time of this writing, and this is the version I'm using to illustrate WCM functionality).

Once you have the zip file, you're ready to proceed with the installation.

Installing Site Studio Content Server Component

Below are the few simple steps you need to complete:

1. Launch your Component Manager. Uncheck **Hide Standard and System Components** and make sure you have DBSearchContainsOpSupport in the **Enabled Components** box. This component is required for Site Studio to work properly, so if you don't have it in place find it in the ZIP file, that contains your Content Server distribution and use Component Manager to install it—before proceeding to the next step (See *Chapter 10, Customizing Oracle UCM,* if you need a refresher on installing components).

2. Unzip the Site Studio main file. Using Component Manger, install a component, found under component/ subdirectory. File name should be similar to sitestudio9.0.0.470.zip as shown in the following screenshot:

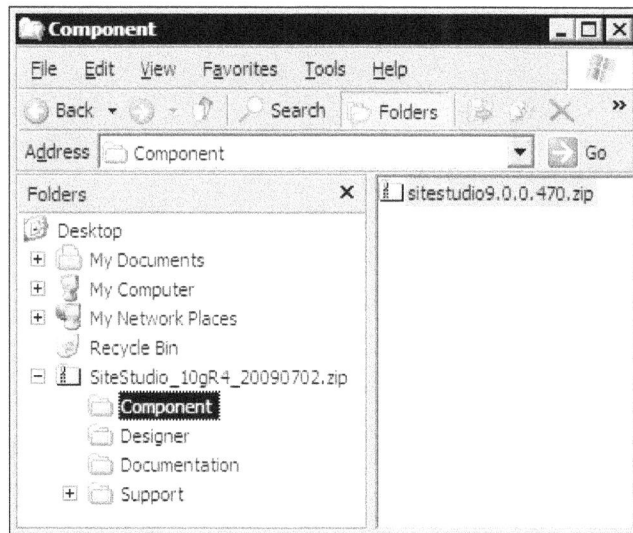

> When installing Site Studio 10g R3 you must enable database full text indexing. See **Content Server Installation Guide** from the UCM documentation library for instructions on how to do that. This is not a requirement for Site Studio 10g R4.

During the install, you will see the **Install Settings** screen as shown in the following screenshot:

Install Settings

Choose a content type to be used for checking in the fragment libraries: `ADACCT ▾`

Choose a content type to be used for checking in the custom element forms: `ADACCT ▾`

Choose a content type to be used for checking in the validation scripts: `ADACCT ▾`

Choose a content type to be used for checking in the sample web site objects: `ADACCT ▾`

Choose a content type to be used for checking in the custom configuration scripts: `ADACCT ▾`

Enter the initial value used to name web site sections: `0`

Continue | Cancel

It gives you an option to pick different Content Types for different types of files that make up your websites. This will help you group them by type and locate easily. Might be well worth your time to click on **Cancel**, go ahead and create five content type, and then come back to installing Site Studio Component (See *Chapter 3, Metadata*, if you need a refresher on creating the Content Types).

3. Enable the component and restart Content Server.

4. Open *Site Studio Installation Guide* and scan the *Post-Installation Tasks and Considerations* section. Depending on your web server configuration, you might need to perform additional steps.

5. If running on Windows then restart your IIS. If you forget, you may not be able to see your Site Studio websites that you will be developing.

That's it! You're now to ready to start building your website, and you'll need Site Studio Designer on your desktop. So let's now install the Site Studio Designer.

Installing Designer application

This one is really easy. Just extract and run `setup.exe` from `/Designer` directory in the Site Studio `ZIP` file. There are no options to pick from and it installs in a flash.

Congratulations! All the pre-work is now behind us and we're ready to create our first website.

Creating your website

I'm sure you've heard that *an ounce of prevention is better than a pound of cure*. Indeed, a solid day or two of planning can save you weeks and even months of frustration, working around the knots in your site framework. Below is a checklist of what you should be clear on—*before* you jump into the implementation:

1. Your **site map** where all your pages and links are clearly defined.

2. Your **site layout and HTML templates**. For instance, if your homepage looks different and the rest of the site has the same layout then you will need two templates—one for the homepage and one for the rest of the site.

   It may be very helpful to create **wireframes**—the rough sketches of what elements make up your pages—for every type of the page that you will need on the site. I'm also a big fan of using pencil and paper or whiteboard for those instead of neat looking Visio diagrams and fancy mock-ups. Why?

   It is quite simple. An impeccable-looking diagram looks, well, perfect. So when your business client looks at it—they tend to like it—before they even had a chance to think of the actual page elements that are shown. And the page layout may not work out in the long run, and all of your planning efforts will be wasted. On the other hand, a pencil sketch or a white board drawing bring attention to the subject itself and invite participation.

   The same goes for the **story boards**—diagrams that show your common browsing patterns and typical user behaviors. Creating story boards will help you structure your content more logically, and can produce massive savings and productivity gains—when you consider how minutes saved of each site interaction multiple with each of the thousands people browsing your site.

3. Your **contribution regions** clearly marked within your templates. These are the blocks of content within the page that your users (contributors) can change directly—without using development tools.

   If you have a newsflash page, that has your top and your left menu, content areas for your president's message, your featured story and page footer then you're looking at two contribution regions—one for your featured news story and one for your president's message. Your marketing folks should be able to update those without coding and calling on your development folks. But they don't need to touch your top and your left menu and your footer.

Site Studio 10gR4 adds a few more levels of indirection to give you even better separation of structure elements and simplify the reuse. Instead of the contribution regions in the template, it uses placeholder tags that can contain a sub-template or a region definition. (See *Site Studio Designer Guide v.10gR4* for more information).

4. Your **dynamic content** needs to be identified. Things like RSS feeds, calendars, dynamic menus, web forms and image galleries. You need to find everything that's not static HTML and not user-changeable content.

    One of the most common types of dynamic content in Site Studio driven websites is simply a result of a Content Server query. Your list of breaking news can simply be a result of the query for Content Type of a `NewsStory` and release date within the last three days (See *Chapter 3, Metadata*, if you need a refresher on Content Server queries).

5. Your reusable fragments. Things such as menus, page footers, and company logos that appear on more than one page and need to all be changed in just one place. Fragments may be static (like the logo) or dynamic (like a menu) but they cannot be changed by contributors.

6. Your **naming convention** the prefix you give to the Content ID and the Title of your site elements — templates, fragments and alike.

    Not only your naming convention is important for grouping your reusable elements by site, organization unit and alike, and making your code look logical and consistent, it also helps you separate your site structure from your site content.

    Remember, your site structure elements, like your templates and your project files are also stored in your Content Server — along with the actual content that goes on your website.

7. **Permissions and metadata** — roles, accounts, content types, and custom metadata that you'll be using on the site structure elements and the site content.

Wow! Looks like a long list, but believe me, a few days spent planning your site is a small price to pay for avoiding pain and agony of mid-project redesigns and wasted weeks of un-necessary content migrations.

The good news is that we're just learning the ropes and you don't have to do all of this thinking right now. I just wanted you to be aware of these things. Better safe, than sorry.

OK. We're now ready to look at the WCM tools. Let me give you a quick primer on core elements of your website structure.

Understanding site structure elements

Let's look at all the files and structures that make up your website in Site Studio:

- **Project File**: This is a master XML file that Site Studio is using to store your site' structure and navigation. It's a glue that holds together your navigation, your templates, and your content. You can easily spot it in the search results that it has a Content ID starting with SS_PROJECT_ .

- **Fragments**: These are reusable blocks of content that cannot be changed by contributors. Fragments are stored in **Fragment Libraries** — each containing an XML file with code for all the fragments and snippets, and a ZIP file with **Fragment Assets** — its images, CSS styles, and other files used by fragment's HTML.

- **Navigation sections:** These are thenodes of the site structure (such as Home, About Us, and Our Products). Each section has a primary page and a page template for rendering other content inside this section.

- **Page Templates** (**Layout Files**): The dynamic Content Server pages (HCSP, JSP, or ASP) that are used to render a page — complete with fragments, contribution regions, elements, and content.

- **Placeholders** (introduced in 10gR4): These are new insertion tags that let you place a contribution region or sub-template into your page template.

- **Subtemplates** (introduced in 10gR4): These are reusable mini-page templates that may have placeholders of they own.

- **Contribution Regions**: These are marked areas on the page template that contain user-changeable content.

- **Elements** within a Region: These are individual units of managed content of the same type. For example, a job title on a job posting site may be a plain text element. A region can contain multiple elements. Other element types include rich text, image, static lists, and Content Server query (Dynamic list).

- **Region Templates** (introduced in 10gR4): These are partial HTML files that let you define the look and feel of the Contribution Region and the Elements.

- **Contributor Data Files**: These are XML files that contain user content inside the Region Elements.

- **Native Documents**: A document (such as MS Word, Excel, PDF, or an AutoCAD drawing) that is placed inside a contribution region. A document gets dynamically converted to HTML when the page is displayed.

Sounds complex? It's actually not. Take a look at the diagram below – it will help you to "drive home" these terms and how they all fit together. You will see how Navigation Sections in a Project File linked to page templates, how multiple templates are used to render different page layouts, and how contribution regions and elements are used to render managed content:

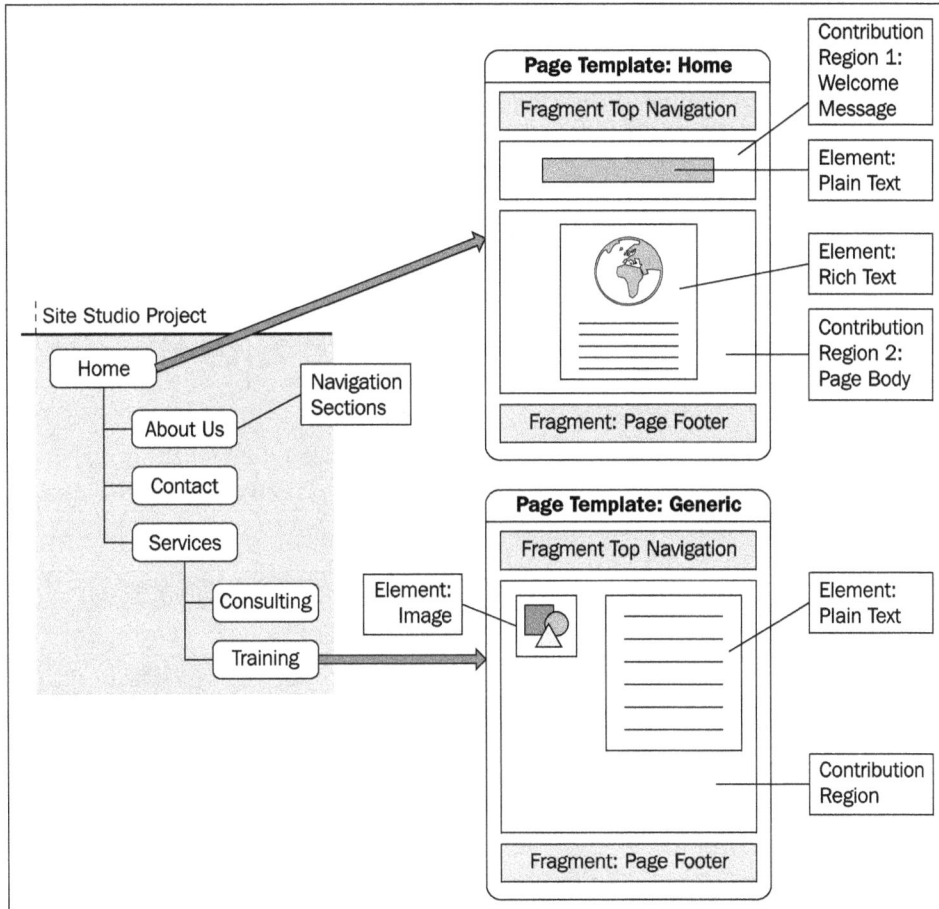

What about the placeholders? This diagram shows you the "traditional" site structure of Site Studio 10gR3 and earlier versions. I've purposely left out the new levels of indirection, introduced in R4, because I want you to keep things simple when you're making your first steps.

Create your first website using this, much simpler "traditional" model, that continues to be supported in 10gR4. Once you get comfortable, it's easy to follow the *Site Studio Designer Guide 10gR4* and add these new powerful features such as the Region Templates and Subtemplates to your mental framework.

And now it's a perfect time to see all of these in action. Next section is a lab that walks you through creating a simple website.

Lab 11: Creating a website with Site Studio Designer

Launch your Designer application. The first thing you see when starting Designer for the first time is **Site Connection Manager** screen as shown in the following screenshot:

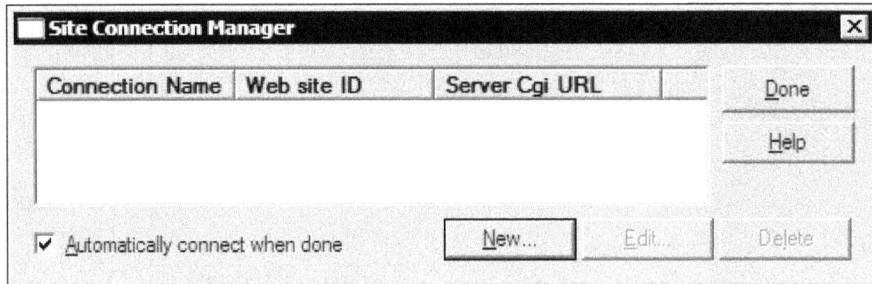

You're now ready to create your new site.

Creating new site

Below are the few simple steps it takes to create a new Site Studio website:

1. Click on the **New** button. **Site Connection Details** dialog displays as shown in the following screenshot:

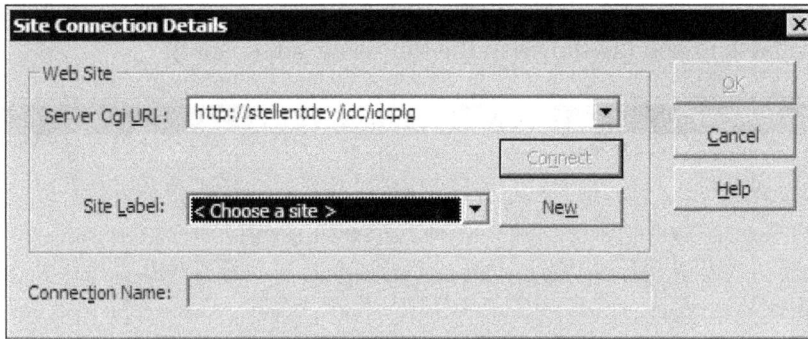

2. Type up your **Server Cgi URL**. If your server name is `stellentdev` and your Content Server instance name is `idc`, your Cgi URL will be: `http://stellentdev/idc/idcplg`.

3. Click on **New** button next to **Site Label**. **Create New Site** dialog displays as shown in the following screenshot:

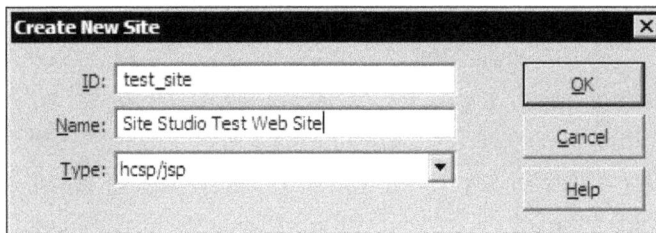

4. Populate Site **ID** (the URL name of your website), **Name** (full, user-friendly name) and dynamic page **Type** you're about to use.

   In most cases, you'd be fine with the default choice, `hcsp/jsp`, in place. The other choice is to create the site based on Active Server Pages (`asp`). ASP sites allow you to reuse your legacy ASP code, but you won't be able to take advantage of full functionality, architecture, and features introduced in Site Studio 10gR3 and 10gR4.

[
Instead of creating an ASP site consider hosting your few hard-to-replace ASP pages inside an iframe in your full-featured HCSP site.
]

5. Voila! Your site is now created, and full Site Studio Designer interface is available to you (as shown in the following screenshot):

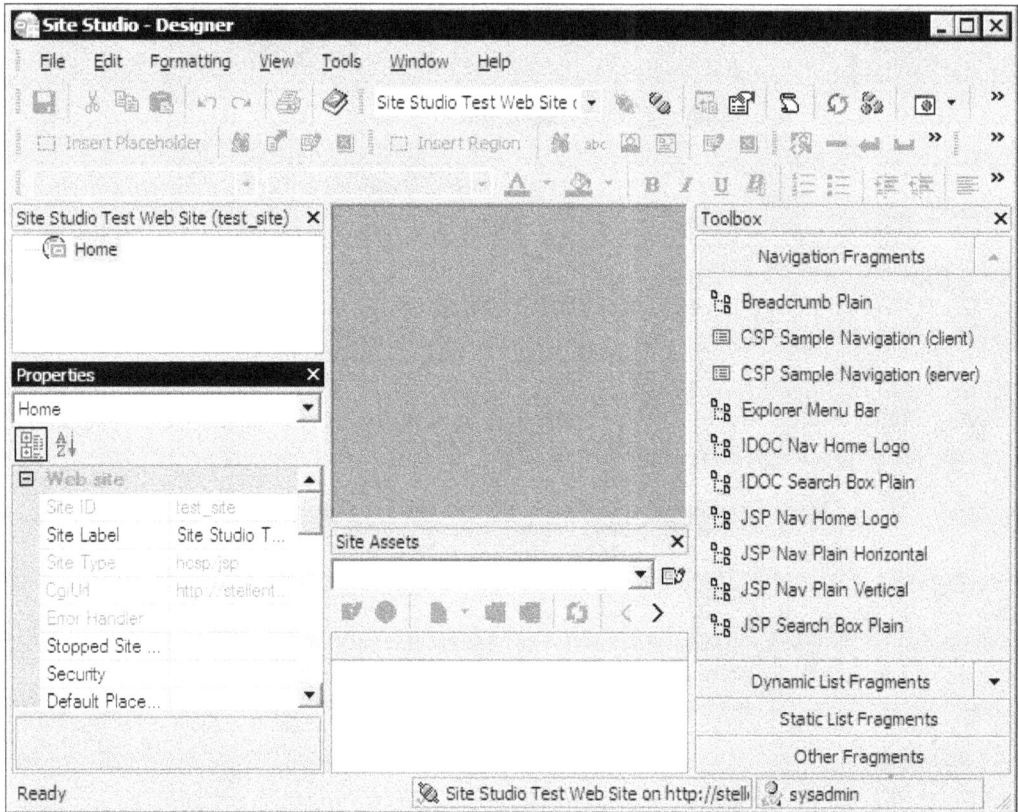

You're now ready to build your site.

Using Page Templates

Right now your site navigation is empty. Let's create your first page:

1. Right click on the **Home** node and pick **Select Home Page** as shown in the following screenshot:

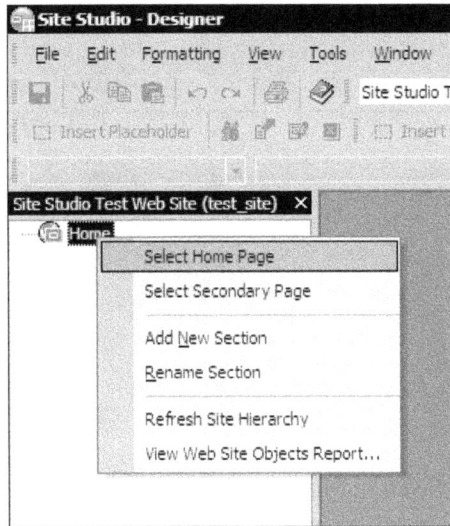

2. **Select Page Template** dialog displays. Pick **Create a new page template** (**hcsp**) and click on **OK** as shown in the following screenshot:

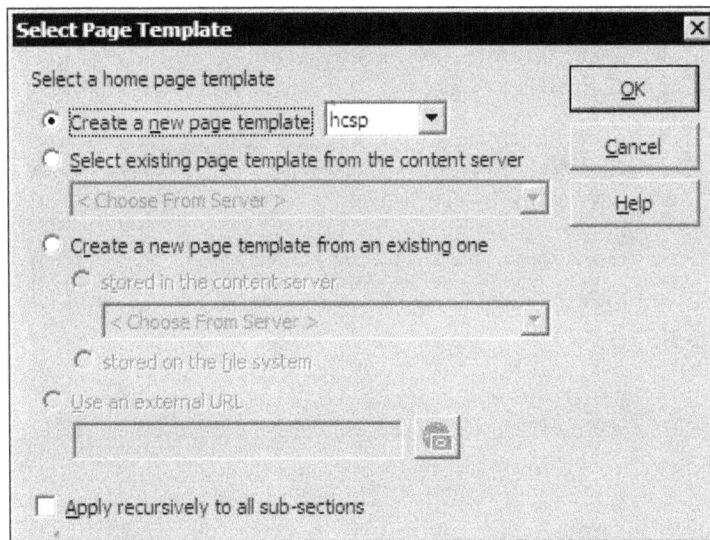

3. **Warning** dialog displays. When working on a live web site, you'll need to be aware of the fact that your changes, like adding pages or including them in navigation, will be instantly reflected and visible to your site's visitors. For now though, we can simply dismiss the warning (see the screenshot below):

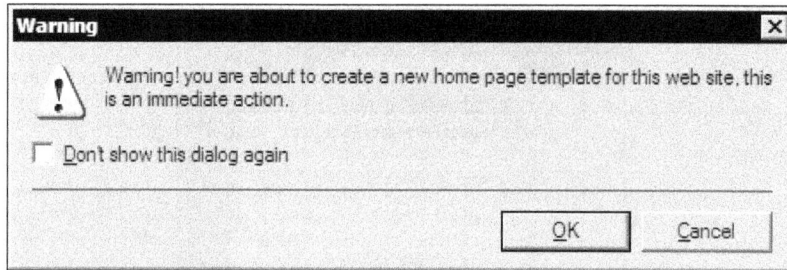

4. Click on OK to acknowledge the warning. **Check In** screen will pop up.

5. Give your template a **Title** and click on **Assign Info** to complete Check In. Your Home Page Template now displays in the site hierarchy pane. Double-click on the template name to open it in the editor.

6. Type some text in the page template and select **File | Save**.

7. Right-click on your new template and pick **View in Browser**. Congratulations! Your site now has its first page and the page is proudly displaying in a browser as shown in the following screenshot:

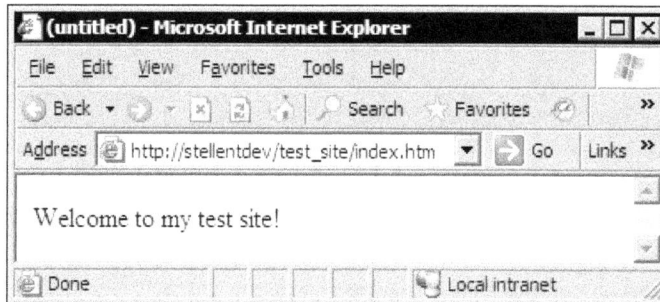

8. You can also go back to familiar Content Server user interface and click on the **Web Sites** tray. Your new website will be there and you can click on the site name to see its homepage (see the following screenshot):

That's great. Your first page is now up. But it doesn't really look like a website. Let's take a next step and add some navigation. The next section shows you how.

Using Fragments

Here's a simple way to add top navigation bar to our site.

1. Move cursor to the top left of the document where the top navigation bar would go. In the **Toolbar** pane select **Navigation Fragments** and click on **Nav Tabs Top** (see the following screenshot):

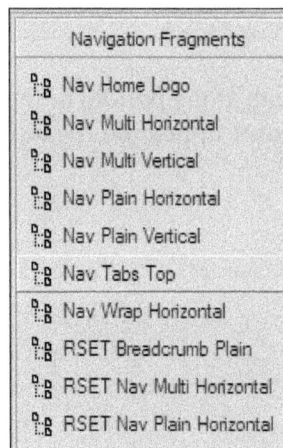

2. **Fragment Parameter Values** dialog displays (see the following screenshot). Pick values for the text color, background color, and so on.

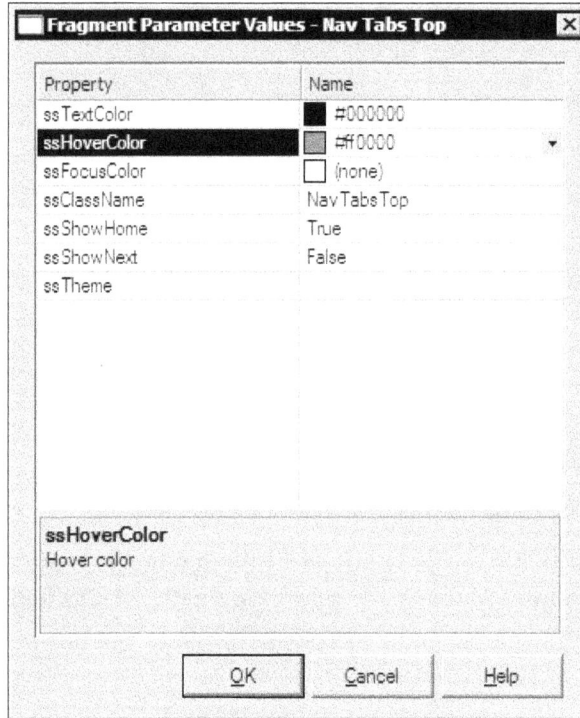

3. Click on the **PREVIEW** tab at the bottom of the main editor window. You can see navigation tab for **Home** appear on the top left of your siteas shown in the following screenshot:

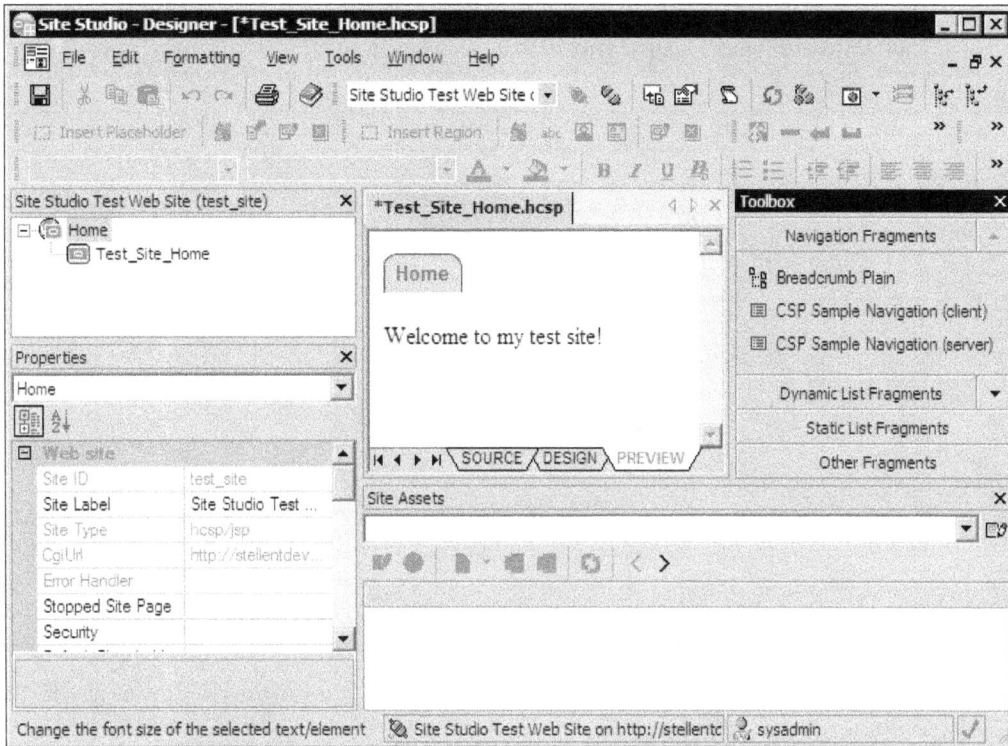

Now let's add Copyright note to the bottom of the page. In fact, let's make it reusable, so any template on any site in our company can use it. And if we want to add something to our copyright note later on, or change our company name — we only want to change it one place. How do we do this?

By creating our own fragment. The easiest way to get started is to copy an existing fragment. Here's how to do it:

4. Click on **Other Fragments** in the toolbox pane. Right-click on **Copyright Example** and select **Copy and Edit...** as shown in the following screenshot:

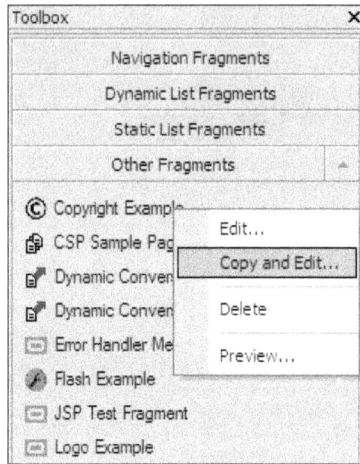

5. Type `fr_TestCo_Copywrite` for Content ID (I like to use a prefix in a name so I can easily distinguish fragments by content ID).

6. **Fragment Editor** now displays in the main editor window as shown in the following screenshot:

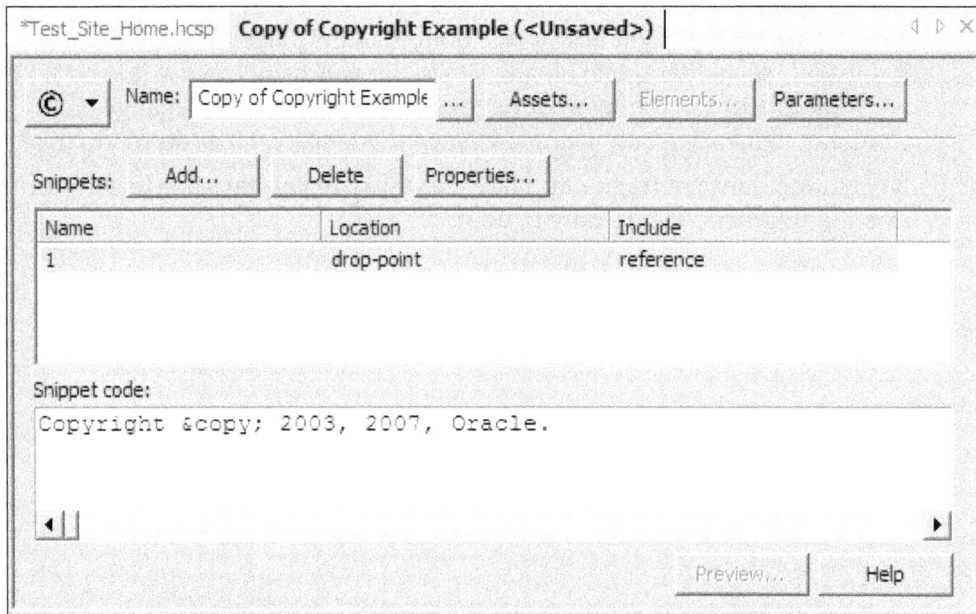

Fragment Editor has two main panes: Snippets pane and Source Code pane. A fragment can contain multiple **snippets** — blocks of code that get added to your template when you add a fragment to it. You can define multiple snippets that can be inserted inside HTML head element, top, and bottom of HTML body tag or simply at the **drop-point** — the point in the document where your cursor was when you clicked on the fragment in the toolbox.

When you select a snippet, its code is displayed in the **Snippet code** window below.

7. Now you can preview your fragment. Click on the **Preview...** button at the bottom of the fragment editor.

8. And now it's time to save our new fragment. Go to **File | Save**. **Save Fragment** dialog displays (See the following screenshot). Click on **New** button to create new fragment library. Let's call it lib_TestCo_Fragments.

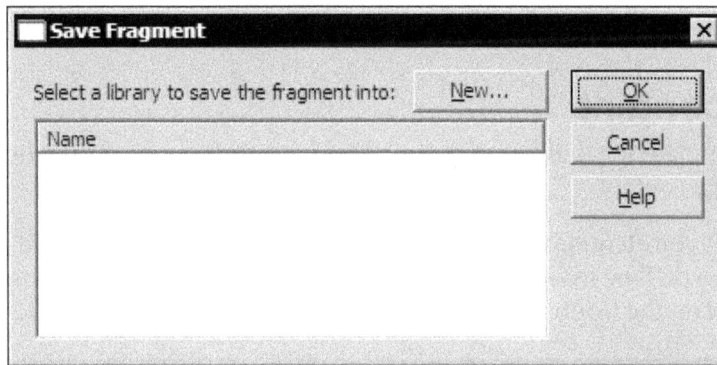

And here comes the fun part! Let's change the snippet code. Why don't we make the copyright year dynamic, so it always has the current year, and we never have to manually update it?

All we need is to use iDoc Script function dateCurrent() and format its output, so we only see a year. Here's how finished Snippet code will look like:

```
Copyright &copy;
<!--$formatDateWithPattern(dateCurrent(),"yyyy")-->,
Test Co Inc.
```

9. Type up the code in the **Snippet code** window and click on **Preview** button at the bottom of the fragment editor window. Voila! Our new dynamic copyright fragment displays correctly as shown in the following screenshot:

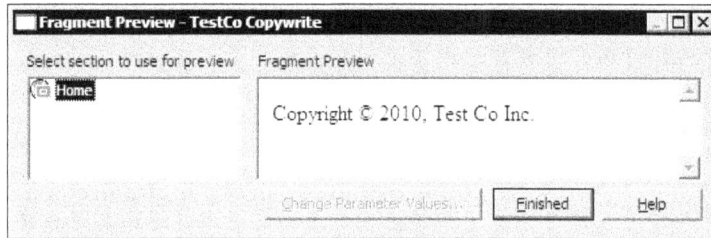

10. Now move the cursor to the bottom of the page and click on our new **Test Co Copyright** fragment to add it to your template.

Perfect! We now have the menu and the footer in place. Seems like a perfect time to drop in some content.

Adding content

Now we'll populate the main area of the page. Let's drop in a region where users can actually change content:

1. Switch your template editor to **DESIGN** tab and move cursor to the place where you'll be inserting a contribution region. Then click on **Insert Region** button on the Contribution Toolbar as shown in the following screenshot:

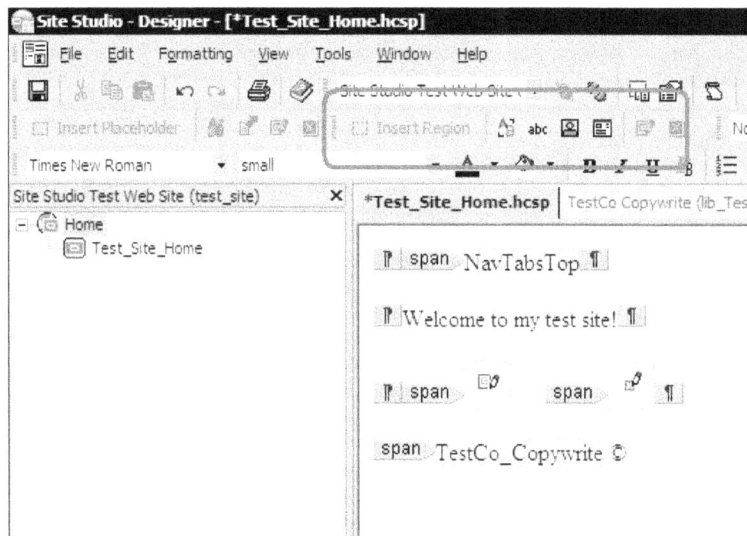

2. **Contribution Region** dialog displays. Give your region a name such as `Main_Page_Content` (see screenshot below). You can also pick the actions you'd like to allow contributors to perform on this content region.

   To continue with this lab, pick the actions exactly as shown below. Here's why:

   - ° **Contributor edit** option allows contributors to launch the web-based editor and update your content.
   - ° **Document info** lets them bring up the Content Information dialog and see metadata values for your contributor data file.
   - ° **Workflow approve** and **Workflow reject** allows designated approvers to approve and reject changes to content items.
   - ° **Switch region content** lets them place another contributor data file in this contribution region.

   I'll tell you more on switching region content — right after the screenshot:

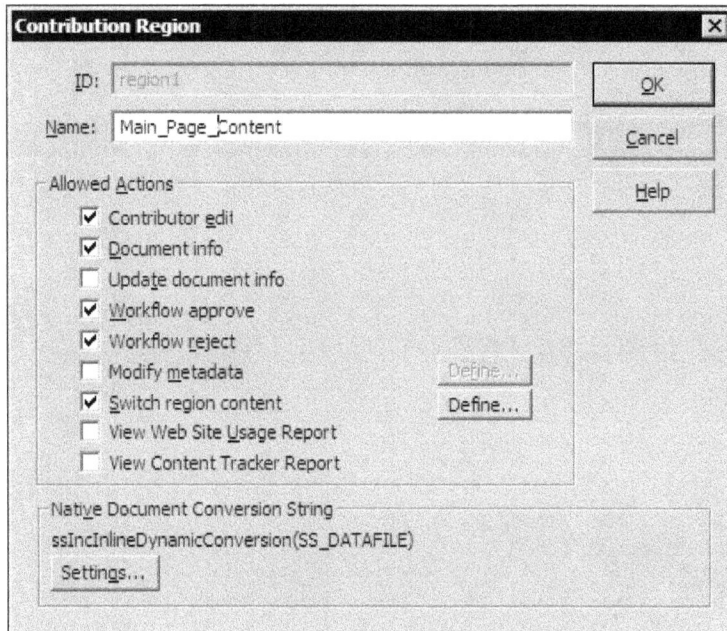

Switch region content option allows users to pick a different Contributor Data File or create a new one. This is useful when some of your pages (on one or more sites) share the same content and you'd like to have just one place to update it. How would you assign the same content to more than one page?

Browse to the page that you'd like to reuse.

When in contributor mode (see later in this chapter on how to get in contributor mode) pick **Document Info** and make a note of the Content ID of contributor data file.

Browse to the page where you'd like to see another copy of this content and pick **Switch Region Content**. Select Existing From Content Server and select the Content ID you memorized in Step 1.

You now have exactly the same contributor data file assigned to more than one region and changes in any one of them will affect all the pages that share it.

3. If you decide to allow your contributors to switch region content, you can further customize the behavior by clicking the **Define** button next to its check box (see the following screenshot):

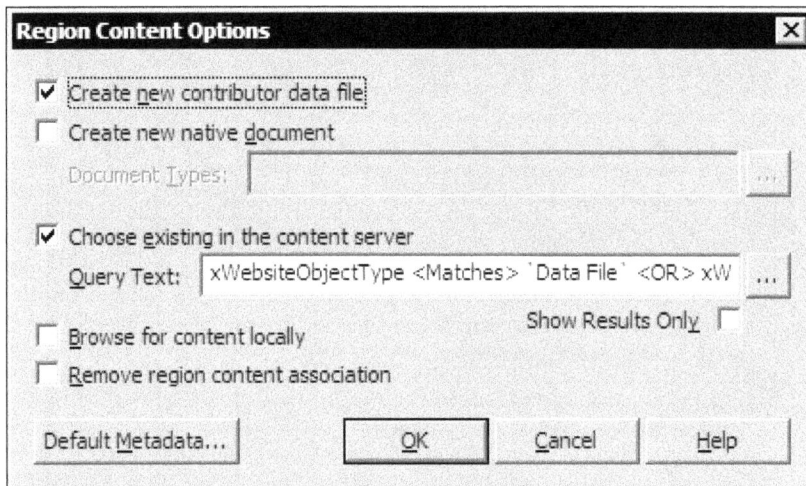

That's great. You now have a contribution region defined, but it takes one more step to let your contributors actually edit the content. You need to insert one or more elements into your region.

4. Place your cursor inside the region and click on **Add Image Element** button on the Contribution toolbar.

5. **Element Definition** dialog pops up. Specify the **Name** (that will show in your template), **Label**, and **Info** (that will show on Contributor interface)- (see the following screenshot):

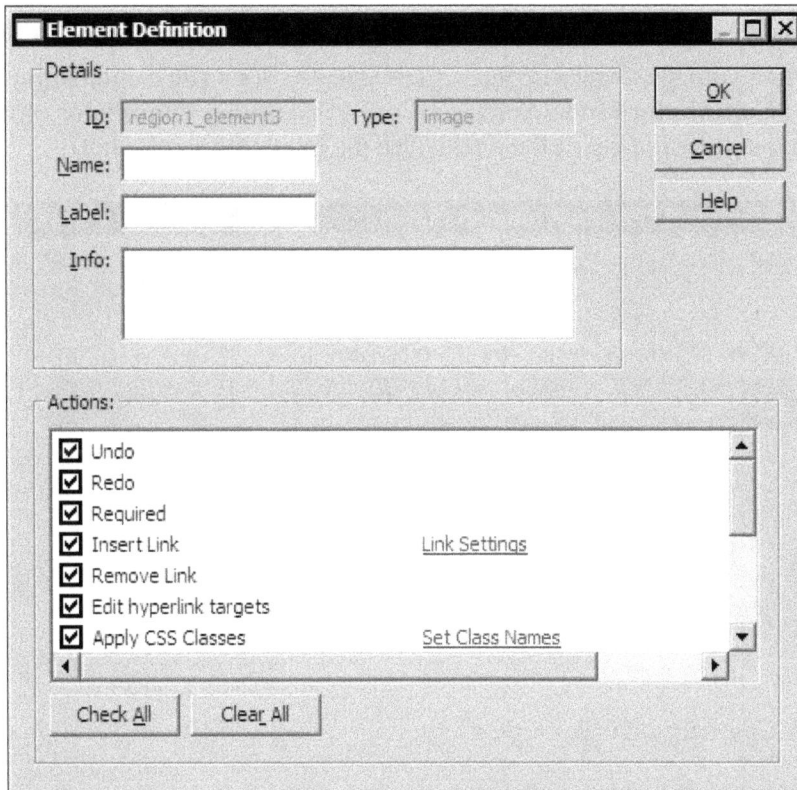

6. **Actions** section of the dialog allows you to enable or disable various actions that contributors can perform from their interface. You can also specify validation rules, such as acceptable image dimensions for the image element.

7. Click on **OK** to continue.

8. Now add a *Plain Text* element right after your Image Element.

We've just hit another milestone. You now have a contribution region defined in your page. Now let's see how it will work from your business user's end.

Using Contributor interface

We're going to view the site from the site's contributor point of view (a contributor is a user who can change content):

1. Save your changes. Right-click on your template and pick **View in Browser**.

2. When your site comes up, click *Ctrl+Shift+F5*. It's a key combination to enter the **Contributor Mode.** You'll see Oracle Site Studio Contributor Mode banner over the top of the screen (see the following screenshot).

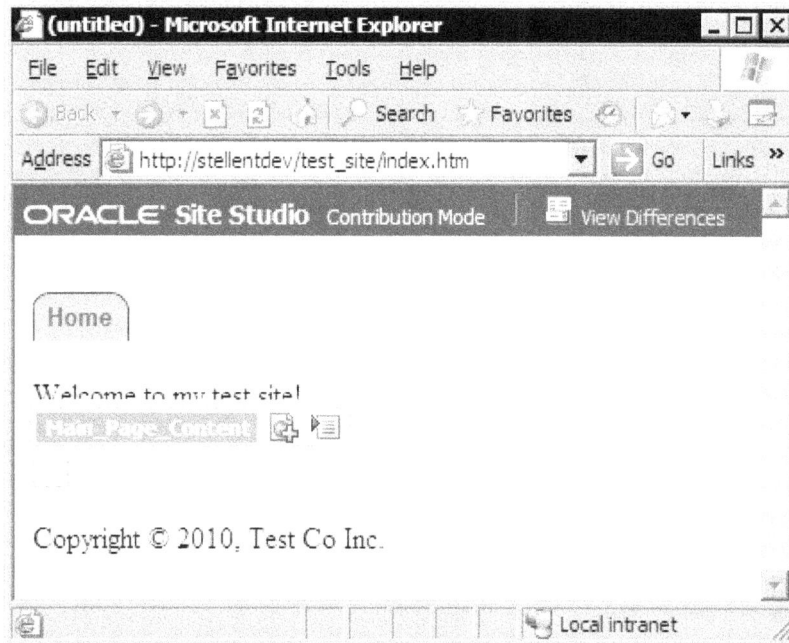

3. Click on the **popup menu** icon (second icon for the region) and pick **Switch Content**.

4. **Switch Content** dialog comes up as shown in the following screenshot:

5. Pick **New Contributor Data File** to create a new file that will hold this region content. Click on **Next** button below. A familiar check in screen comes up. Populate the required fields and click on **Finish** button to complete.

6. You'll now have the **Edit** option appear on the Region Popup Menu. Click on **Edit** to bring up Site Studio Contributor application and add content to your region.

7. Press *Ctrl+Shift+F5* once again to get out of contributor mode. Your page content is now displayed normally (see the following screenshot):

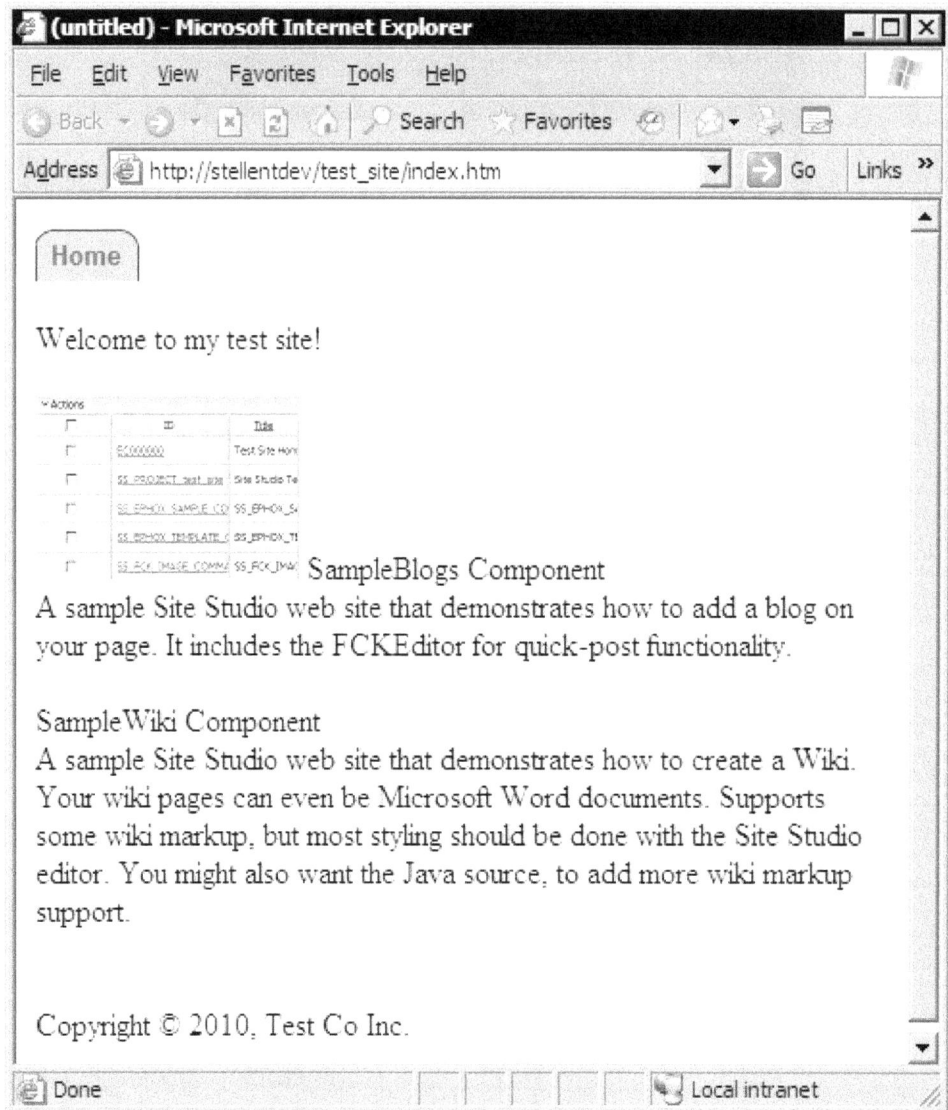

As you can see, the image is inserted in-line with the text. But what if you prefer to lay it out in a table, with image and text each occupying their own column? (see the following screenshot):

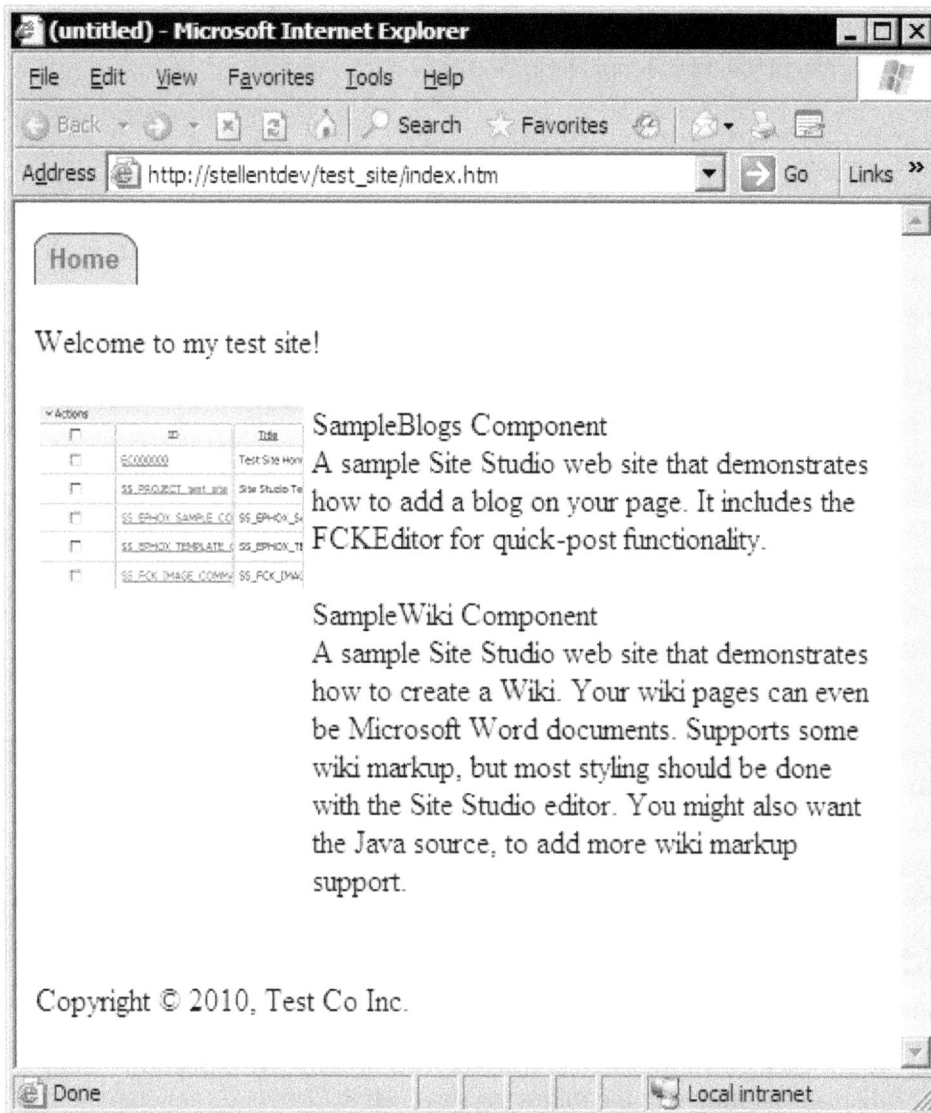

If you try to insert a table in **DESIGN** mode and then move your elements inside the table, you'll get an error message. So how did I do it?

Simple! I just inserted the table in the **SOURCE** view. I found the code that Site Studio inserted for the region (`<!--SS_BEGIN_OPENREGIONMARKER(region1)-->` and so on) and inserted a table inside the region tag, to lay out my contribution elements.

Here's what the finished region code looks like:

```
<!--SS_BEGIN_OPENREGIONMARKER(region1)-->
<!--$SS_REGIONID="region1"-->
<!--$include ss_open_region_definition -->
<!--SS_END_OPENREGIONMARKER(region1)-->

  <table border="0">
      <tr valign="top">
        <td>
            <!--SS_BEGIN_ELEMENT(region1_element1)-->
          <!--$ssIncludeXml(SS_DATAFILE,region1_element1 &
              "/node()")-->
          <!--SS_END_ELEMENT(region1_element1)-->
        </td>
        <td>
            <!--SS_BEGIN_ELEMENT(region1_element2)-->
            <!--$ssIncludeXml(SS_DATAFILE,region1_element2 &
                "/node()")-->
            <!--SS_END_ELEMENT(region1_element2)-->
        </td>
      </tr>
  </table>
<!--SS_BEGIN_CLOSEREGIONMARKER(region1)-->
<!--$include ss_close_region_definition -->
<!--SS_END_CLOSEREGIONMARKER(region1)-->
```

Perfect! And now let's look a little closer at adding new pages.

Adding pages

Let me show you the way that you're likely to be using the most often:

1. Right-click on **Home** node and select **Add Section**. **New Section** Dialog displays as shown in the following screenshot. Give your new navigation section a **Label** and **URL**:

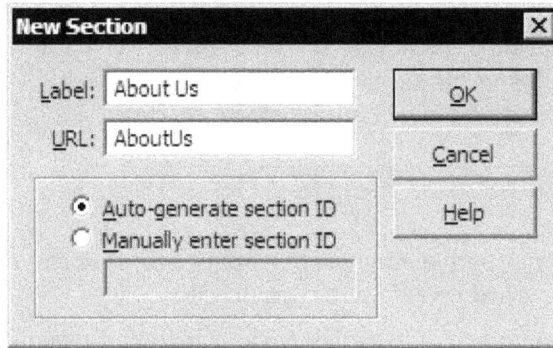

2. Right-click on the new section and pick **Select Primary Page**. **Select Page Template** dialog displays as shown in the following screenshot:

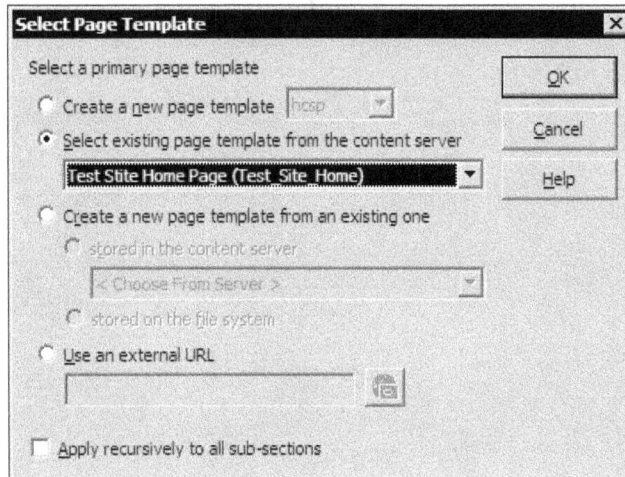

In step seven above I've shown you how to create a new page template, but we haven't explored two other options:

- **Select existing page template from the content server**: This is your most common pick, simply because majority of your website's pages will be sharing a small set of page templates.

- **Create a new page template from an existing page**: This will be your second most common choice, since even when you do need a new page template, you're much better off making a small change to an existing page template, rather than creating a new template from scratch.

Below we're going to try both of these options. Let's begin with the most common one:

1. Pick **Select existing page template from the content server,** pick the template we've just created and click on **OK.**

2. You're almost done. All that's left to do is include this new section in navigation. Until then, it will be hidden and will only show up in the Designer application. Right-click on the new section and pick **Include Section in Navigation** (see the following screenshot)

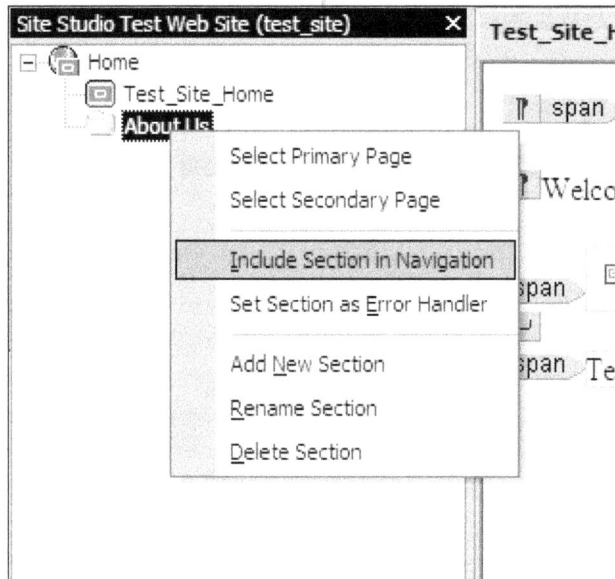

3. Go to **Tools | Update Navigation** and display your new section in a browser (this is a right-mouse context menu on your section's page template). Notice that the top menu fragment now has your new section too (see the following screenshot):

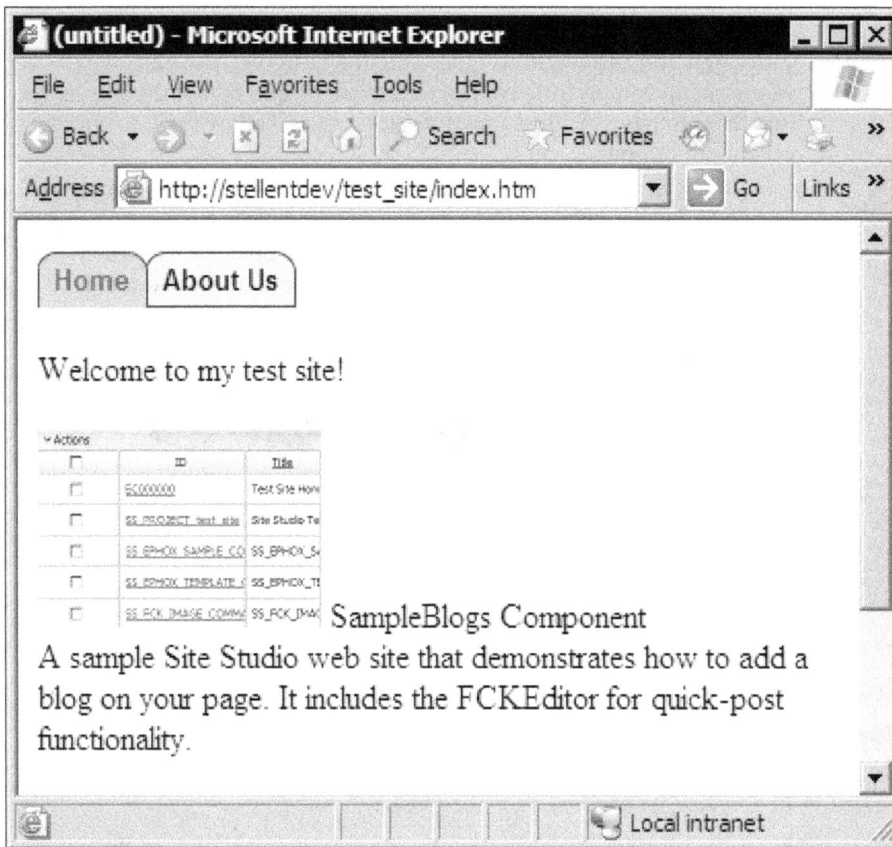

4. And now let's add one more page. This time, let's make a copy and slightly modify our page template. Right-click on **Home** node and add another new section there.

5. Right-click on this new section and pick **Select Primary Page**, but this time, when **Select Page Template** dialog shows up, pick **Create a new page template from an existing page**.

6. Once you're done creating new page template, double-click on it to open it for editing. Delete **Image** and **Plain Text** elements from your contribution region, and instead place a **WYSIWYG** element there (See *Adding Content* section above if you need a refresher on adding regions and elements).

7. Take a moment to study **Element Definition** screen (see the following screenshot). It gives you options to enable or disable each individual control on WYSIWIG Rich Text Editor.

Notice how much power this gives you, the designer. You can give people as much or as little control over the look and feel of the site, as you trust them to have. At the same time, you can still allow them to edit the content of your page.

For instance, if you prefer to control your fonts and styles with the CSS, you can only allow them to type text, insert links and, maybe, make text bold. They won't be able to change the font, insert pictures or in some other way affect the consistency of your look and feel, and your site accessibility.

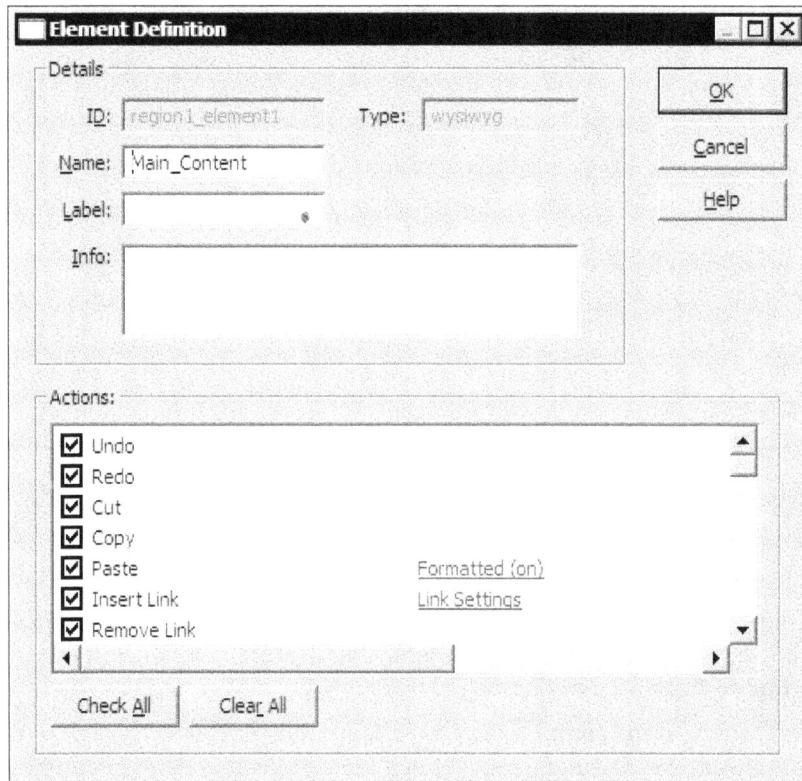

8. Display your new page in a browser. Go into Contributor mode and pick **Assign Content**. Create new Contributor data file and then edit the element.

9. Rich Text Editor will come up, letting you to edit and format text, insert links and pictures, and paste rich text from other applications (see the following screenshot below):

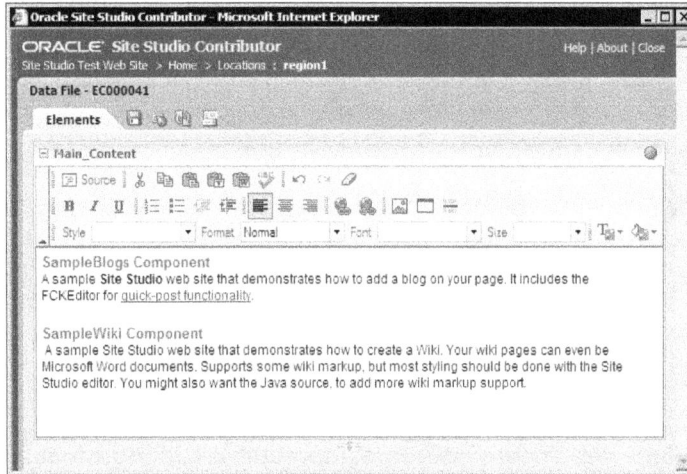

10. Once you done editing, click on the save icon on the top of the dialog (right below the element's content ID). Notice how your rich text content is now part of the page (see the following screenshot):

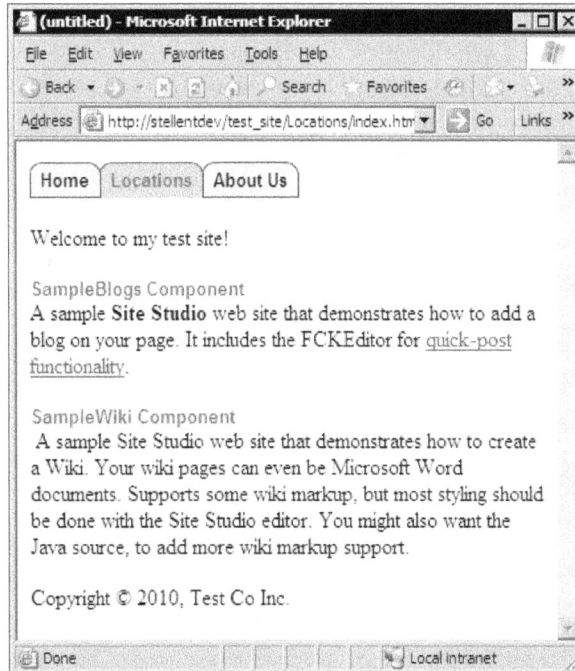

Congratulations! You've completed the Web Content Management tutorial and now ready to begin working on a real-life website of your own. WCM is large enough of a subject to fill up an entire book; so inevitably, you will be bumping onto additional features and ways to do things that we haven't covered in this quick introduction.

But we did accomplish the most important objective—if you followed the chapters of this book, you now understand the core WCM structure elements, how they fit together and how you can use them. With that knowledge under your belt, it will be easy to pick up the rest of WCM features and techniques.

But don't just believe me. Test for yourself. Get comfortable with this tutorial, then scan through the **Oracle Site Studio Designer Guide** and see if any of the features get you baffled. They won't. You'll be well prepared.

When you done with that, the next topic you might consider checking out is the **Technical Reference Guide** for deeper level technical information on Site Studio file structures and iDoc scripting guide.

And we're not done yet. There's one more important WCM topic that I'd like to walk you through. I want you to have a solid understanding of Site Studio Publishing Models.

Understanding the publishing model

Your **Publishing Model** is the framework you choose to have your content delivered. For instance, if you let your end users (your content **consumers**) simply browse your site on the Content Server—you're using *Dynamic Publishing Model*. And if they're browsing a static HTML version of your website, you're looking at *Static Publishing*. Essentially, there are three publishing models; Static, Dynamic, and the Native. Let me show you the features and benefits of each.

Static publishing

There are cases when it can be highly beneficial to have your site published as static HTML. Your contributors can work on a site inside your company's firewall and then have it published onto your public webserver, outside of the firewall. If that public server gets compromised, the hacker will leave empty-handed. There's nothing there, but public content. Your protected sensitive content was not published at all and stayed behind in your Content Server.

There's also another major benefit to this model. Even though a Content Server can be very fast serving content, nothing beats plain and simple static HTML content delivery. So that can also be your choice if you deal with very high traffic sites.

If you decide to explore Static publishing, you'll need to install and use Oracle Site Studio Publisher tool. This is a crawler that scans your site for changes as often as you specify and keeps your static HTML version updated. It can also deliver this copy to another server for you through FTP and other options.

> Site Studio Publisher is being given a big overhaul in soon-to-be-released v.11g, so be sure to claim your free newsletter subscription, and keep up to date on this and many other important UCM features, see the *Preface* or *Appendix A* for instructions on how to subscribe.

And now let's look at Native Publishing Model.

Native publishing

We briefly touched on Native Publishing in our WCM tutorial. If all you're trying to do is simply publish a copy of your existing documents on the Web, Native Publishing can save you a ton of money, rework and frustration. It allows you to eliminate multiple copies of the same document. There's no need to get your webmaster to create and maintain HTML copies of your business documents, just so you can publish them on the Web.

Simply assign your original documents to contribution regions as Native Documents and have Content Server convert them to HTML on the fly for you. (You'll need Oracle Dynamic Converter, an add-on you can download as part of Oracle Document Management bundle).

And now let's take a look at our last (and very popular) publishing model, Dynamic Publishing.

Dynamic publishing

Once again, if you let your site visitors (content consumers) to browse directly off your Content Server, you're running a Dynamic Publishing model. You then must be concerned about security and, if your site is public-facing and attracts thousands of visitors, capacity and performance may also become a concern.

Content Server Planning and Implementation Guide shows you multiple deployment scenarios, that let you come up with the exact Content Server and WCM configuration to suite your organization's needs.

In my opinion, the most popular Dynamic publishing scenario is the **Contribution-Consumption architecture**. Here's how it works.

Using contribution-consumption architecture

Let's say, you website lives in a main Content Server instance, and you need to dynamically publish it to the world. Instead of exposing your Content Server (and your sensitive content) to the world, you can use a second Content Server instance (a **Consumption Server**) that will only have your read — only publically available content for extranet or public web consumption. Your main Content Server (your **Contribution Server**) will have all of your content and will push content onto the Consumption Server with Archiver Replication. This approach offers a number of important benefits:

- It allows you to isolate your public-facing Consumption Server and leave your sensitive content in your Contribution Server behind the firewall.

- It helps you increase performance by reducing the amount of content available in your Consumption Server (only a subset of content is published and only the latest revisions).

- You can further increase your performance and site capacity by installing a reverse proxy in front of your consumption server, and using longer `max age` values. You may not be able to do this on your contribution server, where content contributors must always see the changes that they make right away.

So there you have it. You're now aware of the publishing models. And here's the question that nearly every one of our clients is concerned about: What about Web 2.0?. Features such as RSS Feeds, Blogs, Wiki, Team Calendars, and portlets are now on every organization's wish list.

So, let's see how you too can use these Web 2.0 features on your project.

Adding online collaboration

If you were browsing through fragments in a Designer, looking for RSS feeds, Blogs and Wikis, you were probably disappointed. They are not there! Why?

Years before online collaboration became main stream; Stellent had a product called Collaboration Manager (You can still download and install it. It's a Content Server component). It gives you project workspaces, online discussions and another, more traditional security model.

But now Oracle offers a new, by far more superior product for all of your online collaboration needs. The name of the product is **Oracle WebCenter**. Let's take a closer look.

Using Oracle WebCenter

WebCenter is the new Oracle product that's coming in to replace the old Collaboration Manager. It offers personal and team workspaces, portlets, killer collaboration features such as blogs, wiki, RSS, and more—all out of the box.

And yes, it has UCM integration built in. So if you need to use online collaboration, I encourage you to evaluate WebCenter (An evaluation version is available from Oracle for free download). Even better—WebCenter license may even be included into your UCM Suite license and it might not cost you an extra dime (Check your paperwork or contact Oracle Representative to be sure).

But what if all you need is one simple RSS feed or a blog or just one Wiki library and you're not up to learning a new product just yet? In this case you may consider using these free UCM sample components.

Finding UCM sample components

There is a number of sample Stellent components available for free download. Below are the three most popular.

RSS feeds

This component adds RSS feed support to Content Server searches, workflows and to Site Studio static and dynamic lists. Component comes with samples and documentation. To download it Google: "Sample Components for Universal Content Management", and search for "RSS Feeds".

Then there are blogs and wiki components.

Blogs and wiki components

Blogs and Wiki samples were too once provided by Oracle but are no longer available for download. My guess is that Oracle is trying to encourage people to use WebCenter product instead. But, like I said before, if you need to add a blog or a wiki to your site in a hurry, you may consider these samples (both are well documented). At the time of this writing, Brian (Bex) Huff is still keeping a copy of them at his site at: `http://bezzotech.com/library`.

Below are the actual component names and short functionality descriptions from Brian's site:

- **SampleBlogs Component**: A sample Site Studio website that demonstrates how to add a blog on your page. It includes the CK Editor for quick-post functionality.

- **SampleWiki Component**: A sample Site Studio website that demonstrates how to create a Wiki (Wiki pages can even be Microsoft Word documents). Supports some wiki markup, but most styling should be done with the Site Studio editor. You might also want the Java source, to add more wiki markup support.

And here's another good excuse to go ahead and try these components — they are a great way to master Site Studio development even further.

Below is the third popular source of Oracle UCM components.

Fishbowl Oracle UCM Component Repository

Fishbowl Solutions maintains a library of reusable UCM components. Some are free and some are available at nominal costs. Check them out at: `http://www.fishbowlsolutions.com/StellentSolutions.`

That's it. We've covered all the bases to give you a running start with the Site Studio and Web Content Management. All that's left to see is this brief, important recap of what you've learned.

Summary

In this chapter you learned how to build websites with Web Content Management. You've seen the exact steps to install Site Studio components and how to build your first website. You've learned about the publishing models and seven forgotten but blazingly obvious website planning steps that will make your efforts wickedly effective. We've also surveyed the landscape of Oracle online collaboration tools, and found the quick shortcuts that can get you up and running in a short afternoon.

This concludes our journey. Following this chapter, be sure to review the *Appendix A* that gives you the important big picture of entire Oracle UCM product offering, and your critical next steps that will take you to an even higher level in your Oracle projects and your own career.

A
Exploring Oracle UCM Product Offering

We've just finished looking at the Web Content Management and Site Studio suite of products. In previous chapters we used a lot of tools that help us build, administer, and manage the Content Server. Did we cover all of the UCM?

Nope. But we learned its foundation and its two most popular modules: Document Management (ECM) and Web Content Management (WCM). And the chances are — you won't need to learn any other UCM modules. But even if this is the case, you will still benefit by understanding what other products and modules are included, and the fastest ways to go about mastering them.

So let's look at all of the products that make up Oracle Universal Content Management.

UCM product line up

Essentially, there are five groups of products. We will look at each one in more detail, so you will always be sure that you use the right tool for the job at hand. The first one we should look at is the ECM.

Enterprise content management

The ECM (also known as Document Management) is a set of tools you'll use to add full text search, revisions, granular access control, workflow, easy web publishing, and more to your existing content. Many organizations use it to transition from paper documents in file cabinets, e-mail, file shares, and other legacy document management systems. It helps business users find the right documents fast—just when they need them, and cut down on wasteful paper processes. It also makes their content more secure and better protected against an accidental loss.

Document Management Group includes the following products:

- **Content Integration APIs**: This includes Java toolsets (Custom Components, CIS, RIDC and so on) for extending ECM functionality and for remote communication with UCM, and WSDL Generator for using any SOAP-aware tool to consume UCM services (We looked at these tools in more detail in *Chapter 10, Customizing Oracle UCM*).

- **Desktop Integration Suite**: This allows you to integrate Virtual Folders with Windows Desktop and Microsoft Office (We explored the CIS in *Chapter 6, Understanding Virtual Folders and WebDAV*).

- **Dynamic Converter**: This allows you to convert business documents into web pages for everyone to see, without the need to use applications that created them. You can include MS Office, AutoCAD drawings, and hundreds of other proprietary file formats on your site—and never worry about your end users needing to have an appropriate viewer on their machines to open them. Dynamic Converter is also a core of the *Native Publishing Model* that we discussed in more details in *Chapter 11, Web Content Management and Collaboration*. You can find more info on Oracle Dynamic Converter section on the online UCM Documentation Library.

- **Content Conversion Server** (Also known as **Inbound Refinery**): This is a standalone server product that converts content between different file formats. It can also create preview thumbnails. Unlike dynamic converter, that converts documents on demand, Inbound Refinery performs its conversion during the check-in process. More information is available in *Inbound Refinery Administration Guide*.

- **PDF Converter**: This is a Content Conversion Server add-in that allows you to automatically generate PDF version of a document on check in. (More information available in *PDF Converter Installation and Administration Guide*).

- **PDF Watermark**: This is an optional Content Server add-on to add dynamic, configurable watermarks to the PDF documents generated by the PDF Converter. More information is available from *PDFWatermark Installation and Administration Guide*.

- **Content Categorizer**: This is a Content Server add-on that suggests metadata values for the documents being checked in, based on their content and other business rules. You can also use it to mass-update existing content. You can find more information from *Content Categorizer Administration Guide* – from the UCM Documentation page.

- **Content Tracker**: This is another Content Server add-on that allows you to gather detailed usage information and generate reports – for auditing and monitoring purposes. Learn more about it from *Content Tracker Administration Guide*.

- **Web Parts for SharePoint**: These are there to integrate documents stored in Content Server directly into MS SharePoint interface (Supported SharePoint versions are 2003 and 2007).

- **UCM Need To Know Component (NTK)**: This delivers security enhancements and allows you to alter Content Server security model based on business rules (See *Need to Know Component Administration Guide* for more information).

- **UCM Clean Content Component**: This allows you to scan for and remove unwanted parts of MS Office documents that are known to cause security risks. (Things such as hidden text and slides, database queries, sensitive hyperlinks, weak protections, and others. For more information Google for "Oracle Clean Content SDK").

- **Archiver Replication Exceptions**: This helps you to prevent failed imports from stopping replication. It captures such failed imports into "exceptions" archive and sends out an e-mail to system administrator.

- **Collaboration Manager**: This gives you project workspaces, online discussions and another, more traditional security model. However, Collaboration Manager is an older product and I highly recommend that you look into using the Oracle Web Center instead.

- **File Store Provider** (new in 10gR3): This allows you to store your content in a database, instead of a traditional file system. This new approach gives you several important advantages. See *Chapter 7, Under the hood*, for more information.

- **Folders and WebDAV**: The Content Server extra that adds support for Virtual Folders. Please see *Chapter 6*, for more information.

- **Folder Structure Archive Component**: This allows you to selectively export and migrate just the folders you want, as opposed to exporting an entire virtual folder tree. See *Chapter 9, Migrating Configuration*, for more information.

- **Content Folios**: This adds support for compound documents. They let you handle multiple related documents as one–just like a ZIP file, but with a lot more useful features. See *Content Folios User Guide* for more information.

- **Web Forms Editor**: This provides a visual design environment for Hypertext Content Server Files (HCSFs) and iDoc resource files. See *Chapter 10* for more information on Web Forms Editor.

That's all for the Document Management, and if that's not enough, let's move on to Web Content Management.

Web content management

The WCM allows you to use your content in dynamic websites. It's an add-on module that goes on top of the Content Server. You'll need ECM to run WCM.

It also gives you a full featured HTML editor such as FrontPage or Dreamweaver that allows you to create elaborate, efficient and easy to manage websites. All web pages, images and documents will be stored Content Server (See *Chapter 11* for a detailed introduction to Oracle Web Content Management).

Additional modules we have not covered so far include:

- **Oracle Connection Server** is an efficient tool for publishing (and delivering) content to one or more destinations. It can use FTP and other industry standard protocols, pull and push models, and can apply transformations to content while it's being delivered. More information is available in *Oracle Connection Server Administration Guide*.

- **Oracle Site Studio** is a suite of tools for creating killer dynamic websites, driven by Content Server. Refer to *Chapter 11* for more information on the Site Studio.

- **Oracle Site Studio Publisher** (Site Studio Publishing Utility) is a server product that allows you to publish dynamic Site Studio websites as static HTML, so they can be hosted outside of Content Server. See *Chapter 11* for more information on Static Publishing Model and *Oracle Site Studio Publisher Administration Guide* for more information on SSPU.

- **Oracle Content Publisher** is another alternative for publishing business documents on the Web. Just like the Native publishing model in Oracle Site Studio, it allows you to focus on your business documents and have the Content Publisher generate HTML versions for publishing on the Web. And just like the Site Studio, it also uses Oracle Dynamic Converter to generate web-viewable rendition of over 200 different file formats.

Content Publisher or Site Studio?

Content Publisher that ships with Oracle Content Conversion Sever, is an earlier product and is better suited for less complex websites. Consider using it if all you need is to publish your business documents on the Web.

On the other hand, Site Studio allows contributors to come in and manage their own content directly on the site. And it gives you, the designer, a great degree of flexibility to create powerful dynamic websites and build a library of reusable dynamic fragments.

While Site Studio is almost always my first choice over the Content Publisher but when it comes to Native Publishing, I love the **Tutorial** and **Seven Easy Lessons** guides that come with the Content Publisher product. Remember, both tools use Dynamic Converter and you will be creating Dynamic Converter templates exactly the same way — no matter which tool will you end up using.

- **Content Portlet Suite** is a developer toolkit that allows integrating dynamic content and Content Server workflows into various enterprise portals. CPS supports WebLogic, WebSphere, Sun One, Plumtree, and WSRP (Web Services For Remote Portlets). More information is available from *Oracle Content Portlet Suite Developer Guide.*

- Oracle Web Center is a companion product to the UCM suite that offers best in class online collaboration features, such as team workspaces, blogs, wikis, and portlets. You can find more information about the Web Center at its website — Google for Oracle "Web Center".

- Third-party companion products that compliment UCM and WCM functionality. They address common concerns and slash the time (and the budget) you need for WCM implementations. The most useful, in my humble opinion, is the Site Studio Toolbox™ and other Oracle UCM components available from Fishbowl Solutions (Check their website at: www.fishbowlsolutions.com for the full catalog of components and more information).

That's all for the Web Content Management. The next UCM product group we shall look at is the URM.

Universal records management

The URM allows you to control retention and disposition of a sensitive content that requires life cycle management and long-term preservation. Oracle URM is one of the top players in the Records Management market and is DOD 5015.2 and .4 certified.

Oracle URM contains these modules:

- **Records Manager** (Corporate and DoD Editions) is a Content Server add-on that implements URM functionality for electronic content. Find more information about the Records Manager in *Oracle Universal Records Manager* section in online documentation page.

- **Physical Content Manager** is the URM module that allows you to keep track of physical records, such as file folders, boxes, CD, and tape media and so on. It can be integrated with bar code scanners so you could easily identify the actual physical items. More information is available in *Physical Content Manager Administration Guide*.

- **URM Adapters** help you extend the retention, disposition, and litigation support of the URM to other Enterprise Content Management systems. While content continues to reside in external systems, such as Documentum, FileNet, or SharePoint, its life cycle is now controlled by the URM. The adapters also send information back to the URM server so it can keep track of all record content in the entire enterprise. More information is available in the **Oracle** *Universal Records Manager Adapters* section of online documentation page.

And this completes the Universal Records Management group of products. But we're not through yet. The next UCM product group is Oracle IPM.

Imaging and process management

Imaging and Process Management (IPM) enables image capture via Oracle Document Capture and Oracle Distributed Document Capture. It also offers OCR, full text search, annotation, and mark-up of images, routing, and approvals.

It also provides means of organizing and searching documents across the enterprise—regardless of where are they stored or what application they came from. IPM includes adapters for Oracle E-Business (BPEL), PeopleSoft, and IPM SDK.

You can find more information about Oracle IPM in the *Oracle Imaging and Process Management* section of online documentation site.

And there is one more UCM module left to look at. Let's look at Oracle IRM.

Information rights management

Oracle IRM is there to encrypt and secure sensitive content when it's not in repository — inside or outside the firewall. It allows organizations to retain control over their sensitive information — even after it has been shared, track content that was forwarded to various internal and external audiences, prevent unauthorized access and revoke it when required.

The software itself has two components:

- **IRM Server** that stores decryption keys and information rights.
- **IRM Desktop** — lightweight client that must be installed on every computer that will be using sealed documents, created with Oracle IRM.

You can find more information about IRM in *Oracle Information Rights Management* section of online documentation site.

And now that you've seen an entire Oracle UCM product offering, let's see a few more easy steps you can take to bump your UCM expertise to an even higher bracket.

Your secret to mastering Oracle UCM in just minutes a day

You've just finished the Oracle UCM Handbook and its about the time for me to reveal the biggest of my secrets — the one powerful enough to help you achieve any one of your learning objectives, no matter how ambitious or even outlandish they may seem.

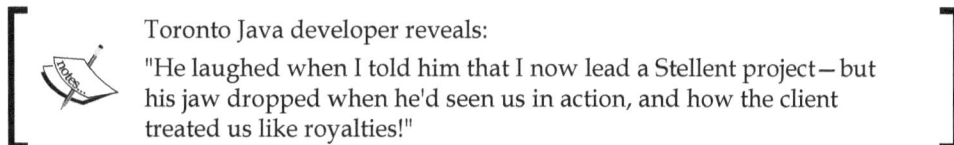

> Toronto Java developer reveals:
>
> "He laughed when I told him that I now lead a Stellent project — but his jaw dropped when he'd seen us in action, and how the client treated us like royalties!"

This may well be one of the most important sections in the entire book. Here's what it is all about.

Many regard me as one of the most respected names in Oracle UCM, but it hasn't always been that way. Listen, just over five short years ago, I've accepted a team lead role at a large Stellent Web Content Management migration project for a local government, without any formal Stellent experience! (I've been somewhat involved with the Content Server for about a month, but that was it.) Oh, and I forgot to tell you that the project was in a serious crisis!

A couple of months after I started, I've bumped into a manager I used to work with at my previous place. He asked what am I up to and I told him. He grinned and said that he heard how much of a "kludge" the Stellent was and how sorry he feels for me. So what did I say?

I took him for lunch the next day but I asked him to meet me in the building! I used an excuse to bring him upstairs and introduced him to my team, my boss, and the client.

Man it was priceless! Just watching his jaw drop alone made all of my sleepless nights well worth it! So how did I do that?

I wasn't tricking him and I couldn't possibly learn that fast just by reading documentation and bugging Stellent Support. So what was my secret?

It wasn't luck and I didn't have to stop sleeping and eating and just work. Nope. My secret took me from an average Java developer from the trenches to the forefront of a foreign field. And the secret is simply this:

I've been learning from the best of the best.

I bet you've heard this one before! So why so few people out there are are using it?

Well, how would you tell the good guys from the charlatans? And how would you sift through the tons of daily blog posts, tweets, and status updates when most of them are not even related to Oracle UCM? Will reading a lengthily post about the health of the guru's cat take you any closer to Stellent mastery?

I took a massive step forward to help you answer the first question—identify the "good guys". In *Appendix B*, the Oracle UCM Resource Directory, I've compiled a list of some 42 blogs, article directories, websites, and magazines you can rely on for continuous flow of insider information, but who can follow 42 sites on a regular basis?

Well, I wouldn't be writing this section, a week before the book's publication, at 2:00 in the AM if I didn't have a real working shortcut you can take.

So here's what I've done to thank you for investing in this book, I've set aside your own private and personal spot in the Independent Oracle UCM Knowledge Center. Claim it and you will accomplish these three important objectives:

- You will receive important updates to this book's content—especially timely and critical now, when the new UCM 11g is finally out, and everyone is anxious to see what has changed.
- You will stay abreast of the new tools, features, and techniques, no matter whether or not they were covered in this book at all.

- You will stay motivated about mastering Oracle UCM and reaping the maximum benefit it can give your organization and your career.

It's tough to make yourself learn something new every day, and many people run out of enthusiasm almost immediately. So why not try the other way? Why not simply subscribe to an e-mail list and let the publisher do the hard work? All you need to do is look over the tips, tricks, and trade secrets you receive right in your in-box, and use them to your advantage.

One day I'll ask you to read a short article. The other day, it will be a three minute screen cast video, and before you know it, you will find yourself in the top ranks of Oracle UCM.

Stop by `www.stellentexperts.com/handbook` and pick up your free subscription.

I promise, you won't see any family stories, stock market updates, or rants about my new car. Just the short, to-the-point tips and tricks — hot from the frontline trenches of Oracle UCM. Tips and tricks you can immediately apply and benefit, just the meat and no filler material.

So don't delay. Grab your subscription while you're still thinking about it. You will be glad you did.

Sincerely,

Dmitri Khanine

P.S. You are not risking anything by subscribing to this free exclusive newsletter. Your e-mail address will never be sold, traded or misused, and you can unsubscribe at any time. You have nothing to lose and everything to gain. Don't risk missing out on this great career booster. Subscribe now, while this information is still fresh in your mind.

B

Detailed Oracle UCM Resource Directory

If you ever wanted to achieve your professional goals with a technology (any technology, not just Oracle UCM) a good book can help you hit the ground running, but you will need to tap into a constant flow of insider information to get on top and stay there. You may simply rely on your free newsletter subscription at: `www.stellentexperts.com/handbook` or, if you prefer to form an independent opinion and don't mind doing a bit of extra work—below I'm giving you a complete (to the best of my knowledge) list of Oracle UCM resources—everything from industry's most respected names to trusted service providers. More specifically, I'm giving you:

- **Free online resources**: Blogs and article sites that you can scan for tips and tricks, early insights and technology reviews. I'm further dividing those into UCM-specific resources, general Oracle resources, and those covering an entire field of Information Management.

- **Publications and periodicals**: A (much shorter) list of UCM-related books, magazines, and whitepapers you may want to consider reading.

- **Trusted service providers**: An even shorter list of system integrators and training providers that has been around and consistently receiving good feedback from their clients.

All lists are alphabetical.

Let's start with the free online resources.

Free online resources

Once again, I'm splitting this category into UCM-specific resources — blogs, article sites, and discussion forums that focus on Oracle UCM and related technologies, Generic Oracle resources and, an even broader category of those, who lead the way in Information Management.

Obviously, I'd like to begin with the UCM-specific sites.

Oracle UCM—specific resources

Below is an alphabetic list of resources with my brief comments and/or publisher's own descriptions.

Name and URL	Description
Bex Huff http://bexhuff.com	Brian "Bex" Huff is the author of the first Developer's book on Stellent UCM (back in 2006, when it was not owned by Oracle, I'm recommending this book later in this chapter). Brian's site offers a great collection of resources on Oracle UCM, Oracle Fusion Middleware, and some life hacks too.
C4 Blog http://cfour. fishbowlsolutions.com	C4 stands for Content, Collaboration, Context, and Community. This is a blog run by Fishbowl Solutions. With over a decade of Oracle Universal Content Management (Stellent) expertise, Fishbowl is happy to share some of that expertise with you! Many of its best and brightest consultants are contributing to this blog, so that you can make better decisions, faster, and continue to do more.
Content Management Simplified blog http://cmstechie.blogspot.com	From time to time, this blogs offers some good, from-the-trenches tips for Oracle UCM developers.
David Roe' Content on Content Management http:// contentoncontentmanagement. com	David's primary focus is implementing Oracle Content Server. His blog is a great resource for developers, who focus on customization and system integration.

Name and URL	Description

EnterpriseTwoDotOh
 	
`http://blogs.oracle.com/`
`EnterpriseTwoDotOh`
	This blog offers great insider tips from the trenches, by an Oracle Employee and UCM practitioner.

FusionECM blog
 	
`http://blogs.oracle.com/`
`fusionecm`
	Another Oracle blog run by John Brunswick. John is an Enterprise 2.0 Solution Consultant at Oracle, specializing in enterprise portal and content management solutions. He is passionate about both business and technology.
	
	This blog provides technical strategy and tips to help customers make the most of their technology investments.

Independent Oracle UCM Knowledge Center
 	
`http://stellentexperts.com/`
`blog`
	Right and wrong UCM strategies — and little pointers that keep your projects on track.

John Sim' Blue Studios
 	
`http://www.bluestudios.co.uk/`
`blog`
	John offers frequent technical posts on Oracle UCM, WebCenter, and some free Content Server components.

Kyle Hatlestad's blog `http://blogs.oracle.com/kyle`	Kyle Hatlestad works in the Enterprise Solutions Group at Oracle and focuses on Content Management and Enterprise 2.0 products. Kyle is an old-timer who came to Oracle through the acquisition of Stellent in 2007.

Michael Caruana's WebMonkeyMagic blog
 	
`http://webmonkeymagic.`
`blogspot.com`
	WebMonkeyMagic is a blog that helps web developers who are using Oracle UCM with SiteStudio. It's like a journal of tips and tricks that Michael discovered firsthand. He also talks about Content Server administration and offers plenty of advice for maintaining and configuring the system.

Oracle ECM Alerts blog
 	
`http://blogs.oracle.com/`
`ecmalerts`
	This is an internal Oracle blog, run (in part) by Shahid Rashid from the ECM (UCM) Product Management Team.
	
	This blog's areas of coverage include records management across the US, Europe, and Asia, SharePoint integration, email, eDiscovery, compliance, and partnerships.

Name and URL	Description

Oracle Fusion Middleware Technology blog
 	
`http://blogs.oracle.com/`
`garyniu`
	Another Oracle blog, run by Gary Niu—focusing on UCM and Oracle WebCenter.

Redstone CMS blogs
 	
`http://www.corecontentonly.`
`com` and
 	
`http://businessvalue.`
`corecontentonly.com`
	This is a technical blog with a primary focus in Oracle UCM, Enterprise 2.0 and Portals, and Service-Oriented Architecture.
	
	Redstone's business blog that covers the topics of interest to the business user community.

Software Development and Technical Expertise for ECM blogs
`http://`
`softwaredevelopmentforecm.`
`wordpress.com`
and
`http://ecmtechnicalexpertise.`
`wordpress.com`
	These blogs run by software developers at Image Source Consultancy with posts mostly focusing on Oracle Imaging and Business Process Management (IPM), and general Web Development tools and techniques.

Oracle UCM Discussion Forums

Below is an alphabetic listing of places where you can post your UCM-related questions and participate in technical discussions online.

Name and URL	Description
AIIM Communities `http://aiimcommunities.org`	AIIM is the community that provides education, research, and best practices to help organizations find control, and optimize their information. They also organize and sponsor a number of popular industry events. This site is focused on Enterprise 2.0, Electronic Records Management, and more. You will find wiki, blogs, buyer's guides, and online discussions here.

Name and URL	Description
IOUG' Oracle Content Management SIG http://www.ioug.org	Shortly after Stellent acquisition by Oracle, Independent Oracle User Group (IOUG) set up the Oracle Content Management Special Interest Group (Stellent SIG). It provides a forum and open discussion, related to UCM products. This is a mailing list you can subscribe to — for gaining an insight about the top IOUG Stellent-related events, and you can ask questions too! Just go to: www.ioug.org and search for Stellent.
Minnesota Stellent User Group http://www.mnsug.com	Minnesota Stellent User Group (MNSUG) is a forum designed for the exchange of knowledge and ideas to enhance the Stellent user's experience. It is one of the oldest user groups for Stellent and Oracle UCM products.
Oracle Forums http://forums.oracle.com	This is the Oracle's own online community. Go to **User Interaction and Content Management** and click on **More...** link to access the **Enterprise Content Management** forum.
Oracle MIX http://mix.oracle.com	Oracle Mix provides social networking, idea sharing, groups, and more for the Oracle community. I suggest you check out the **Enterprise Content Management** (ECM) and **Enterprise 2.0** (E2.0) groups. ECM Group is for people interested in Oracle Enterprise Content Management such as UCM, Oracle Content Server, Beehive, DAM, and IRM — for sharing their knowledge, ideas, complains, problems, and challenges. Enterprise 2.0 group is for those interested in applying collaboration and web 2.0 techniques in the corporate world.
Yahoo intradoc_users · Stellent Users Group http://tech.groups.yahoo.com/group/intradoc_users	This is the oldest (dating back to 1999) Stellent and Oracle UCM online discussion forum I know about. The group facilitates an open discussion on all technical aspects of UCM implementation, development, and customization.

Social networking groups

Below is a partial listing of UCM-related discussion groups formed inside many popular social networks. Some of those are UCM-specific and some have more general focus.

Name and URL	Description
AIIM Linked In group http://www.linkedin.com/groups?gid=3698	This group is focused on helping organizations find, control, and optimize their information — intelligent information management. Focus areas: document management, imaging, records management, web content management, workflow, and collaboration.
Content Management Professionals Facebook group http://www.facebook.com/group.php?gid=2380373544	Content Management Professionals is the worldwide organization for people who want to learn more about content management from other professionals.
Oracle UCM Facebook group http://www.facebook.com/group.php?gid=6301164132	A group for people who know and use Oracle UCM and would like to leverage the network of information. Also a good way to keep tabs on people and projects that are happening around the world of UCM.
Stellent and Oracle UCM Linked in group http://www.linkedin.com/groups?gid=51413	This group is for architects and developers with experience using Oracle UCM.
WebCenter Linked In group http://www.linkedin.com/groups?gid=2256274	This is a place where you can discuss all the aspects of Oracle WebCenter Suite.

Resources on Oracle technologies

Name and URL	Description
Angelo Santagata's Blog http://blogs.oracle.com/angelo	Angelo is an architect and technology evangelist at Oracle. His blog is focused on Web Center and Fusion Middleware.

Name and URL	Description
Bob Rhubart's ArchBeat blog `http://blogs.oracle.com/archbeat`	This is another Oracle blog, that shows you what's happening in and around the Oracle Technology Network (OTN) Architect Community.
Brian Dirking' Content@Work blog `http://bdirking.blogspot.com`	Brian's blog is more marketing-focused. He tells you about recent events, business problems, and customer experiences.
Dirk Nachbar's blog `http://dirknachbar.blogspot.com`	Dirk is a practicing Oracle Application Server and Fusion Middleware expert, Oracle DBA and Oracle Certified Trainer. He shares his battle-hardened tactics, common pitfalls, tips and tricks, and implementation secrets that he learns in his daily consulting work. He shares things, that are not so obvious from Oracle product documentation, and saves his readers hours, days, and even weeks of trial and error.
IOUG `http://www.ioug.org`	The Independent Oracle User Group (IOUG) represents the voice of Oracle technology and database professionals, and focuses on topics including implementing, upgrading and tuning Oracle Database 10g and 11g, data warehousing and security, application development, business intelligence and analytics, service oriented architecture, and products including Essbase, Stellent, Real Application Clusters, and Fusion Middleware.
OAUG `http://www.oaug.org`	The Oracle Applications Users Group (OAUG) is a global organization that enhances the capabilities of Oracle users in their day-to-day use and management of the growing family of Oracle Applications. Formed in 1990, the OAUG is one of the software industry's most successful user groups and speaks with one voice for the family of Oracle Applications users.
Oracle AppsLab blog `http://theappslab.com`	Oracle AppsLab is a think-tank developed to drive adoption of new web patterns and technologies across Oracle's business and products. This blog is a space for sharing ideas of this small group, dedicated to living and breathing new technologies.

Name and URL	Description
OTN Blog `http://blogs.oracle.com/otn`	Oracle Technology Network (OTN) is the world's largest interactive community of developers, DBAs, admins, and architects using Oracle products along with industry-standard technologies. This is the official blog of the Oracle Technology Network team. It's a great place to get insider information.
Quest International User Group `http://www.questdirect.org`	Quest is a not-for-profit association supporting Oracle applications users, including PeopleSoft, JD Edwards, UCM and Oracle Utilities and the ecosystem, from the underlying ERP solutions to the numerous complementary products and services.
Web Oriented Architecture 2.0 Blog `http://blogs.oracle.com/woa`	This blog is run by Emiliano Pecis, Oracle Sales Consultant, specialized on Middleware Solutions and related technologies, with a focus on Enterprise 2.0 and distributed data grid. This is it for my list of Oracle resources. And now here's the list of general Information Management resources that you need to check out.

Information management resources

In this section I will give you my favorite free online resources that help you follow the trends in general Info Management space. You'll notice that I've broken my usual alphabetical order. Why? I did this to bring more focus to my favorite site, CMSWire that gives you a wealth of friendly, easy to digest and to-the-point trend watching and product reviews.

Name and URL	Description
CMSWire http://www.cmswire.com	CMSWire is a rapidly growing web magazine dedicated to all things content management and a few other things they considered related. The CMSWire audience consists of CIOs, technologists, decision makers, vendors, and analysts with a focus on information management practices, content, document and asset management technologies, web publishing, enterprise collaboration, and a dash of social media. The content and information management marketplace remains a dynamic and broad field of great innovation, and one of interest to many disciplines. CMSWire team does its best to keep you informed of the latest twists, turns, and trends this industry presents.
CMS Watch blogs http://www.cmswatch.com/Blog	CMS Watch is a buyer's advocate for enterprises, looking to invest in content technologies. They publish independent research that helps you sort out suitable technology choices for your particular needs. Their research is known for its technical depth, readability, and absolute neutrality.
Ironworks blogs http://fitandfinish.ironworks.com and http://underthehood.ironworks.com	"Fit and Finish" is the User Experience blog published by Ironworks, System Integrator Consultancy. They're sharing ideas, best practices, creativity, humor, and useful resources. "Under the Hood" is Ironworks' Coder and API blog that covers various technology-related topics, from high-level application architecture all the way down to those pesky 1s and 0s that keep the world moving these days. This is it! Wasn't this an ocean of free online resources to follow? And now let me give you some pointers that you might find helpful when looking for an Oracle UCM consulting help.

Service providers

In this section I'm giving you some consulting and training providers, and how to find others if you need to. Consulting providers are first—please see below.

Consulting

Selecting a consulting vendor is a matter of chemistry, personal preferences, and many other factors, so I'll only give you a short list. You can always find additional vendors at **Find Oracle Partner** Page: `http://solutions.oracle.com`.

But before you go there, I suggest you check out Fishbowl Solutions (`http://www.fishbowlsolutions.com`), one of the oldest and most reputable solutions providers in the Oracle UCM space.

Another one that provides refreshingly low prices and unbeatable true lifetime warranty on all customizations is the `StellentExperts.com`.

And now let's look at your options for custom UCM training.

Training

Almost every Oracle UCM consulting vendor can provide you with the custom training, but you need to be aware of the common pitfalls. Check out the last section of *Chapter 10, Customizing Oracle UCM*, before you ask yours about it.

Your other option is to go to the source and consider engaging me personally. From time to time I'm available for a limited number of training and consulting engagements. Check out *About Author* section for details on how to contact me.

And if you insist on formal education or you need to get your folks certified—check out Oracle University (`http://education.oracle.com`) and look for the UCM courses.

And now let's conclude our Resource Directory by looking at books, magazines, and major whitepapers.

Publications and periodicals

Let's start by looking at the few books that cover Oracle UCM and related technologies.

Books

At the time of this writing there are only three. Let's look at them one by one.

Reshaping Your Business with Web 2.0

(By Billy Cripe, Vince Casarez, Jean Sini, and Philipp Weckerle, McGraw-Hill, 2008)

The book shows you how to integrate Web 2.0 trends and technologies into the enterprise.

Below is the full book's description taken from Amazon.com.

> *Written by a team of experts from the Web 2.0 community and Oracle Corporation, this innovative guide provides a blueprint for leveraging the new culture of participation in an enterprise environment. Reshaping Your Business with Web 2.0 offers proven strategies, for the successful adoption of an enterprise 2.0 paradigm, and covers the technical solutions that best apply in specific situations. You will find clear guidelines for using Web 2.0 technologies and standards in a productive way to align with business goals, increase efficiency, and provide measurable bottom line growth. Faster collaboration and accelerate information dissemination with blogs and wikis, Implement folksonomic strategies to achieve business intelligence, analytics, and semantic web goals Capture and broadcast connection graphs and activity streams via social networks. Bring together application data, business analytics, unstructured information, and collaborative interactions in enterprise mashups Enable rich Internet applications with Ajax, Ruby on Rails, Flash, FLEX, and other technologies Connect your Web 2.0 ecosystem through Web services such as REST and JSON Ensure security, and compliance management.*

The next one is another strategy book.

Transforming Infoglut! A Pragmatic Strategy for Oracle Enterprise Content Management

(By Andy MacMillan and Brian Huff, Osborne Oracle Press 2008)

And here's an Amazon.com description:

> *Glean actionable business information from your "digital landfill" by deploying a flexible, cost-effective content management framework across your entire organization. Transforming Infoglut!: A Pragmatic Strategy for Oracle Enterprise Content Management details, step-by-step, how to rein in the current data explosion and gain the competitive edge. Get tips for building an enterprise content management (ECM) team, centralizing storage, finding and managing information, incorporating legacy systems, and handling unstructured content. You'll also learn how to secure your system, optimize performance, and ensure regulatory compliance.*

And here's the last one — the only in-depth UCM technical reference book (prior to the one you're reading now).

The Definitive Guide to Stellent Content Server Development

(By Brian Huff, Apress, 2006)

As the title suggests, this book is focused on Content Server customization and integration. Most of the information is still valid and some is a bit dated. The book is available in hardcover and e-book formats and as a free preview from Google Books (`http://books.google.com`). Below is the book's description from Amazon.com:

> *The Definitive Guide to Stellent Content Server Development is the most complete book available for this Enterprise Content Management application. It gives an introduction to Content Management, followed by an in-depth discussion of Stellent's core service-oriented architecture.*
>
> *It details how its flexible, component-driven model makes it easy to customize the appearance and behavior of the server. Focusing on the developer, this book gives step-by-step examples for creating data entry forms, designing skins, adding services, customizing the web interface, integrating with other applications, and modifying the behavior with Java. Throughout the book the author reveals tips and tricks on security, performance, metadata design, maintenance, undocumented features, and general best practices.*

It is complete with appendices detailing the inner working of the Content Server. This includes a full discussion about the IdocScript language, the JSP integration layer, and some of the internal Java APIs. You will find this a vital resource whether you're just considering Stellent, or you own it and want to customize it to fit your exact needs.

And now let's look at one more valuable source of Oracle UCM expertise, industry trends and insider information, Oracle magazines and whitepapers.

Magazines and whitepapers

Below are the two well-known magazines and three must-read whitepapers you ought to see.

Oracle magazine

`http://www.oracle.com/oramag`

Oracle Magazine needs no introduction. This is an official Oracle voice that presents Oracle news, customer stories, hands-on technology articles, podcasts, and much more.

KMWorld magazine

`http://www.kmworld.com`

KMWorld serves the content, document, and knowledge management markets. It's the key information provider for a broad array of industry leaders who use business content in all its forms to drive productivity, gain competitive advantage, and create new opportunities for revenue and innovation in their organizations.

KMWorld focuses on Business Process Management, Collaboration, Document Management, Portals, Enterprise Content Management, Records Management and Regulatory Compliance, Smart Enterprise Suites, Workflow and E-Process, and Imaging and Forms Processing just to name a few.

And now let me show you the three important whitepapers that cover the basics of Information Management. They help you get a broader prospective—the kind of insight that comes so handy at those critical points, every UCM project goes through.

Fishbowl content management whitepapers

http://www.fishbowlsolutions.com/StellentSolutions/
ContentManagementResources

This page offers you a wealth of resources (many of which I've already mentioned). What I urge you to do is go to the **White Papers** and **Ebooks** sections to the bottom of the screen and read these three important ones by Billy Cripe:

- **Two Types of Collaboration and Ten Requirements for Using Them** — an eye-peeling eBook that makes you aware of the often-overlooked Accidental Collaboration and how to reap sizable benefits by intentionally facilitating it.

- **Information Architecture for Enterprise 2.0: Enabling Access, Intelligence and Participation** — a whitepaper that outlines the key points of what Enterprise 2.0 deployments should include and how it should be implemented within the organization.

- **The Agile Enterprise-Requirements in the Post-Modern Economy** — another landmark whitepaper that helps you achieve massive savings by capitalizing on UCM's inherent agile-friendly capabilities. It walks you through a few practical steps that help you maximize your value and avoid the quicksand of typical problems.

There you have it — my very best shot at giving you the most complete, most up-to-date Oracle UCM Resource Directory you can possibly get.

You're now reading the last page of The Oracle UCM Handbook, and it would be a perfect time to take one last moment and summarize everything you have just accomplished.

Index

E

ECM. *See* Document Management
Enterprise content management. *See*
    Document Management
EnterpriseTwoDotOh
  URL 313
environment packager, content server
    administration control 55
external authentication providers
  integrating with 58

F

fields
  putting on forum 79, 80
File Store Provider 303
filesystem
  backing up 190
  content, moving to another server 191
  inactive content, removing 192
  metadata, mass-updating 192
Fishbowl content management whitepapers
    324
Fishbowl Oracle UCM Component
    Repository 300
folder archiving 216
folder behavior, customizing
  folder user interface features, customizing
    152, 153
  user default metadata values, defining 152
folder configuration, content server
    administration control 50, 52
Folder Structure Archive Component
    261, 303
folder structures, migrating
  in one shot 224, 225
  selected content, migrating 226-229
  selected folders, migrating 226-229
folder user interface features, customizing
    152, 153
fragments 277-282
FusionECM blog
  URL 313

G

global settings, virtual folders
  System Default Information Fields link 150
  System Defaults page 150

H

HCSP (Hypertext Content Server Page) 253
HCST (Hypertext Content Server Form) 253
HDA files
  about 178
  LocalData section 178
  OptionList section 178
  OptionList sections 178
  ResultSet sections 178, 179
  sample 178
host machine 14
Hyper Data. *See* HDA files
Hypertext Content Server Template (HCST)
    pages 249

I

idcCommand 210
Idcplg directory 172
idcserver_stop 191
iDoc files 253
Imaging and Process Management (IPM)
    306
Independent Oracle UCM Knowledge
    Center
  CenterURL 313
  URL 213
Information management resources
  CMS Watch blogs 319
  CMSWire 319
  Ironworks blogs 319
Information Rights Management (IRM)
  about 307
  components 307
  IRM Desktop 307
  IRM Server 307
inheritance, virtual folders
  about 147
  propagate feature, using 147-149
install directory 172

Q

Quest International User Group
  URL 318

R

real-time content replication
  setting up 203, 204
Records Management (URM) 263
Records Manager 306
Redstone CMS blogs
  URL 314
relationships
  defining 76, 77
Remote IntraDoc Client API (RIDC API)
  237
repository manager, admin applets 46
ResultSet section, HDA files 178, 179
role-based component
  about 99
  accounts component 104
  content groups, working with 101-103
  permissions 100, 101
  security group 99
  user roles 99, 100
  user roles, working with 101-103
RSS feeds 299

S

SampleBlogs Component 299
SampleWiki Component 300
scripting
  adding, to workflow 127-129
security group 99
security model
  about 96
  auditing 96
  authorization component 96
  multiple dimensions 97
  paradigm shift 96, 97
  planning 111
  UCM security, components 98
security model, planning
  content categories 111
  degree of control 111
  UCM products 112

use cases 112
security, virtual folders 149
server output, admin server 50
server providers
  consulting vendor, selecting 320
  training 320
service 176, 177
Service Oriented Architecture 176, 177
Simple Object Access Protocol (SOAP) 235
site structure elements
  contribution regions 270
  contributor data files 270
  elements 270
  fragments 270
  native documents 270
  navigation sections 270
  page templates 270
  placeholders 270
  project file 270
  region templates 270
  subtemplates 270
site studio content
  consuming, in third-party web applications
    238, 240
Site Studio Content Server Component 264
  installing 266, 267
Site Studio Contributor 264
Site Studio Designer 264
  installing 267
  website, creating with 272
Site Studio Manager 264
skins, content server interface 257, 258
SOA. *See* Service Oriented Architecture
social networking groups
  AIIM Linked In group 316
  Content Management Professionals
    Facebook group 316
  Oracle UCM Facebook group 316
  Stellent and Oracle UCM Linked in group
    316
  WebCenter Linked In group 316
Software Development and Technical
    Expertise for ECM blogs
  URL 314
standard metadata
  about 64
  database, exploring 64-66

URM Adapters 306
use cases, security model 112
user admin, admin applets 45
user admin applet
  customizing 58
user default metadata values
  defining 152
user roles
  about 99, 100
  working with 101-103
users
  adding 55, 56
  external authentication providers,
    integrating with 58
  group, adding 57
  managing 55
  user admin applet, customizing 58

V

vault directory 175, 176
view providers, admin server 50
Views
  creating 75, 76
virtual environment 14
virtual folders
  about 144
  exploring 144
virtual folders, exploring
  folder, security 149
  global settings 150, 151
  inheritance, working 147
  major controls 144-146
  propagate feature, using 147-149
Virtual Hard Disk (VHD) 16
Virtual Machine. *See* VM
VM
  about 14
  host machine 14

W

WCM. *See* Web Content Management
WebCenter 299, 305
WebCenter Linked In group
  URL 316

Web Content Management (WCM)
  about 301, 304
  components, downloading 265
  modules 304
  Oracle Site Studio 264
  Oracle Site Studio, installing 265
  Site Studio Content Server Component,
    installing 266, 267
Web Content Management (WCM),
  modules
  Content Portlet Suite 305
  Oracle Connection Server 304
  Oracle Content Publisher 304
  Oracle Site Studio 304
  Oracle Site Studio Publisher 304
  Oracle Web Center 305
  Third-party companion products 305
WebDAV
  about 151
  folder behavior, customizing 151
  folder user interface features, customizing
    152, 153
  used, for contributing content 158
  user default metadata values, defining 152
web form editor
  downloading 254, 255
  using 254
WebLayout directory
  about 173, 174
  physical content storage, options exploring
    for 174
web layout editor, admin applets 44, 45
Web Oriented Architecture 2.0 Blog
  URL 318
Web Services Definition Language (WSDL)
  235
website, creating
  about 269
  content, adding 282-285
  contributor interface, using 286-289
  fragments, using 277-282
  new site, creating 272-274
  pages, adding 290-296
  page templates, using 274-277
  publishing model 296
  structure elements 270-272

with Site Studio Designer 272
whitepapers
  Fishbowl content management whitepapers
    324
wiki components 299, 300
Windows Explorer
  content server, contributing to 158-160
  documents, contributing from Word 162
  Outlook, working 160-162
  used, for contributing content 158
Word
  documents, contributing from 162
workflow
  automatic workflow 115
  basic workflows 134
  basic workflow templates 137
  content life cycle 125
  criteria workflow 115, 116
  enabling 120-122
  Manager_Approval workflow 123
  manual workflows 135, 136
  scripting, adding 127-129
  steps, adding 118, 119
  Sub workflows 134
  Workflow Admin application 114, 115
  Workflow Assignments page 124

workflow admin, admin applets
  about 46
Workflow Admin application
  about 114
  criteria tab 114
  templates tab 114
  workflows tab 114
**workflows tab, Workflow Admin
    application 114**
WSDL Generator component 235

X

xCollectionID field 69
xComments field 69
xWebsites 138

Y

Yahoo intradoc_users · Stellent Users Group
  URL 315

Thank you for buying
The Oracle Universal Content Management Handbook

About Packt Publishing

Packt, pronounced 'packed', published its first book "Mastering phpMyAdmin for Effective MySQL Management" in April 2004 and subsequently continued to specialize in publishing highly focused books on specific technologies and solutions.

Our books and publications share the experiences of your fellow IT professionals in adapting and customizing today's systems, applications, and frameworks. Our solution based books give you the knowledge and power to customize the software and technologies you're using to get the job done. Packt books are more specific and less general than the IT books you have seen in the past. Our unique business model allows us to bring you more focused information, giving you more of what you need to know, and less of what you don't.

Packt is a modern, yet unique publishing company, which focuses on producing quality, cutting-edge books for communities of developers, administrators, and newbies alike. For more information, please visit our website: www.packtpub.com.

About Packt Enterprise

In 2010, Packt launched two new brands, Packt Enterprise and Packt Open Source, in order to continue its focus on specialization. This book is part of the Packt Enterprise brand, home to books published on enterprise software – software created by major vendors, including (but not limited to) IBM, Microsoft and Oracle, often for use in other corporations. Its titles will offer information relevant to a range of users of this software, including administrators, developers, architects, and end users.

Writing for Packt

We welcome all inquiries from people who are interested in authoring. Book proposals should be sent to author@packtpub.com. If your book idea is still at an early stage and you would like to discuss it first before writing a formal book proposal, contact us; one of our commissioning editors will get in touch with you.

We're not just looking for published authors; if you have strong technical skills but no writing experience, our experienced editors can help you develop a writing career, or simply get some additional reward for your expertise.

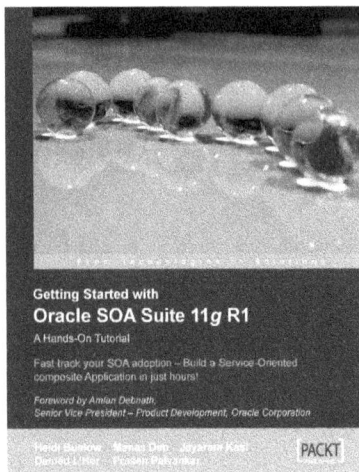

Getting Started With Oracle SOA Suite 11g R1 – A Hands-On Tutorial

ISBN: 978-1-847199-78-2   Paperback: 482 pages

Fast track your SOA adoption – Build a service-oriented composite application in just hours!

1. Offers an accelerated learning path for the much anticipated Oracle SOA Suite 11g release

2. Beginning with a discussion of the evolution of SOA, this book sets the stage for your SOA learning experience

3. Includes a comprehensive overview of the Oracle SOA Suite 11g Product Architecture

Web 2.0 Solutions with Oracle WebCenter 11g

ISBN: 978-1-847195-80-7   Paperback: 412 pages

Learn WebCenter 11g fundamentals and develop real-world enterprise applications in an online work environment

1. Create task-oriented, rich, interactive online work environments with the help of the comprehensive Oracle WebCenter Suite 11g

2. Accelerate the development of Enterprise 2.0 solutions by leveraging the Oracle tools

3. Apply the basic concepts of Enterprise 2.0 for your business solutions by understanding them completely

Please check **www.PacktPub.com** for information on our titles